12.–

بسم الله الرحمن الرحيم

Other books by the same author:

The Ideology of Peace

In Search of God

Indian Muslims

Islam and Peace

Islam As It Is

Islam Rediscovered

Islam: Creator of the Modern Age

Islam: The Voice of Human Nature

The Moral Vision

Principles of Islam

Prophet Muhammad: A Simple Guide to His Life

The Quran for All Humanity

The Quran: An Abiding Wonder

Religion and Science

Simple Wisdom (PB)

Tabligh Movement

A Treasury of the Quran

The True Jihad

Woman Between Islam and Western Society

Woman in Islamic Shari'ah

Words of the Prophet Muhammad

MUHAMMAD ﷺ

A PROPHET FOR ALL

HUMANITY

Maulana Wahiduddin Khan

GOODWORD BOOKS

Translated by Farida Khanam
Urdu version: Paighambar-e-Inquilab
Marathi version: Muhammad: Karantiche Preshit
Previously titled: Muhammad: The Prophet of Revolution

First published 1999
Reprinted 2014

Goodword Books
1, Nizamuddin West Market, New Delhi-110 013
Tel. +9111-4182-7083, Mob. +91-8588822672
email: info@goodwordbooks.com
www.goodwordbooks.com

Goodword Books, Chennai
324, Triplicane High Road,
Triplicane, Chennai-600005
Tel. +9144-4352-4599
Mob. +91-9790853944, 9600105558
email: chennaigoodword@gmail.com

Islamic Vision Ltd.
426-434 Coventry Road, Small Heath
Birmingham B10 0UG, U.K.
Tel. 121-773-0137
Fax: 121-766-8577
e-mail: info@ipci-iv.co.uk
www.islamicvision.co.uk

IB Publisher Inc.
81 Bloomingdale Rd, Hicksville, NY 11801, USA
Tel. 516-933-1000
Fax: 516-933-1200
Toll Free: 1-888-560-3222
email: info@ibpublisher.com
www.ibpublisher.com

Printed in India

Contents

Introduction

In an American publication entitled *The Hundred,* the author mentions the one hundred people he believes to have exerted the greatest influence on human history. The author, Dr Michael Hart, was born into a Christian family, and received a scientific education. But at the top of his roll of honour he has placed neither Christ's name, nor Newton's. There was one person, he believes, whose achievements excelled all others: that person was the Prophet Muḥammad. No one else has had such an impact on the history of man. "He was the only man in history," he writes, "who was supremely successful on both the religious and secular levels."[1]

Just as to the American, Michael Hart, he is the most outstanding figure of human history, to the English historian, Thomas Carlyle, he is "the hero of the Prophets."

In ancient times, when Abraham and Ishmael were building the House in Makkah. they prayed for a prophet among their descendants. 2500 years later, this "hero," the Prophet Muḥammad, arose from the People of Makkah bringing with him special divine succour. The prayer of Abraham was fulfilled, and with it the purpose of the prophets' coming to the world was achieved.

Before Muḥammad, history did not carefully record the lives of the prophets. From a strictly academic and historical point of view, then, their prophethood was difficult to establish. The Prophet Jesus was the last of the ancient line of prophets and has a following of millions, yet so tenuous is his historical position that Bertrand Russell has had occasion to remark: "Historically it is quite doubtful whether Christ ever existed at all." This is not the case with the Prophet Muḥammad, the last of the prophets. His life is so well-documented and clearly laid down in history that anyone who studies his life is forced to agree with Professor Philip Hitti that, "Muḥammad was born in the full light of history."[2]

The factor which makes the greatest contribution to the permanence of Muḥammad's prophethood is the Qur'ān, that enduring miracle which was revealed to him by God. If this miracle had been of the same order as those bestowed upon his prophetic predecessors, its effects would not have outlived him, and his prophethood would not have been accepted in the way that it was by subsequent generations. A miracle is a wondrous event which man, on his own, is unable to produce. This definition applies in full measure to the Qur'ān: it is beyond man even to emulate it. There is no doubt that the Qur'ān is a miracle wrought by the Almighty.

Muḥammad's role was exceptional in that he was to be the last of the prophets. It had been so ordained by God. The final revelation of God's will was to be conveyed to the people by him and, for posterity, the scriptures had to be preserved by him and subsequently by his devoted followers throughout the centuries. To ensure this train of events, the Prophet had to bring about a great revolution that would give him a following the world over.

> Muḥammad is the father of no man among you. He is the Prophet of God and the last of the prophets. God has knowledge of all things.[3]

The Prophet was chosen by God to give the kind of guidance to people which they needed if they were to lead upright, virtuous lives. If people seemingly have complete control over what they do, it is because, in this world, they are on trial. If the illusion of free will causes them to act as they choose, it is because they are being tested. The Prophets, in spite of their divine mission, cannot force people to change their ways. All they can do is communicate the message with which God has entrusted them:

> Yet what should Messengers do but give plain warning?[4]

God has done the maximum to ensure that we should not go astray in our journey through life. He has given us a conscience, enabling us to differentiate between what is right and wrong, and has placed us in a world based on justice. But whenever man has failed to listen to his conscience, or was deaf to the silent message emanating from every object of God's creation, God sent His prophets to bring him the truth, and so that these God-sent messages should not be incomprehensible to the people of many different lands, they were communicated to them in their own languages.

In pre-Islamic times religious institutions had become debased by the veneration of mere mortals; whereas the prophet Muḥammad admitted of no other form of religion but that based on the worship of the immortal God. Religious beliefs had very frequently been founded on superstition; but by him they were established on the foundation of reality. It was he who taught people to conquer nature instead of worshipping it, thus paving the way for the scientific era. And where political power had been in the hands of one hereditary monarch, he showed the way to government by the people. While learning had been based on conjecture and assumption, he taught people to learn from observation of reality. In cases where human society had been vitiated by cruelty and oppression, he showed people how to live together in justice and peace. These are all achievements of the Prophet Muḥammad. He changed the tide of human history.

From whatever angle one looks at history, ever-broadening reverberations of his impact will be manifest. All that is best in human values, all the important advances of human civilization, are direct or indirect results of the revolution he brought about.

His own personal life was a perfect example for mankind. Because he himself was made to experience all kinds of special conditions, he was able to provide a model for living both at the individual and social levels. He showed us the life that God would like us to live on earth, for in all matters each and every one of his actions was in accordance with the will of God. Not only did he establish the perfect pattern for the worship of God, but he also showed how God helps those who truly devote their lives to His service. We can see from his life how, if one fears God, there is nothing else that one need fear. If one remains patient in the face of provocation, He will pour oil on troubled waters. If one rises above negative impulses, one can win over everyone, even enemies. If one sacrifices this world for the next, one will eventually have the best of both worlds.

Just as the farmer who cultivates his land by divinely inspired methods reaps the best crop, so, at any time, can the followers of the Prophet prevail over others. God has provided all of the conditions necessary for and conducive to the dominance of His, the divine religion. By understanding and utilizing them, adherents of this religion can bring Islamic thought into pre-eminence.

Between the time of the Prophet Abraham and the coming of the Prophet Muḥammad, two thousand five hundred years elapsed. Throughout this period the stage was being set for the coming of the Prophet. The Prophet, acting at God's behest, played the role for which he was cast. That was why his mission was supremely successful.

In making the Prophet Muḥammad the greatest figure, and consequently one of the most resplendent landmarks in human history, God has bestowed his greatest favour on mankind. Whoever seeks a guide for himself cannot fail to see him, for he stands out like a tower, a mountain on the horizon, radiating light like a beacon, beckoning all to the true path. It is inevitable that a seeker of truth will be drawn up to the magnificent pinnacle on which he stands.

During the fourteen hundred years that have passed since the times of the Prophet Muḥammad, the historical changes that have occurred, the massive advances in human knowledge that have taken place, have all combined in support of Islam. The religion that the Prophet taught can still take pride of place over other religions. But, for this to be achieved, divinely-inspired methods have to be adopted. This rule, which applied to the Prophet, equally applies to his followers.

NOTES

1. Dr. Michael Hart, *The Hundred,* New York, 1978.
2. Philip K Hitti, *History of the Arabs,* London, 1978.
3. Qur'ān, 33:40.
4. Qur'ān, 16:35.

PART ONE

1

From Adam to the Messiah

All of the prophets who came into this world had an identical mission. They taught that man's life on earth was but an infinitesimal part of his eternal life.

In this world he was put to the test. Reward or punishment would come in the next. After death, if he had followed the Lord's path, he would find his eternal abode in heaven. But, if he had strayed from it, he would be plunged straight into hell. His damnation would be everlasting. This was the reality of life taught by each and every one of the prophets.

Adam was the first man on earth and also the first prophet. He was succeeded by a long line of prophets right up to the time of the Messiah. Altogether there have been some 124,000 messengers of God, of whom 315 have been prophets. They appeared in different lands and among different peoples, preaching the word of God and exhorting people to live in fear of Him. But very few of those they addressed have ever proved willing to give up their freedom for the sake of God. Few people, for instance, followed the Prophet Yaḥyā (John the Baptist) and he died a martyr's death. When Lot left his people, only two of his daughters accompanied him. According to the Old Testament, only eight people entered the ark along with Noah. When Abraham left his native country, Iraq, the only people to accompany him were his wife Sarah and his nephew Lot, although they were later joined by his two sons, Ishmael and Isaac. Even after great missionary effort on the part of Jesus, the priests and religious authorities who heard his teachings did not follow him, and even his twelve friends temporarily forsook him at the moment of truth.

This was the unhappy lot of most of the prophets. The ties of kith and kin sometimes brought a handful of followers to the more fortunate, but as often as not, would-be prophets were forced by the inattention and insensitivity of those around them to live out their lives in solitude and persecution. This verse of the Qur'ān very aptly sums up common attitudes to prophethood throughout the history of mankind: "Alas for the servants! They laugh to scorn every prophet that comes to them."[1]

In God's sight, the prophets stand head and shoulders above the human race. How extraordinary it is, then, that they are the very ones to whom the least historical importance has been attached. History has fully chronicled the lives of kings and soldiers, but not one single prophet's life has been given its due place in the annals of history. Aristotle (384-322 B.C.), who was born one thousand years after the Prophet Moses, was not even acquainted with Moses' name. The reason is not far to seek: most of the prophets were rejected by their peoples; their homes were demolished; they were treated as outcasts from society; they appeared so unimportant that no one deemed it necessary even to make any mention of them.

Why were the prophets treated in this manner? There was just one reason for this, and that was their criticism of current practices, especially of the established religious authorities, the priesthood. People love nothing more than being praised; and they loathe nothing more than being criticised. The prophets exposed the difference between right and wrong, making no compromise with their peoples. They were persistently pointing out the faults in people's beliefs and actions. Consequently, people turned against them. If the prophets had taught what everyone wanted to hear, they would never have been treated in this manner.

Although this was the fate of most of the prophets, a few of them were spared, Joseph, Solomon and David being names that immediately spring to mind. But the power and prestige that these prophets acquired was not due to the popularity of their teachings; they had an entirely separate origin.

David was a young soldier in the army of the Israelites under King Saul, during the time that the Israelites and Philistines went to war with each other. Among the army of Philistines was the giant Goliath. So powerful a fighter was he that no one was prepared to do battle with him. King Saul then announced that he would give his daughter in marriage to anyone who slew Goliath. David came forward, challenged the giant, and killed him. In this way he became the son-in-law of the King of Israel. In a subsequent war, both King Saul and his heir apparent were killed in battle. David was thereupon crowned King of Israel. Solomon was David's son, and succeeded to his father's throne. As for Joseph, he was endowed by God with the ability to interpret dreams and the King of Egypt, impressed by his ability, went so far as to entrust the affairs of state to him. But the King still remained head of state and he and his subjects continued to adhere to their pagan religion.

This hostile treatment meted out to the prophets throughout the ages, deprived people of true guidance and, what was even more serious, made the preservation of the scriptures and teachings of the prophets impossible. Only a prophet's followers can preserve his teachings after him; but the prophets either had no followers, or so few as to be unable to counter the challenges of their society to the preservation of the Holy Scriptures.

The knowledge of God is eternal. He sees the future just as He does the past. He was aware, before the sending of the prophets, that this would be the fate of the human race. So He had decreed that He would remedy this situation at the end of the prophetic era by sending His own special envoy to the world: a prophet whose task would be not only to preach religion, but also to exalt it above all others on earth. He would be granted special succour from God, enabling him to compel his people to bow to the truth. God would keep him on earth until he had rectified the perversions of the society around him.

God's own might would assist the Prophet to vanquish his enemies. In this way the true religion would be established on solid foundations and God's word would be perpetuated, as it says in the Bible, "for the earth shall be filled with the knowledge of the glory of God, as the waters cover the sea."[2]

Translations and additions have taken the present-day Bible very far from the original. But it still contains multiple references to the coming of the Prophet Muḥammad. If one studies the Bible objectively, one will find certain references that cannot be applied to anyone else. The very purpose of the mission of the Prophet Jesus was to announce to the world, and to the Jewish nation in particular, the coming of the final prophet. The "New Testament" to which he referred was, in truth, Islam, for it marked the end of Jewish religious hegemony and projected the Children of Ishmael as the true recipients of the word of God. Hence the rise of the Prophet Muḥammad.

The Prophet Jesus came to the world six hundred years before the last of the Prophets. In one reference to Jesus, the Qur'ān has this to say:

> And remember the Prophet Jesus, who said to the Children of Israel: "I am sent forth to you by God to confirm the Torah already revealed and to give news of an apostle that will come after me whose name is Aḥmad."[3]

The words "Aḥmad" and "Muḥammad" have the same meaning: the praised one. In the Gospel of Barnabas the name of the coming prophet is given quite clearly as Muḥammad. But since Christians consider the Gospel of

Barnabas to be apocryphal, we do not consider it proper to quote from that source. We cannot even be sure whether Jesus, in his prophecy, referred to Aḥmad or Muḥammad. Most probably he used a word with the same meaning as these names.

In his biography of the Prophet, Ibn Hishām quotes the historian, Muḥammad ibn Isḥāq, the most authentic source on the Prophet's life, as saying that when Jesus spoke in his mother tongue, Syrian, the word that he used of the coming prophet was "Munhamann" meaning "the praised one." This traditionally accepted appellation was probably passed on to him by Palestinian Christians who had come under Islamic rule. When the Bible was translated into Greek, the word became "Paraclete".

NOTES

1. Qur'ān, 36:30.
2. Bible, Habakkuk, 2.14.
3. Qur'ān, 61:6.

2

The Emergence and Legacy of the Prophet Muhammad

Poised between Africa, Asia and Europe, the Arabian peninsula lay at the very heart of the ancient world. Yet no ambitious conqueror had invaded the territory; no ruler had sought to bring it under his domain. All military campaigns had been limited to the area bordering Arabia—Iraq, Syria, Palestine and Lebanon. As for the Arabian peninsula, no one had considered it worth fighting for. True, its shores were lapped by three seas, but its interior offered little beyond inhospitable desert and barren mountains.

Makkah was the central township of this land, it was in this "uncultivable valley" in which it lay that the Prophet of Islam, Muḥammad, on whom be peace, was born. His father, 'Abdullah ibn 'Abdul Muṭṭalib, died a few months before the birth of the Prophet. He was only six years of age when his mother, Āminah, also passed away. For two years he was cared for by his grandfather, 'Abdul Muṭṭalib, and, when he too died, the Prophet's uncle, Abū Ṭālib, became his guardian. Abū Ṭālib's demise occurred three years before the emigration of the Prophet to Madinah. The Prophet then, at the most difficult stage of his life, was left without a protector. But nature had endowed the Prophet with a remarkable personality. Those who saw him in his youth used to remark: "This boy has a great future." His dignified and impressive personality grew with age. 'Alī,[1] once commented, "Those who saw him for the first time were filled with awe, and those who came close to him grew to love him." The Prophet's noble character was undisputed, yet when in his fortieth year, he announced his prophetic mission, people's attitude to him changed. They poured scorn on his claim to prophethood. "Look at this village boy who reckons he's in contact with the heavens," they would say.

His preaching mission extended over a mere twenty-three years. It was during this short time that he brought about a revolution among the Arab tribes, the like of which the world had never seen. Within one hundred years this revolution had vanquished both the Sassanian and the Byzantine Empires. With the fall of these two great empires of the world, Islam annexed the territory extending from Iran and Iraq to Bukhara in the east, while in the west, Syria, Palestine, Egypt, and then the whole of north Africa also fell to Islam. And the torrent did not halt there. In A.D. 711 Islam surged forward across the Straits of Gibraltar into the Iberian Peninsula. In 732 a Frankish prince, Charles Martel, arrested the advance of Islam at Tours. Then followed the Crusades, stretching over two centuries, and after the

Crusades the horrific onslaughts of the Tartar tribes. But despite these attacks from outside, the Islamic Empire held its own until the 15th century, when, due to infighting among the Muslims themselves, Spain was lost.

It was then the turn of the Turks and the Mughals to be aroused by the spirit of Islam. In 1453 the Turks conquered Constantinople and advanced into Eastern Europe as far as Yugoslavia. A Turkish army remained encamped outside Vienna until 1683. In the 16th century the Mughals established Islamic rule in India and Afghanistan. Over the last thirteen centuries Muslims have spread to every corner of the globe. Close on four dozen countries of Asia and Africa have come to constitute a Muslim world. According to the *World Muslim Gazetter*[2] there are 900 million Muslims in the world today.

This was all the result of a twenty-three year effort conducted in Arabia under the Prophet's guidance. In this short space of time, the Islamic revolution not only assured itself of a permanent place in human history; it also created a new history of its own. Humans alone do not have it in them to accomplish such a gigantic task; it can only be done by God. The Islamic revolution was truly the work of God. When the Muslims were returning from their victory at the Battle of Badr, they were met at a place called Rauha by some well-wishers, who congratulated them on the outcome of the fighting. "Why do you congratulate us?" asked Salmah ibn Salamah. "The enemy were just like tethered camels, and we duly slaughtered them."[3]

All of this was evidently pre-ordained by God. From the

bare Arabian desert He raised up a people of extraordinary tenacity, a people whose characters had been tempered by their environment. They knew only acceptance or denial; for them there was no third alternative. In them were preserved all the natural qualities needed for dedication to a cause. Added to this there was the fact that the two great powers of the day lay on the borders of their country. It was only natural that the mighty empires of Rome and Persia should not take kindly to the emergence of a new power on their doorstep. In their attempt to arrest the rise of Islam, they waged war against the Muslims. In so doing, they forced the Muslims to fight back. This gave the Muslims the chance to conquer the empires of Rome and Persia, whose borders, at that time, extended to the farthest reaches of the known world. There is no doubting the fact that the conquests of Islam were not wars of aggression against others; rather they were a response to aggression from others. They were wars of self-defence and never, in any country of the world, have there been two minds on the justification for such wars.

Over and above the political significance of these events was the fact that the Islamic revolution opened out hitherto unexplored opportunities for humanity. It made God's revealed religion a historical reality, something that it had not been before.

It ushered in the age of the press, ensuring the preservation of the Qur'ān for all time. It brought the age of democracy and freedom of speech to the world, removing all artificial barriers that had obstructed preachers in their call to truth. It made new discoveries possible in the world of science, enabling religious truths to be proved and explained on a rational, intellectual level.

An even more important aspect of this revolution was that, through the Prophet, God showed the world what would happen in the hereafter. His life and mission provided us with a preview of the events of the next world. Those who accepted and patterned their lives upon the truth that he brought to them were made supreme, and that is how they will remain forever in the hereafter, if God wills. The wicked, meanwhile, were made to taste the humiliation that they would forever be a prey to in the world to come.

History shows that those who devote their lives to God always appear in a passive and depressed condition, while those devoted to wealth and power always seem to have their way in the world. Such is the sombre evidence of the history of saints and prophets. This state of affairs is quite contrary to reality, for, eventually, God will bestow everlasting honour and glory upon His true servants, while self-worshippers and worshippers of the world will forever be assigned to a pit of humiliation and disgrace.

This world is for our trial. Here, people have the chance to act as they please. That is why God does not hold anyone in check in this world. But once, at least, by means of the prophet of Islam, God has shown on earth the situation that will prevail in its most complete and permanent form in the next world.

The companions of the Prophet, whose homes were

demolished, for whom the earth had become a place of unmitigated oppression, who were robbed of their properties, who were so victimized and terrorized that they lived in constant fear of extermination—these very people were raised to a position of great honour. The Quraysh and the Jews, the Romans and the Iranians, the Yemenis and the Ghassanis[4]—those who took pride in their wealth and power—were meanwhile reduced to ignominy and disgrace.

Every prophet who comes from God provides a criterion of divine justice. Through him God announces to humanity the decisions that He Himself will announce in the next world. But the Prophet of Islam gave such a display of divine justice that it became a world experience; it became an accepted historical reality. We could see with our own eyes how God honoured His faithful servants and degraded those who rebelled against Him. Heaven and hell were realities that would be made manifest in the next world. But we had been given a preliminary glimpse of them in this world so that we might take heed.

What really emerged with the prophethood of Muḥammad was the divinity of God Himself. That is why the New Testament foretells of his prophethood as the "Kingdom of God." There is no doubting the fact that the revolution of the Prophet had great political and strategic implications. But its main importance is as an earthly manifestation of God's glory, a revelation of divine justice. The revolution of the Prophet Muḥammad showed us in advance the realities that would come upon us in stark and absolute form in the hereafter.

NOTES

1 The Prophet's cousin and son-in-law.
2. *World Muslim Gazetter published* by *Mu'tamar al-'Ālam al-Islamī*, 1971
3. Ibn Hishām, *Sīrah*, p. 153.
4. Arabian kingdom prominent as a Byzantine ally in the 6th century A.D.

3

Exemplary Conduct

The Prophet of Islam, Muḥammad, upon whom be peace, was born in Arabia on 22 April A.D. 570, and died on 8 June A.D. 632. He was a very handsome and powerfully built man. His childhood gave indications of the sublime and dynamic personality that was to emerge. As he grew up, the nobility of his personality used to have an effect on anyone beholding him, but he was so soft-spoken and of such genial disposition that anyone coming into close contact with him would learn to love him. A perfectly balanced personality—tolerant, truthful, perspicacious and magnanimous—he presented the highest example of human nobility. According to Dā'ūd ibn Ḥusayn, he became known as he grew older as the most chivalrous among his people, tolerant and forebearing, truthful and trustworthy, always the good neighbour. He would stay aloof from all quarrels and quibbles and never indulged in foul utterances, abuse or invective. People even left their valuables in his custody, for they knew that he would never betray them. His unimpeachable trustworthiness won for him the title of "*al-Amīn*," a faithful custodian, an unfailing trustee.

When he married at the age of twenty-five, his uncle Abū Ṭālib performed the marriage service. "There is no one to compare with my nephew, Muḥammad ibn 'Abdullah," he said. "He outshines everyone in nobility, gentility, eminence and wisdom. By God, he has a great future and will reach a very high station." Abū Ṭālib did not utter these words in the sense in which later events proved them to be true. He meant them in a worldly sense. Nature had endowed his nephew with a magnetic and versatile personality. His people would surely appreciate his qualities, and raise him to a high position. Abū Ṭālib envisaged a future of worldly success and accomplishment for his nephew; this was the "great future" which he referred to in his sermon.

Without doubt the Prophet had every opportunity for worldly advancement. He was born into a noble family of Makkah and his virtues guaranteed his success in life. True, he had inherited just one camel and one servant from his father, but his inborn high qualities had impressed the richest woman in Makkah, Khadījah, a forty-year-old widow belonging to a family of merchants. When the Prophet was twenty-five, she offered herself to him in marriage. Not only did marriage with Khadījah provide the Prophet with wealth and property; it also threw open to him a vast field of business in Arabia and beyond. The Prophet had every opportunity, then, of leading a successful and comfortable life. But he forsook all these things and chose something quite different for himself. Quite intentionally, he took a road that could lead only to worldly ruin. Before his marriage, the Prophet had earned his living in different ways. Now he relinquished all such activity, and dedicated himself to his lifelong vocation—the pursuit of truth. He used to sit for hours and ponder over the mysteries of creation. Instead of socializing and trying to gain a position for himself among the nobles of Makkah, he would wander in the hills and dales of the desert. Often he used to retire to the loneliness of a cave in Mount Ḥira'—three miles from Makkah—and stay there until his meagre supply of food and water was exhausted. He would return home to replenish his supplies, and then go back to the solitude of nature for prayer and meditation. He would beseech the Maker of the heavens and the earth for answers to the questions surging in his mind. What is our true role in life? What does the Lord require of us, as His servants? Whence do we come and whither will we go after death? Unable to find answers to these questions in the centres of human activity, he betook himself to the stillness of the desert; perhaps, there, the answer would be forthcoming.

The Romanian orientalist Konstan Virgil George (b. 1916) writes in his book, *The Prophet of Islam:*

> Until one has spent some time in the wilds of Arabia and the Middle East, one cannot begin to understand how the vastness and tranquillity of the desert expands the human intellect and fortifies the imagination. There is a great difference between European and Arabian plants. There is no plant in the arid reaches of the desert that does not exude a sweet fragrance; even the acacia trees of this land are aromatic. The desert stretches for 3,000,000 square kilometres. Here it is as though man comes into direct contact with God. Other countries are like

> buildings in which massive walls obstruct one's view; but there is nothing blocking one's vision of reality in the vast open reaches of Arabia. Wherever one looks, one sees endless sands and fathomless sky. Here, there is nothing to stop one from consorting with God and His angels.[1]

It was no small matter that a young man should be taking up this course in the prime of his life. He was renouncing worldly happiness and choosing a way fraught with difficulties and sorrow. He had all conceivable means and opportunities for a comfortable life, but his turbulent soul did not find satisfaction in them. He attached no value to them and could not rest content until he had unravelled the mysteries of life. He sought to delve beyond external appearances, and seek out the reality of life. Worldly gain and loss, comfort and distress, did not concern him; what mattered to him was the all important question of truth and falsehood.

This phase of the Prophet's life is referred to thus in the Qur'ān:

> Did He not find you wandering and guide you?[2]

The word used in this verse for "wandering" ("*dhallan*") can also be used to describe a tree standing alone in an empty desert. The Prophet, then, was like a lone tree standing amidst the vast wilderness of ignorance that was Arabia of the time. The idea of consolidating his position in this society was abhorrent to him. He sought the truth, and nothing less than the truth could satisfy his soul. His quest had reached a point when life had become an unbearable burden. The Qur'ān looks back on that time:

> Have We not lifted up and expanded your heart and relieved you of the burden which weighed down your back?[3]

God, indeed, relieved him of his burden. He turned in mercy to His Prophet, illuminating his path and guiding him on his journey. On February 12, A.D. 610, the Prophet was sitting alone in his cave. The angel of the Lord appeared before him in human form and taught him the words which appear at the beginning of the ninety sixth chapter of the Qur'ān. The Prophet's quest had finally been rewarded. His restless soul had joined in communion with the Lord. Not only did God grant him guidance; He also chose Muḥammad as His Prophet and special envoy to the world. The mission of the Prophet extended over the next twenty-three years. During this period the entire content of the Qur'ān—the final divine scripture—was revealed to him.

The Prophet of Islam discovered Truth in the fortieth year of his arduous life. It was an attainment that was not to usher in ease and comfort, for this Truth was that he stood face to face with an Almighty God. It was discovery of his own helplessness before the might of God, of his own nothingness before the supernatural magnitude of the Almighty. With this discovery it became clear that God's faithful servant had nothing but responsibilities in this world; he had no rights.

The meaning that life took on for the Prophet after the Truth came to him can be ascertained from these words:

> Nine things the Lord has commanded me.
> Fear of God in private and in public;

Justness, whether in anger or in calmness;
Moderation in both poverty and affluence;
That I should join hands with those who break away from me;
and give to those who deprive me;
and forgive those who wrong me;
and that my silence should be meditation;
and my words remembrance of God;
and my vision keen observation.[4]

These were no just glib words; they were a reflection of the Prophet's very life. Poignant and wondrously effective words of this nature could not emanate from an empty soul; they themselves indicate the status of the speaker; they are an outpouring of his inner being, an unquenchable spirit revealed in verbal form.

Even before the dawn of his prophethood, the Prophet's life had followed the same pattern. The motivation, however, had been subconscious; now it came on to the level of consciousness. Actions which had previously been based on instinctive impulses now became the well-conceived results of profound thinking. This is the state of one who reduces material needs to a minimum; whose life assumes a unique pattern; who in body lives in this world, but in spirit dwells on another plane.

The Prophet once said,

A discerning person should have some special moments:
a moment of communion with God;
a moment of self-examination;
a moment of reflection over the mysteries of creation;
and a moment which he puts aside for eating and drinking.[5]

In other words, this is how God's faithful servant passes the day. Sometimes the yearning of his soul brings him so close to God that he finds something in communion with the Lord. Sometimes fear of the day when he will be brought before the Lord for reckoning makes him reckon with himself. Sometimes he is so overawed by the marvels of God's creation that he starts seeing the splendours of the Creator reflected therein. Thus he spends his time encountering the Lord, his own self, and the world around him, while also finding time to cater for his physical needs.

These words are not a description of some remote being; they are a reflection of the Prophet's own personality, a flash from the light of faith that illuminated his own heart. These "moments" were an integral part of the Prophet's life. One who has not experienced these states can never describe them in such a lofty manner. The soul from which these words emanated was itself in the state that they describe; through words that state of spiritual perfection was communicated to others.

Before he received the word of God, this world—with all its shortcomings and limitations—appeared meaningless to the Prophet. But now that God had revealed to him that besides this world there was another perfect and eternal world, which was the real abode of man, life and the universe took on new meaning. He now found a level on which his soul could subsist, a life in which he could involve himself, heart and soul. The Prophet now found a real world into which he could put his heart and soul, a target for all his hopes and aspirations, a goal for all his life's endeavours.

This reality is discovered not merely on an intellectual level. When it takes root, it transforms one completely, and raises one's level of existence. The Prophet of Islam provides us with a superlative example of this way of life. The greatest lesson imparted by his life is that, unless one changes one's plane of existence, one cannot change one's plane of actions.

When the Prophet Muḥammad discovered the reality of the world hereafter, it came to dominate his whole life. He himself became most desirous of the heaven of which he gave tidings to others, and he himself was most fearful of the hell of which he warned others. Deep concern for the life to come was always welling up inside him. Sometimes it would surge to his lips in the form of supplication, and sometimes in the form of heartfelt contrition. He lived on a completely different plane from that of ordinary human beings. This is illustrated by many incidents a few of which are mentioned here.

Once the Prophet was at home with Umm Salamah. He called the maid-servant, who took some time in coming. Seeing signs of anger on the Prophet's face, Umm Salamah went to the window and saw that the maid was playing. When she came, the Prophet had a *miswāk*[6] in his hand. "If it wasn't for the fear of retribution on the Day of Judgement," he told the maid, "I would have hit you with this *miswāk*." Even this mildest of punishments was to be eschewed.

The men taken prisoner in the Battle of Badr were the Prophet's bitterest enemies, but still his treatment of them was impeccable. One of these prisoners was a man by the name of Suhayl ibn 'Amr. A fiery speaker, he used to denounce the Prophet virulently in public to incite people against him and his mission. 'Umar ibn al-Khaṭṭāb suggested that two of his lower teeth be pulled out to dampen his oratorical zeal. The Prophet was shocked by 'Umar's suggestion. "God would disfigure me for this on the Day of Judgement, even though I am his messenger," he said to 'Umar.

This is what is meant by the world being a planting-ground for the hereafter. One who realizes this fact lives a life oriented towards the hereafter—a life in which all efforts are aimed at achieving success in the next, eternal world; a life in which real value is attached—not to this ephemeral world—but to the life beyond death. One becomes aware that this world is not the final destination; it is only a road towards the destination, a starting-point of preparation for the future life. Just as every action of a worldly person is performed with worldly interests in mind, so every action of God's faithful servant is focused on the hereafter. Their reactions to every situation in life reflect this attitude of looking at every matter in the perspective of the life after death, and of how it will affect their interests in the next world. Whether it be an occasion of happiness or sorrow, success or failure, domination or depression, praise or condemnation, love or anger—in every state they are guided by thoughts of the hereafter, until finally these thoughts become a part of their unconscious minds. They do not cease to be mortal, but their minds come to function only on matters related to the world of immortality, making them almost forget their interest in worldly matters.

HUMILITY AND FORBEARANCE

The Prophet was a man like other men. Joyous things would please him while sad things would sadden him. Realization of the fact that he was first and foremost God's servant, however, prevented him from placing more importance on his own feelings than upon the will of God.

Towards the end of the Prophet's life Māriah Qibṭiyah bore him a beautiful and vivacious son. The Prophet named him Ibrāhīm, after his most illustrious ancestor. It was Abū Rāfi' who broke the good news to the Prophet. He was so overjoyed that he presented Abū Rāfi' with a slave. He used to take the child in his lap and play with him fondly. According to Arab custom, Ibrāhīm was given to a wet nurse, Umm Burdah bint al-Mundhir ibn Zayd Anṣārī, to be breast fed. She was the wife of a blacksmith, and her small house was usually full of smoke. Still, the Prophet used to go to the blacksmith's house to visit his son, putting up—in spite of his delicate disposition—with the smoke that used to fill his eyes and nostrils. Ibrāhīm, was just one and half years old when, in the tenth year of the Hijrah (January A.D. 632), he died. The Prophet wept on the death of his only son, as any father would. In this respect the Prophet appears like any other human being. His happiness and his grief were that of a normal father. But with all that, he fixed his heart firmly on the will of God. Even in his grief, these were the words he uttered:

> God knows, Ibrāhīm, how we sorrow at your parting. The eye weeps and the heart grieves, but we will say nothing that may displease the Lord.

It so happened that the death of Ibrāhīm coincided with a solar eclipse. From ancient times people had believed that solar and lunar eclipses were caused by the death of some important person. The people of Madinah began attributing the eclipse to the death of the Prophet's son. This caused the Prophet immense displeasure, for it suggested this predictable astronomical event was caused out of respect for his infant son. He collected the people and addressed them as follows:

> Eclipses of the sun and moon are not due to the death of any human being; they are just two of God's signs. When you see an eclipse, then you should pray to God.

On one of his journeys, the Prophet asked his companions to roast a goat. One volunteered to slaughter the animal, another to skin it, and another to cook it. The Prophet said that he would collect wood. "Messenger of God," his companions protested, "we will do all the work." "I know that you will do it," the Prophet replied, "but that would amount to discrimination, which I don't approve of. God does not like His servants to assert any superiority over their companions."

So humble was the Prophet himself that he once said:

> By God, I really do not know, even though I am God's messenger, what will become of me and what will become of you.[7]

One day Abū Dharr al-Ghifārī was sitting next to a Muslim who was black. Abū Dharr addressed him as "black man." The Prophet was very displeased on hearing this, and told Abū Dharr to make amends "Whites are not superior to blacks," he added. As soon as the Prophet admonished him, Abū Dharr became conscious of his error. He cast himself to the ground in remorse, and said to the person he had offended: "Stand up, and rub your feet on my face."

The Prophet once saw a wealthy Muslim gathering up his loose garment to maintain a distance from a poor Muslim sitting next to him. "Are you scared of his poverty clinging to you?" the Prophet remarked.

Once the Prophet had to borrow some money from a Jew by the name of Zayd ibn Sa'nah. A few days before the date fixed for the repayment of the debt, the Jew came to demand his money back. He went up to the Prophet, caught hold of his clothes, and said to him harshly: "Muḥammad, why don't you pay me my due? From what I know of the descendants of Muṭṭalib, they all put off paying their debts." 'Umar ibn al-Khaṭṭāb was with the Prophet at the time. He became very angry, scolded the Jew and was on the point of beating him up. But the Prophet just kept smiling. All he said to the Jew was: "There are still three days left for me to fulfill my promise." Then he addressed 'Umar "Zayd and I deserved better treatment from you," he said. "You should have told me to be better at paying my debts, and him to be better at demanding them. Take him with you, 'Umar, and pay him his due; in fact, give him 20 *ṣa'ahs* (about forty kilos) of dates extra because you have alarmed him with your threats." The most remarkable thing about this episode is that the Prophet could still behave with such forbearance and humility even after being established as head of the Muslim state of Madinah.

So successful was the Prophet's life that, during his lifetime, he became the ruler of the whole of Arabia right up to Palestine. Whatever he said, as the messenger of God, was accepted as law. He was revered by his people as no other man has ever been revered. When 'Urwah ibn Mas'ūd was sent to him as an envoy of the Quraysh (A.H. 6), he was amazed to see that the Muslims would not let any water used by the Prophet for ablution fall on the ground, but would catch it in their hands, and rub it on their bodies. Such was their veneration for him. Anas ibn Mālik, the Prophet's close companion says that in spite of the great love they had for the Prophet, out of respect they could not look him full in the face. According to Mughīrah, if any of the Prophet's companions had to call on him, they would first tap on the door with their fingernails. One night, when the moon was full, the Prophet lay asleep, covered in a red sheet. Jābir ibn Samrah says that sometimes he would look at the moon and sometimes at the Prophet. Eventually he came to the conclusion that the Prophet was the more beautiful of the two.

Arrows rained down on the Prophet from the enemy ranks, but his followers formed a ring around him, letting the arrows strike their own bodies. It was as though they were made of wood, not flesh and blood; indeed the arrows hung from the bodies of some of them like the thorns of a cactus tree.

Devotion and veneration of this nature can produce

vanity in a man and engender a feeling of superiority, but this was not the case with the Prophet. He lived among others as an equal. No bitter criticism or provocation would make him lose his composure. Once a desert-dweller came up to him and pulled so hard at the sheet he was wearing that it left a mark on his neck. "Muḥammad!" he said. "Give me two camel-loads of goods, for the money in your possession is not yours, nor was it your father's." "Everything belongs to God," the Prophet said, "and I am His servant." He then asked the desert-dweller, "hasn't it made you afraid, the way you treated me?" He said not. The Prophet asked him why. "Because I know that you do not requite evil with evil," the man answered. The Prophet smiled on hearing this, and had one camel-load of barley and another of dates given to him.

The Prophet lived in such awe of God that he was always a picture of humility and meekness. He spoke little and even the way he walked suggested reverence for God. Criticism never angered him. When he used to put on his clothes, he would say: "I am God's servant, and I dress as befits a servant of God." He would sit in a reverential posture to partake of food, and would say that this is how a servant of God should eat.

He was very sensitive on this issue. Once a companion started to say, "If it be the will of God, and the will of the Prophet..." The Prophet's face changed colour in anger when he heard this. "Are you trying to equate me with God?" he asked the man severely. Rather say: "If God, alone, wills." On another occasion a companion of the

Prophet said: "He that obeys God and His Prophet is rightly guided, and he who disobeys them has gone astray." "You are the worst of speakers," the Prophet observed, disliking a reference which placed him in the same pronoun as the Almighty.

Three sons were born to the Prophet, all of whom died in infancy. His four daughters, all by his first wife, Khadījah, grew to adulthood. Fāṭimah was the Prophet's youngest daughter, and he was extremely attached to her. When he returned from any journey the first thing he would do, after praying two *rak'āt*[8] in the mosque, was to visit Fāṭimah and kiss her hand and forehead. Jumai' ibn 'Umayr once asked 'Ā'ishah whom the Prophet loved most. "Fāṭimah," she replied.

But the Prophet's whole life was moulded by thoughts of the hereafter. He loved his children, but not in any worldly way. 'Alī ibn Abī Ṭālib, Fāṭimah's husband, once told Ibn 'Abdul Wāḥid a story about the Prophet's most beloved daughter. Fāṭimah's hands, he said, were blistered from constant grinding; her neck had become sore from carrying water; her clothes would become dirty from sweeping the floor. When the Prophet had received an influx of servants from some place, 'Alī suggested to his wife that she approach her father and ask for a servant. She went, but could not speak to the Prophet because of the crowd. Next day, he came to their house, and asked Fāṭimah what she had wanted to see him about. 'Alī told the Prophet the whole story, and said that he had sent her. "Fear God, Fāṭimah," the Prophet said, "Fulfill your obligations to the

Lord, and continue with your housework. And when you go to bed at night, praise God thirty-three times, and glorify Him the same number of times; exalt His name thirty-four times, and that will make a full hundred. This would be much better than having a servant.' "If that is the will of God and His Prophet," Fāṭimah replied "then so be it." This was the Prophet's only reply. He did not give her a servant.

The truth revealed to the Prophet was that this world did not spring up by itself, but was created by one God, who continues to watch over it. All men are His servants, and responsible to Him for their actions. Death is not the end of man's life; rather it is the beginning of another, permanent world, where the good will enjoy the bliss of paradise and the wicked will be cast into a raging hell. With the revelation of this truth also came the commandment to propagate it far and near. Accordingly, ascending the height of the rock of Ṣafā, the Prophet called the people together. First he made mention of the greatness of God. Then he went on to say:

> By God, as you sleep so will you die, and as you awaken so will you be raised after death: you will be taken to account for your deeds. The good will be rewarded with good and the evil with evil. And, for all eternity, the good will remain in heaven and the evil will remain in hell.

One who goes against the times in his personal life is faced with difficulties at almost every step, but these difficulties are not of an injurious nature. They may wound one's feelings, but not one's body. At the most, they are a test requiring quiet forbearance. But the position is quite different when one makes it one's mission to publicly oppose convention—when one starts telling people what they are required to do and what not to do. The Prophet was not just a believer; he was also entrusted with conveying the word of God to others. It was this latter role that brought him into headlong collision with his countrymen. All forms of adversity—from the pain of hunger to the trepidation of battle—were inflicted on him. Yet throughout the twenty-three years of his mission, he always remained just and circumspect in his actions. It was not that he had no human feelings in him and, therefore, incapable of bitterness; it was simply that his conduct was governed by the fear of God.

Three years after the Prophet's migration to Madinah, Makkan opponents mounted an assault on Madinah and the Battle of Uḥud took place. At the beginning, the Muslims held sway; but later on a mistake made by some of the Prophet's companions gave the enemy the chance to attack from the rear and sway the tide of battle in their favour. It was a desperate situation and many of the companions started fleeing from the field. The Prophet was left alone, encircled by the armed forces of the enemy. Like hungry wolves, they advanced upon him. The Prophet started calling to his companions. "Come back to me, O servants of God,' he cried. "Isn't there anyone who will sacrifice his life for my sake, who will fend these oppressors off from me and be my companion in paradise?'

Imagine how dreadful the situation must have been, with the Prophet crying for help in this manner. Some of his companions responded to his call, but such confusion reigned at the time that even these gallant soldiers were not able to protect him fully. 'Utbah ibn Abī Waqqāṣ hurled a stone at the Prophet's face, knocking out some of his lower teeth. A famed warrior of the Quraysh, 'Abdullah ibn Qumayyah, attacked him with a battle-axe, causing two links of his helmet to penetrate his face. They were so deeply embedded that Abū 'Ubaydah broke two teeth in his attempt to extract them. Then it was the turn of 'Abdullah ibn Shahāb Zuhrī, who threw a stone at the Prophet and injured his face. Bleeding profusely, he fell into a pit. When for a long period the Prophet was not seen on the field of battle, the word went around that he had been martyred. Then one of the Prophet's companions spotted him lying in the pit. Seeing him to be alive, he cried jubilantly, "The Prophet is here!" The Prophet motioned to him to be silent, so that the enemy should not know where he was lying.

In this dire situation, the Prophet uttered some curses against certain leaders of the Quraysh, especially Safwān, Suhayl and Ḥārith. How can a people who wound their prophet ever prosper!' he exclaimed. Even this was not to God's liking, and Gabriel came with this revelation:

> It is no concern of yours whether He will forgive or punish them. They are wrongdoers.[9]

This admonition was enough for the Prophet and his anger subsided. Crippled with wounds, he started praying for the very people who had wounded him. Abdullah ibn Mas'ud later recalled how the Prophet was wiping the blood from his forehead, and at the same time praying:

> Lord, forgive my people, for they know not what they do.[10]

Biographies of the Prophet are full of incidents of this nature, which show his life to be a perfect model for mankind. They show that we are God's servants, and servants we should remain in every condition. Being God's humble servants, we should always remain in a state of trepidation before our Lord and the life hereafter. Everything in the universe should serve to remind us of God. In every event we should see the hand of the Almighty, and, for us, every object should portray God's signs. In all matters of a worldly nature, we should remember that everything will finally be referred to God. Fear of hell should make us live humbly among our fellows, and longing for paradise should impress on us the significance of this world. So conscious should we be of God's greatness that any idea of demonstrating our own greatness should appear ridiculous. No criticism should provoke us and no praise should make us vain. This is the ideal human character which God displayed to us in the conduct of His Prophet.

NOTES

1. Konstan Virgil George (b 1917), *The Prophet of Islam*.
2. Qur'ān, 93:7.
3. Qur'ān, 94:1-3.
4. Hadīth of Razīn.
5. Hadīth of Ibn Hibban.
6. *Miswāk*, a stick used as a dentifrice.

7. Hadīth of al-Bukhārī.
8. *Rak'āt*, section of prayer.
9. Qur'ān, 3:128.
10. Hadīth of Muslim.

4

Sublime Character

In the Qur'ān the Prophet Muḥammad is described as being of "sublime character."[1] Here are two sayings of the Prophet which throw light on what this "sublime character" consists of:

> Never debase your character by saying that if people treat you well, you will treat them well, and if they harm you, then you will do worse to them. Rather, become accustomed to being good to those who are good to you, and not wronging those who harm you.[2]
>
> Join hands with those who break away from you, forgive those who wrong you, and be good to those who harm you.[3]

The sublime character described here was displayed—in its noblest form—by the Prophet himself. Such character is required of ordinary Muslims as an accessory, but with the Prophet it was a basic requisite.

There are two levels of character, an ordinary and a superior level. An ordinary character is based on the principle: do as you have been done by. Such a character might be termed a "knee-jerk character," for those possessed of such a character offer only reflex responses to treatment by others, breaking with those who break with them, wronging those who wrong them, and harming those who harm them.

But the higher level of character is based on the principle: do as you would be done by. Those possessed of such a character deal with both friend and foe in the same principled manner, irrespective of how they have been treated. They are reconciliatory, even joining with those who break with them. They are compassionate, even to those who seek to harm them. They are forbearing, even towards those who wrong them.

According to the French philosopher, Voltaire (1694-1778), "No one is a hero to his valet." The reason for this is that a valet has access to a person's private life, and in private life no one is perfect. Those close to a person usually do not hold him in such high esteem as those who are further off. That is why they cannot come to think of him as a hero. But this does not hold true for the Prophet Muḥammad. History shows that the closer one came to him, the more one was impressed by his fine qualities.

Once some members of the tribe of Banū Qayn ibn Jasr attacked the camp of the Banū Ma'an, a branch of the Ṭay' tribe. In the midst of plundering they captured an eight-year-old boy called Zayd, whom they subsequently sold as a slave at the fair of 'Ukāz. It so happened that the latter came into the service of the Prophet, having been presented by his buyers to Khadījah shortly before her marriage to the Prophet. The boy's father and uncle soon learnt of his whereabouts, and came to Makkah to recover him and take him home with them. They met the Prophet, and said that they would give any compensation that he required, so long as he returned the child to them. The Prophet said that he did not want any compensation; if Zayd wanted to go with them, they could take him. He called Zayd, and asked him if he knew these people. Zayd said that he did: they were his father and uncle. "They want to take you with them.' "I won't leave you to go anywhere,' Zayd replied. His father and uncle were incensed on hearing this. "What, do you prefer slavery to freedom?' they asked. "Do you want to forsake your own folk, and live amongst others?' "I cannot prefer anyone to Muḥammad.' Zayd replied, "not after seeing the qualities that he has.' They had no choice then but to go back home without him. Such was the charisma of the Prophet.

This incident, which occurred before the commencement of the Prophet's mission, reveals the tenderness that was inherent in his nature. The Qur'ān has referred to this characteristic of his in the following words:

> It was thanks to God's mercy that you were lenient to them. Had you been cruel and hard-hearted, they would surely have deserted you.[4]

It was this magnanimity of the Prophet that gave him the power to capture people's hearts: the closer one came to him, the more one would be won over by his noble character.

The Prophet once said: "Honouring ties of relationship does not mean honouring your ties with those who honour their ties with you; it means honouring your ties with those who sever their ties with you.' The well-known case of 'Ā'ishah, wife of the Prophet and daughter of Abū Bakr, being accused of adultery, is an apt illustration of this principle.

This accusation—brought against 'Ā'ishah when she was accidently left behind while returning from the expedition to Banu al-Mustaliq (A.H. 6), then rescued by a young companion of the Prophet by the name of Ṣafwān ibn al-Mu'aṭṭal—was absolutely slanderous. Indeed, the episode has become famous in Islamic history as the "case of the slander.' One of the persons responsible for fabricating it and then spreading it far and wide was a relative of Abū Bakr named Misṭaḥ. When Abū Bakr learnt that Misṭaḥ was one of those who had defamed his innocent daughter, he cut off the allowance that he used to grant Misṭaḥ as a needy relative. When Abū Bakr took this step, God revealed this verse of the Qur'ān to His Prophet:

> Let not the honourable and rich among you swear not to give to their kindred, the poor, and those who have migrated for the cause of God. Rather, let them pardon and forgive. Do you not wish God to forgive you? He is Forgiving, Merciful.[5]

That is, a person who is in need should not be denied financial assistance because of his misconduct. Rather one should pardon him and continue to help him.

A man came up and insulted Abū Bakr one day when he was sitting with the Prophet. Abū Bakr listened but remained silent. The man continued to abuse him. Again

Abū Bakr still held his peace. When the man kept on repeating his foul tirade, Abū Bakr could contain himself no longer, and answered back. On hearing this, the Prophet immediately got up and left. "Why have you left your place, Prophet of God?' Abū Bakr enquired. "As long as you remained silent, Abū Bakr,' the Prophet replied, "God's angel was answering for you. But as soon as you burst out, the angel left.' Thus the Prophet illustrated that God requites any wrong done to one, as long as one does not oneself retaliate. To one who seeks revenge God turns a deaf ear. Obviously retribution will be more complete if it is left to God.

The Prophet once borrowed some money from a Jewish scholar. After a few days the Jew came to demand payment of his debt. "At the moment, I have nothing to pay you with,' the Prophet told him. "I won't let you go until you have paid me back,' the Jew retorted. And so he stayed there, from morning until night, holding the Prophet captive. At this time the Prophet was the established ruler of Madinah: he had the power to take measures against the Jew. His companions, indeed, wanted to rebuke the man and chase him away. But the Prophet forbade them to take any action. "A Jew is holding you captive,' protested one of them. "True,' the Prophet replied, "but the Lord has forbidden us to wrong anyone." Night turned to morning. With the light of dawn, the Jew's eyes opened. He was profoundly moved on seeing the Prophet's tolerance, notwithstanding the latter's power to take action, and he thereupon embraced Islam. This Jew, a rich man, had detained the Prophet the day before on account of a few pence; but the Prophet's noble conduct had such an impact on him that now he was willing to give all his wealth to the Prophet, saying, "Spend it as you please.'

'Abdullah ibn Abī al-Hasma' was once engaged in a transaction with the Prophet. It had not yet been completed when he had to go home on some urgent business. "Wait here,' he said to the Prophet. "We'll settle this affair when I come back.' When he reached home, he became so engrossed in certain tasks that he forgot his promise. He remembered it three days later and went back to that place where he found the Prophet still waiting. All he said to 'Abdullah ibn Abī al-Ḥasma' was: "You have given me a lot of trouble; I have been waiting here for three days.' Such conduct has a powerful magnetism, which even the most obdurate person cannot resist.

Once a group of Rabbis came to the Prophet. When they entered, instead of giving the normal '*Assalāmu 'alaykum*' greeting (Peace be upon you), they said "*Assāmu 'alaykum*', meaning "death to you.' 'Ā'ishah heard this, and was not able to contain herself. "Death to you instead,' she said. "May God damn you.' The Prophet told 'Ā'ishah not to answer back in this manner. "God is gentle,' he said, "and He likes gentleness in every matter.' In truth, there is no more effective method of winning a person's heart than by returning soft words for harsh. It is possible to withstand armed onslaught, but noble conduct is a force in itself that no one can resist. It is sure to prevail in all situations.

What a terrible thing it must have been for a man such as the Prophet when, as night was falling, he found the urchins of Ṭā'if chasing him out of town and pelting him with stones. Ṭā'if was the place where the Ḥijāz aristocracy used to while away their summer days and the Prophet had made the fifty-mile trip from Makkah to call them to Islam. But the lords of Ṭā'if did not listen to his well-meaning words; instead they set the street-urchins on him, and they kept on chasing him until night had cast a veil between them and God's Prophet. His body was covered in wounds. Bleeding from head to foot and utterly exhausted, he took refuge in a vineyard. This, even for the most ordinary of men, would have been a traumatic experience. The Prophet once told his wife, 'Ā'ishah, that it had been the hardest night of his life. But even at this gravest of moments, the Prophet did not wish his enemies any harm. All he said was: "Lord, guide them, for they know not what they do.' Such was the noble character of the Prophet, and it was this nobility which finally subdued his opponents and brought the whole of Arabia within the Islamic fold. The force of his sublime spirit was enough to conquer all in its path. No prejudice, antagonism or contumacy could withstand the magical power of good that was embodied in his person.

ABSENCE OF ACRIMONY

The Prophet had made peace with the Quraysh at Ḥudaybiyyah (A.H. 6) on three conditions: one was that if any Makkan accepted Islam and wanted to settle in Madinah, he must be surrendered to the Quraysh. But if any of the Madinan Muslims should go to Makkah, the Makkans would not send them back to Madinah. No sooner had this treaty been made than a Makkan youth by the name of Abū Jandal escaped from Makkah and came to Ḥudaybiyyah , his body bearing weals and bruises where chains had abraded his skin. "Save me from the enemy!' he cried to the Muslims. This was an extremely sensitive moment. The companions of the Prophet drew their swords. The sight of Abū Jandal had aroused their feelings to such a degree that most of them wanted to break the treaty and save his life. The Quraysh meanwhile reminded the Prophet that this was an occasion on which he would be obliged to abide by the pact that had been made between them. Finally the Prophet decided that he could not go back on the terms that had been agreed upon. Painful as this decision was for the Muslims, Abū Jandal was returned to the Quraysh. Ostensibly the Prophet was putting an innocent victim of oppression back into the clutches of his oppressors. But, in effect, he was acting on the highest of moral principles. The oppressors in turn were confounded and awestruck by such uniquely moral conduct, and then it became no ordinary matter for them to take Abū Jandal away and imprison him; rather the event became symbolic of their own degradation in contrast to the moral ascendancy of Islam. The result of this was that the people of Makkah were won over by the high ethical standards of Islam which many of them started to embrace. Abū Jandal's very presence in Makkah became a living testament to truth of the Prophet's faith. Even as a prisoner, Abū Jandal began to appear to his captives as a threat to their national security. Eventually they deemed it prudent to free him and deport him from Makkah.

While the Prophet was living in Madinah, where he had attained religious and political leadership, he sent some riders to Najd, the inhabitants of which were his sworn enemies. On the way, they came across the ruler of the city of Yamāmah, Thamāmah ibn Uthāl. They took him captive and brought him to Madinah, where they tied him up against a pillar of the mosque. The Prophet came to enquire after him. "If you kill me," Thamāmah said, "my people will avenge my blood; and if you release me, I will always be indebted to you. If it's money you want, then I am ready to give you as much as you desire." The Prophet did not kill Thamāmah physically, but by his humane treatment he conquered the man's soul. After his release, Thamāmah went to a nearby garden, had a bath, and then returned to the mosque. People wondered what he had come back for. But when he proclaimed his conversion to Islam by pronouncing the testimony of faith in a loud voice, people realized that, by releasing Thamāmah, the Prophet had in effect taken him captive for all time. Thamāmah then went on a pilgrimage to Makkah. When the people of Makkah heard of his conversion, they told him that he had lost his faith. "I have not lost my faith," Thamāmah answered. "Rather I have adopted the faith of God and His Prophet." Thamāmah, moreover, became a source of strength to Islam. Yamāmah was one of the main places from which the people of Makkah used to collect grain.

Thamāmah told them that without the permission of the Prophet Muḥammad, he would not provide them with a single grain. The case of Thamāmah shows that noble conduct—though it may appear to have no practical value—is something which can win the world.

Adopting a high code of ethics mean practising what one preaches; treating the weak with the same courtesy and deference as one shows to the strong; setting the same standards for oneself as one sets for others; never budging from one's principles; maintaining a high moral bearing even when others stoop to the depths of degradation. From this point of view, the prophet of Islam stood at the highest pinnacle of human ethics, never abandoning the lofty standards that he preached. Expediency or dispute could not make him resort to unethical conduct. No evidence could be more substantial in this regard than that of his closest companions.

Sa'īd ibn Ḥishām belonged to the generation immediately following that of the Prophet Muḥammad, on whom be peace. He once asked 'Ā'ishah, the Prophet's widow, about her late husband's character. "He was a personification of the Qur'ān', 'Ā'ishah replied. That is to say, the Prophet moulded his own life in accordance with the ideal pattern of life which he presented to others in the form of the Qur'ān. Anas ibn Mālik served the Prophet for ten years. He says that the Prophet never even rebuked him. "When I did something, he never questioned my manner of doing it; and when I did not do something, he never questioned my failure to do it. He was the most good-natured of all men." According to 'Ā'ishah, the Prophet never beat a servant, a woman or anyone else. To be sure, he fought for what was righteous. Yet, when he had to choose between two alternatives, he would take the easier course, provided it did not involve sin: no one was more careful to avoid sin than he. He never sought revenge—on his own behalf—of any wrong done to him personally. Only if divine commandments had been broken would he mete out retribution for the sake of God.

It was this conduct on the part of the Prophet which made him respected even in the eyes of his enemies. His followers stood by him through all kinds of hardship and misfortune. He was as loved in times of oppression as in times of victory and supremacy. His immediate followers found him without blemish—just as he appeared from afar. He provided mankind with an inimitable model of exemplary conduct. The principles on which the Prophet based his life were in the same mould as his sublime disposition. These principles never wavered. They formed a permanent part of his life. He applied them in equal measure to those who followed his path and to those who had harmed or aggrieved him.

Even in pre-Islamic times—known as the Age of Ignorance—the office of gate-keeper of the Ka'bah had been held in high esteem. From ancient times the task had been allotted to one particular family. In the time of the Prophet Muḥammad a member of that family, 'Uthmān ibn Ṭalḥah retained it in his custody.

Al-Bukhārī, the greatest compiler of traditions of the

Prophet, has related how the Prophet, before his emigration to Madinah, once desired to go inside the Ka'bah for worship. He asked 'Uthmān for the keys, so that he could open the gate. 'Uthmān refused and insulted the Prophet. 'Uthmān,' the Prophet said, 'perhaps you will see that one day I will have these keys in my hands. I will have the power to dispose of them as I will.' "It will be a day of disgrace and woe for the Quraysh when the keys of the Ka'bah are handed over to one like you,' 'Uthmān retorted.

Then the time came when the Prophet conquered Makkah and reigned supreme there. The first thing he did on entering the holy city was to go to the House of God. Seven times he circumambulated the Ka'bah. Then he summoned 'Uthmān ibn Ṭalḥah. According to one account, 'Uthmān had become a Muslim during the period in between the peace of Ḥudaybiyyah and the Conquest of Makkah. The Prophet took the keys from him, opened the gate of the Ka'bah, and went inside. He remained there for a while, demolishing the idols that remained standing within its walls.

Then he came outside, holding the keys in his hands. On his lips was this verse of the Qur'ān:

> God commands you to hand back your trusts to their rightful owners.[6]

It was then that 'Alī ibn Abī Ṭālib, the Prophet's cousin and son-in-law, stood up: "God bless you,' he said to the Prophet, "but we Banū Ḥāshim have always been entrusted with the task of bearing water for pilgrims. Now is the time to take over the office of gatekeeper as well.' The Prophet did not reply to 'Alī, and asked where 'Uthmān ibn Ṭalḥah was. When he came forward, the Prophet handed the keys over to him. 'Uthmān,' he said, "here are your keys. This is a day of righteousness and fulfilment of promises. They will remain in your family from generation to generation. It is only a wrongdoer who will take them away from you.'

This action of the Prophet illustrates that Muslims should be meticulous in fulfilling obligations and returning trusts. Even if they have been treated acrimoniously by those with whom they are dealing, they should still pay them their full due. However much it may hurt them, they should never deny people their rights.

When worldly people gain power, the first thing they do is punish their opponents, removing them from their posts and installing their own henchmen instead. All people who come to power think in terms of supporters or opponents. Promoting supporters and demoting opponents is an essential part of their policy. But when the Prophet of Islam gained power in Arabia, he did quite the opposite. He did not look at matters in terms of supporters and opponents; he considered only what was right and fair. He buried all grudges and dealt with everyone as justice and compassion would demand.

NOTES

1. Qur'ān, 68:5
2. Ḥadīth quoted in *Mishkāt al-Maṣābīḥ*.
3. Ḥadīth of Razīn.
4. Qur'ān, 3:159.
5. Qur'ān, 24:22.
6. Qur'ān, 4:58

5

Lessons of the Prophet's Life

THE REWARDS OF RESTRAINT

In the Qur'ān, these words have been addressed to the faithful:

> You have a good example in God's Apostle for anyone who looks to God and the Last Day and remembers God always.[1]

It is clear from this verse that, in the life of the Prophet Muḥammad, there is a perfect example for every human being. But the only real beneficiaries will be those whose apprehension of God is already profound, whose hopes and aspirations centre on God, whose lives are lived in fear of the punishment of the Lord. Those who cherish the thought of eternal bliss and truly yearn for it with every fibre of their beings will be the ones to learn from the Prophet's example.

Why should this be so? The reason is that one has to be sincere in one's search for truth if one is going to find it. If one "looks to God and the Last Day," one will be sincere with regard to them. Sincerity will enable one to see the life of the Prophet in true perspective, and draw the right lessons from it.

This point can be understood from one example. The following saying of the Prophet is related in the Ḥadīth:

> One killed in defence of his property is a martyr. One killed in defence of his life is a martyr. One killed in defence of his religion is a martyr. One killed in defence of his family is a martyr.[2]

As is clear from the text, this *ḥadīth* is about being "killed," not about fighting as such. The Prophet did not mean that whenever there is a threat to one's property, life, religion or family, one should immediately resort to arms, even if one is slain as a result. What he meant was that if, on any of these grounds, a believer is slain, then his or her death is one of martyrdom. The *ḥadīth*, then, is not an incitement to fight; it is a promise of martyrdom to those who are slain.

Those who are not sincere in their attitude to religion, however, who are more concerned with giving their own personal whims the stamp of prophetic sanction, will take the words of the *ḥadīth* and use them to justify their selfish quarrels and nationalistic conflicts. Islam, they will say, teaches you to stand up for your rights like a man; it urges you to fight in defence of your faith, your life and property, your family and relatives. If you are victorious, then you have achieved your ends; and if you are defeated, then you are a martyr, and it is only a fortunate minority who attain the heights of martyrdom.

But those who fears God will look at the matter

soberly. After intense mind-searching they will ask themselves: if you are required to fight in defence of your property, life, religion and family, why then are there cases in the Prophet's life of his not doing so? Why, in the face of manifest oppression, did the Prophet—on many occasions—adopt a passive attitude and exhort others to do the same?

The following incident, for instance, has been recorded by Ibn Hishām on the authority of Abū 'Uthmān al-Nahdī. When Ṣuhayb decided to emigrate to Madinah, the Quraysh said to him: "You came to us in an abject and destitute state. You became rich while with us, until eventually you reached your present state of wealth. Do you think we will let you run away and take everything with you? If so you are mistaken!" Ṣuhayb enquired, "If I hand over all of my wealth to you will you let me go then?" They said they would, so Ṣuhayb gave them everything he had. When the Prophet heard about this, he said: "Good for Ṣuhayb! He has made a fine profit."

If the previously mentioned *ḥadīth* means—in an absolute sense—that one should fight and give one's life in defence of one's property under any conditions whatsoever, the Prophet should then have condemned Ṣuhayb's failure rather than felicitated him on his success.

The case of Abū Jandal (see Part I, Chapter IV) also illustrates this point. When, at Ḥudaybiyyah, in the year of A.H. 6 during peace negotiations with the Quraysh young Abū Jandal, bloodstained and in chains, pleaded with the Muslims not to send him back to the idolaters now that he had accepted Islam, the Prophet ordered that, according to the terms of the treaty which had been agreed upon, he be sent back to Makkah. "Abū Jandal," he said, "be patient. God will grant you, and those persecuted along with you, release from your suffering."

If the previously mentioned *ḥadīth* enjoined on one to fight and be martyred irrespective of the conditions, the Prophet would not have urged patient resignation on Abū Jandal; rather he would have told him to seek martyrdom; he and his companions would have fought with great zeal at Abū Jandal's side.

During the same Ḥudaybiyyah encounter, the Quraysh told the Prophet that they would not let him enter Makkah that year. Accepting this, the Prophet returned to Madinah, without insisting on visiting the House of God. This was an entirely religious affair; indeed, the Prophet had acted on divine inspiration in setting out for Makkah with his companions. Even so, he withdrew. If the previously mentioned *ḥadīth* had referred to fighting and being martyred in an absolute sense, the Prophet would have insisted on visiting the House of God that year, whether he had succeeded in his purpose or been martyred in the process.

'Ammar ibn Yāsir and his parents were slaves of the Banū Makhzūm tribe in Makkah when they accepted Islam. Their conversion was complete anathema to the Banū Makhzūm. They would take the family out to the desert in the heat of noon and lay them down on the blazing sand, where they would savagely torture them. They even went so far as to murder ʻAmmār's mother. Relating this incident, this is what the Prophet's biographer, Ibn Hishām, writes:

> When the Prophet passed them by, from what I have heard, he would say to them: "Be patient, family of Yāsir, heaven is your promised land."[3]

If the *ḥadīth* mentioned above was meant in an absolute sense, then the Prophet's advice to Yāsir would have been tantamount to encouraging cowardice. The Prophet would then have never given such advice. Rather he would have urged Yāsir to fight and be martyred. He himself would have taken up this holy cause, whether the result had been Yāsir's release, or his own martyrdom.

The truth is that the example of the Prophet is open to more than one interpretation, and it may happen that the wrong—or right—interpretation is made. Only if one is sincere will one interpret the situation correctly, and this can only be achieved through the realism that comes from the fear of God.

When sincere people consider these incidents in the Prophet's life, questions such as those posed here are bound to crop up in their minds. They are not just seeking a meaning which will serve their ends; rather they are seeking to ascertain the exact nature of the example imparted by the Prophet. This approach keeps them from misinterpretation. They will look at the matter objectively, and God's grace will enable them to arrive at the heart of the matter. They will see that the secret lies in realizing one thing: that trifling losses must be endured for the sake of great gain.

The consideration that should be uppermost in a believer's mind is what serves the interests of Islam, not their own personal interests. Their preoccupation must be with preaching the message of Islam. If there is a clash between personal and preaching interests, then preaching of the faith must come first. It was in the interest of his preaching mission that the Prophet advised patience in the situations mentioned above. The Prophet endured all kinds of personal, financial and domestic losses in his life, just to ensure the continuation of his efforts to spread the faith. He knew that the Muslims' success in this life and the next lay in their pressing on with missionary work.

When one has a purpose in life, that purpose assumes overriding importance. One will bear losses in life in order to achieve it. In the absence of such a purpose one becomes preoccupied with every trivial matter. Seeking to avoid small losses, one has to put up with even greater ones. The preachers of God's word are the most purposeful people in the world: they endure small losses in pursuit of their greater aim. They avoid clashing with others on any issue, for this would be detrimental to their missionary work. They only act when forced to do so in self-defence, for this does not interfere with their greater goal.

Bearing this in mind, let us look at some incidents of great moral significance, which occurred during the life of the Prophet Muḥammad.

NEVER YIELDING TO DESPAIR

The tribal system prevalent in the time of the Prophet was one which afforded protection to individuals. It was seldom that anyone could survive without it. At the beginning of the period he spent in Makkah, the Prophet Muḥammad, on whom be peace, enjoyed the protection of his uncle, Abū Ṭālib, chieftain of the Banu Hashim. In the tenth year of his mission, Abū Ṭālib died, and his mantle descended upon Abū Lahab. Since Abū Lahab refused to extend any protection to him, the Prophet began seeking the protection of some other tribe, so that he could continue his preaching work. It was for this purpose that he went to Ṭā'if.

Along with Zayd ibn Ḥārithah, the Prophet made the 65 mile journey to Ṭā'if, a fertile oasis south-east of Makkah. He had some relatives in the town, but at that time power rested with three individuals: 'Abd Yalayl, Mas'ūd and Ḥabīb. The Prophet met all three of them, and all three refused to join him, or even extend their protection. "I will tear the curtain of the holy Ka'bah, if God has made you His Prophet," one of them said. "Couldn't God find anyone else to send as His Prophet," added another sneeringly. "I swear that I won't speak to you!" said the third. "It would be an insult to you for me to do so if you are a true prophet, and an insult to myself if you are false in your claims."[4]

Dispirited, the Prophet set out on the return journey. But still the people of Ṭā'if did not leave him alone. They set the urchins upon him, and a volley of stone-throwing and abuse drove him out of town. Zayd tried to shield the Prophet with his blanket, but with no success: he was wounded from head to foot.

Some way out of town, there was a vineyard belonging

to two brothers by the name of 'Utbah and Shaybah. It was dusk when the Prophet reached there, and he took refuge in it. His body was covered in wounds, but on his lips were prayers. "Lord," he cried, "help me; do not leave me to fend for myself."

'Utbah and Shaybah were both idolators; but when they saw the Prophet's condition, they took pity on him. They had a Christian slave by the name of 'Addās. They told him to fetch a few bunches of grapes, and take them in a bowl before their guest. 'Addās did as he was told: he brought some grapes to the Prophet and requested him to partake of them. The Prophet recited the name of God as he took them in his hand to eat. 'Addās looked at the Prophet's face. "By God," he said, "it is not usual for people in this land to utter these words." The Prophet asked 'Addās where he came from, and what his religion was. 'Addās replied that he was a Christian, and hailed from Nineveh in Iraq. "So you are from the town of the good Jonah, son of Matthew," the Prophet observed. "How do you know Jonah, son of Matthew?" 'Addās retorted. "He was a prophet, and so am I," the Prophet said. On hearing this, 'Addās bowed before the Prophet, kissing his head, hands and feet.

'Utbah and Shaybah were looking on. "Look," they said to one another. "This fellow has corrupted our servant." "Shame on you." they said to 'Addās when he returned. "What were you kissing the fellow's head, hands and feet for?" "Master," 'Addās replied. "There is nothing greater than him on the face of the earth. He told me something that no one but a Prophet can reveal." "Shame on you!"

they repeated. "Be careful that he does not turn you away from your religion; for your religion is better than his."

In a single journey, God's Prophet was treated in three different ways by three different groups of people: one pelted him with stones; a second extended hospitality to him; a third acknowledged his prophethood.

There is a great lesson to be learnt from this event—namely, that there is no end to possibilities in this world. If you stand in an open plain, there is sure to be a tree's shade in which you can find rest. If you are treated cruelly by some, do not despair, for if you adhere to the path of truth, and do not respond in a negative way to such treatment by others, God will surely come to your assistance. Some may not rally to your cause, but you are sure to find a place in the hearts of others.

THE PROPHET FORCED INTO EXILE

The Prophet Muḥammad met with dire opposition when he started his preaching mission in Makkah in the year A.D. 609. When he presented the message of Islam before the disbelievers of Makkah, they proudly pointed out that they were already involved in great religious work. "Why should we become Muslims," they protested, "when we already look after the Sacred Mosque, and give water to the pilgrims?" This verse of the Qur'ān was revealed in condemnation of their argument:

> Do you pretend that He who gives a drink to the pilgrims and pays a visit to the Sacred Mosque is as worthy as a man who believes in God and the Last

> Day and strives for God's cause? These are not held equal by God. He does not guide the wrongdoers. Those that have embraced the faith and migrated from their homes and striven for God's cause with their wealth and their persons are held in higher regard by God. It is they who shall triumph.[5]

Initially, the message of the Prophet of Islam had nothing but conceptual truth behind it. It was an abstract message, with no material grandeur attached. The Ka'bah in Makkah, on the other hand, had assumed the status of an institution, backed up by grand architecture and glorious historical traditions. To associate oneself with the Ka'bah was socially acceptable; it had even become a symbol of pride. To associate oneself with the message of the Prophet of Islam, meanwhile, amounted to belief in a religion which had not yet come into its own and had no material benefits to offer.

The people of Makkah, therefore, did whatever they could to thwart him and he was subjected to torment upon torment. But his mission continued to gain ground, and finally the message of Islam reached the people of Madinah, the majority of whom accepted Islam. Together with the Prophet, other Muslims were also persecuted in Makkah. The Prophet told them to go to Madinah, where they would be received by their Muslim brethren, who were ready to give them succour. One by one, the Muslims started emigrating to Madinah. When the Quraysh heard about this scheme, they made efforts to prevent the Muslims from leaving Makkah: some they beat up, some they took captive; but somehow most of the Muslims managed to reach their refuge in Madinah.

Finally (A.D. 622) came the Prophet's turn. The Quraysh realized that, with the rest of the Muslims safely installed in Madinah, it would not be long before the Prophet himself joined them. Leaders of all the tribes of the Quraysh, except the Banū Hashim, met in the great hall of Quṣayy ibn Kilāb's house, where all such meetings were held. Various proposals were put forward, but finally all agreed that a person from every tribe should attack and kill Muḥammad: his blood would thus be divided over all eleven tribes; the Banu Hashim, the tribe to which the Prophet belonged, being unable to fight with all of them, would accept compensation instead. The next night, they surrounded the Prophet's house, waiting for the Prophet to emerge so that they could pounce on him and kill him.

The Prophet knew exactly what was going on. Quietly, he continued his preparations. That night, according to plan, he left Makkah along with Abū Bakr. The Prophet realized that when news of his departure reached the Quraysh, they would send search parties in pursuit of him. So he and Abū Bakr hid in a cave of Mount Thawr, four miles out of Makkah. They planned to stay there a few days, until the Quraysh called off their search, and the two could continue their journey to Madinah.

The Quraysh horsemen started looking everywhere for the Prophet. It was not long before one brigade reached his hideout in Mount Thawr. There they were, armed and standing at the mouth of the cave: the Prophet and Abū Bakr could even see their feet. Abū Bakr, sensing the critical danger they were in, said to the Prophet: "The enemy are upon us." "Don't worry," the Prophet reassured him: "God is with us. We are only two," he continued calmly, "but how do you rate two men who have God as a third companion?"

ABSOLUTE TRUST IN GOD

Another such incident occurred during an expedition made by the Prophet known as Dhāt al-Riqā' (A.H. 4). Recorded in al-Bukhārī, as well as in biographies of the Prophet, it is related by Jābir.

> "Would you like me to kill Muḥammad?" This terrible question was put by a member of the Banū Ghaṭfān tribe, Ghaurath ibn al-Ḥārith, to his tribes people. The answer was overwhelmingly in the affirmative, but they wanted to know how it would be possible. Ghaurath replied with confidence, "I shall catch him unawares and kill him!" And this is exactly what he set out to do. When he reached the camp of Muḥammad and his companions, he chose his moment well. He waited until the Prophet and his companions had settled down to rest, unarmed, in the shade of the trees. The Prophet lay all alone, and his sword dangled from the branches above him. Ghaurath darted forward, snatched the weapon, then bore down on the Prophet. "Who will save you from me?" he challenged, no doubt savouring this moment. "God," the Prophet replied quite simply. Daunted, Ghaurath said, "Take a look at the sword I am holding! Don't you fear it?" "Of course not," the Prophet said. "Why should I fear it, when I know that God will save me?" The supreme confidence of the Prophet's reply proved too much

> for Ghaurath, and his courage left him. Instead of attacking the Prophet, he put the sword back in its sheath and returned it to him. The Prophet then made him sit down, and called his companions. When they arrived, he told them the whole story. Ghaurath was petrified, expecting to be killed at any moment. But the Prophet let him go without inflicting any punishment on him.[6]

Those who put absolute trust in God do not fear anything or anyone. The faith that God, a Live and All-Powerful Being, is always there to help you, makes you bold in the face of every other power. A person's greatest strength, when faced with an enemy, is fearlessness. Have no fear of any foe, and the foe will start fearing you.

REACHING A CONSENSUS

Shortly before the Battle of Badr (A.H. 2), the Quraysh had sent a huge caravan of merchandise, along with sixty men, to Syria. Although the Quraysh were subsequently defeated by the Muslims at Badr, their commander, Abū Sufyān, successfully managed to steer this caravan, in which the people of Makkah had placed all their capital, home to Makkah by a coastal route. Defeat at Badr had left the Quraysh thirsty for revenge, Muḥammad and his followers, and their leaders met in Dār al-Nadwah (The Hall of Convention), where it was unanimously decided that the partners in the caravan should take their capital only, leaving the profits to be devoted to preparations for war. The profits amounted to 50,000 dinars, a huge sum in those days.

The Quraysh made elaborate preparations, and in A.H. 3, advanced on Madinah.

It was then that the Battle of Uḥud took place, just three years after the Prophet's migration to Madinah. When news of the Quraysh's advance reached the Prophet, he called his companions together. Most of them were inclined to meet the attack from within the city. The youthful element among them, however, were strongly opposed to this. If we remain in the city, they contended, then the enemy will interpret it as a sign of cowardice and weakness: the fight should be taken to them, outside the city. 'Abdullah ibn Ubayy, however, concurred, with the opinion of the leading companions.[7]

There were good grounds for the view that the attack should be met from within the city. The geography of Madinah had all the makings of a natural defence system. To the south were orchards of date-palms, so thickly clustered as to make an attack impossible from that side. To the east and west high mountains provided a natural barrier to any invader. There was only one front, then, from which Madinah could be attacked. The city itself was a natural fortress. To leave it amounted to exposing oneself to enemy attack on all four sides, whereas from within the city there was only one front that would have to be defended. And indeed Madinah's favourable location was subsequently taken advantage of in the battle which later came to be known as the Battle of the Trench, in which the entire city was protected by the simple expedient of digging a trench on the open front to the north-west of the town.

Although most of the leading companions, as well as 'Abdullah ibn Ubayy, were in favour of meeting the attack from within the city, the Prophet decided to accede to the wishes of the younger Muslims: along with an army of one thousand, he left the city and set off for Uḥud. 'Abdullah ibn Ubayy was deeply offended to find that his obviously wise and proper advice, had been overruled. With a heavy heart, he went along with the army, but before the Muslims reached Uḥud, he, along with 300 followers, turned back. "He agreed with them and not with me." 'Abdullah ibn Ubayy lamented, "so I fail to see why we should destroy ourselves on this field of battle."[8]

The Muslims' defeat at Uḥud vindicated the opinion of those who had been in favour of meeting the attack from within the city. Accordingly, this strategy was duly adopted at the Battle of the Trench (A.H. 5). All the leading companions of the Prophet, however, forgot their disagreement and remained in the Muslim army. Despite incurring heavy losses from having to bear the brunt of the battle, they fought valiantly alongside the Prophet. Only 'Abdullah ibn Ubayy separated himself from the Muslim force, and for this reason he became known as the "Leader of the Hypocrites." In principle, 'Abdullah ibn Ubayy's opinion had been correct; it was also borne out by experience on the field of battle; but, although he was in the right, his disobedience incurred God's displeasure, and was considered a form of transgression.

Islam attaches great importance to consultation. Everyone has a right to put forward his or her point of view. But no policy can be effectively pursued if everyone expects their own view to prevail, no matter what the circumstances. Only one course has to be followed, so when there is disagreement over what that course should be, not everybody's view can be accommodated. True Muslims, then, should, after offering their opinion, forget about what they think, and follow the directives of decision-makers as if their decisions were their own.

There is no greater sacrifice than that of one's own opinion. Like a building, which can only be constructed if a considerable number of bricks are buried in the ground, so a strong society can only come into being if individuals are ready to bury their own personal opinions—to act in unity with others despite their disagreements. This is the only foundation on which a community of individuals can be formed; it is as necessary to the foundation of human society as bricks are to the foundation of a building.

During the year A.H. 8, an expedition was made to Muta. Part of Muḥammad ibn Jarīr al-Ṭabarī's description of the expedition runs like this:

> Abū Qatadah tells us that the Prophet sent an army to Muta. He appointed Zayd ibn Ḥārithah as commander; if he was martyred then Ja'far ibn Abū Ṭālib was to take over; and if he in turn was killed in action the choice should fall on 'Abdullah ibn Rawahah. Ja'far jumped up when he heard the Prophet's decision, and said that he would not serve under Zayd. The Prophet told him to go along, "for you do not know what is best for you." Then the army set off.[9]

A believer is no angel; he is a mortal human being like any other. Still, there is an enormous difference between a believer and any other human being. Non-believers do not know how to go back on mistaken and perverse notions once they have them fixed in their minds. Right or wrong, they stick to their opinions. They follow their own desires rather than sound reason.

A believer's attitude, on the other hand, should be quite different. True believers are those who set themselves straight when they are shown to be on a wrong course, who correct themselves when their mistakes are pointed out. Rather than being set in their opinions, they should always be open to criticism, always ready to rectify themselves, even when this means doing something that they do not want to do.

A believer, then, is one who submits to truth, while disbelievers submit to nothing but their own selves.

AVOIDING CONFRONTATION

The year after the Battle of the Trench, in A.H. 6, the Prophet Muḥammad, on whom be peace, had a dream in Madinah. In it he saw himself and his companions visiting the House of God in Makkah. His companions were very pleased to hear this, for it meant that, after a lapse of six years, they would soon be going to Makkah and visiting the Holy Ka'bah. In accordance with this dream, the Prophet set out for the holy city with 1400 of his companions. When they reached Ghadīr Ashṭaṭ, they heard that the news of their journey had reached the Quraysh. Indignant at the idea of the Muslims visiting the House of God, they had amassed an army, and vowed to prevent Muḥammad and his companions from entering Makkah, although it was absolutely contrary to Arab tradition to prevent anyone from visiting the Ka'bah. The Prophet was acting under divine inspiration: perhaps that is why he remained calm when he heard of the Quraysh's reaction. He was informed by his spies that Khālid ibn al-Walīd, intent on blocking the Muslims' path, had advanced with two hundred cavalrymen to Ghamīm. On hearing this, the Prophet changed route, deviating from a well-frequented path to a little-known and arduous route, which led him to Ḥudaybiyyah. In this way he avoided clashing with Khālid's army. This is how the historian Ibn Hishām describes the events:

> "Who can show us a path not occupied by the Quraysh?" the Prophet asked. Someone volunteered to do so. He then proceeded to guide the Muslims by a route which led through arduous, rocky and mountainous passes. The Muslims had great difficulty in crossing these passes, but when they had done so, and emerged upon an open plain, the Prophet called on them to seek forgiveness of God, and turn to Him. This they did, and the Prophet said that this was the word of forgiveness which the Israelites had been called upon to utter, but they had failed to do so.[10]

This was indeed a trying time for the Muslims, but they had to face their trial with patience and forebearance. This was the path laid down for them by God. Even the slightest hesitation to follow that path was to be considered a transgression, for which forgiveness had to be sought. That is why the Prophet urged his followers to repent and seek forgiveness for any weakness or irritability they may have shown at that taxing time. Difficulties were to be faced with fortitude. No impulse was to cause one to deviate from the path of God.

In order to survey the situation the Prophet made a halt at Ḥudaybiyyah which is situated nine miles from Makkah. From Ḥudaybiyyah he sent one Kharāsh ibn Umayyah on camelback to inform the Makkans that the Muslims had come to visit the House of God, not to do battle. On reaching Makkah, Kharāsh's camel was slaughtered, and attempts were made to murder him as well, but somehow he managed to escape and return to Ḥudaybiyyah. The Prophet then sent 'Uthmān to appeal to the Makkans to refrain from hostilities, and tell them that the Muslims would return quietly to Madinah after performing the rites of 'Umrah.[11] The Makkans paid no heed, and took him prisoner. Later Mikraz ibn Ḥafṣ along with fifty men attacked the Muslims camp at night, raining stones and arrows down on the pilgrims. Mikraz was captured, but no action was taken against him: he was released unconditionally. Then, as the Muslims were praying in the early morning, eighty men attacked them from Tan'īm. They were also taken captive and then allowed to go free unconditionally.

Lengthy negotiations with the Quraysh ensued. Finally, a truce was made between the two sides. At first sight this truce amounted to an outright victory for the Quraysh and defeat for the Muslims. The Prophet's followers could not understand how, when God had given them tidings of a visit to the House of God, the Prophet could have agreed to return to Madinah without performing the visit. They would be allowed to come the following year, but would have to leave the city after a stay of only three days. Humiliating clauses such as this, exacerbating as they were for the Muslims, were all accepted unquestioningly by the Prophet. It seemed to be an acceptance of defeat.

The Quraysh deliberately acted in an aggressive manner in order to offend the Prophet. They wanted to provoke him into initiating hostilities, so that they could find an excuse for fighting him. To prevent a visit to the Ka'bah was in itself quite contrary to Arab tradition. Moreover, it was the month of Dhu'l-Qa'dah, which was one of four months considered sacred in Arab lore, in which fighting was prohibited. The Quraysh wanted to fight the Muslims, but they did not want to be accused of having desecrated the holy month; they wanted to be able to lay the blame at the door of the Muslims, who were few in number at that time, and not even equipped for battle. There they were, stranded 250 miles from home, right on the border of enemy territory. It was a perfect opportunity for the Quraysh to unleash a savage onslaught on the Muslims, and give full vent to their antagonism. They did everything they could to provoke the Muslims into starting a fight, but the Prophet ignored every provocation; he scrupulously avoided falling into their trap.

The situation was so grave that Abū Bakr was the only one of the companions not to feel that, in accepting humiliating peace terms, they had bowed before the aggressor. They were even more astonished when a verse of the Qur'ān was revealed which referred to the agreement as an "obvious victory." "What kind of victory is this?" one of them protested. "We have been prevented from visiting the House of God. Our camels for sacrifice have not been allowed to proceed. God's Prophet has been forced to turn back from Ḥudaybiyyah . Two of our persecuted brethren, Abū Jandal and Abū Baṣīr, have been handed over to their persecutors..." Yet it was this humiliating treaty that paved the way for a great Muslim victory.

The Treaty of Ḥudaybiyyah appeared to be a capitulation before the enemy; but in fact it gave the Muslims an opportunity to strengthen themselves, and consolidate their position. The Prophet accepted all the Quraysh's demands, in return for a single assurance from them, namely, that they would cease all hostilities against the Muslims for ten years. Continual raids and threats of warfare had prevented the Muslims from pursuing constructive missionary work. As soon as the Prophet returned from Ḥudaybiyyah, he intensified missionary work in and around Arabia, the groundwork having been done beforehand. Now that peace prevailed, the message of Islam started spreading like wildfire.

People in their thousands, tribe after tribe, thronged to join the fold of Islam. Islam began spreading beyond the borders of Arabia too. Safe from the idolators of Makkah, the Prophet was able to take action against, and drive out, the Jews of Khaybar, who had missed no opportunity of helping the enemies of Islam. He also turned his attention to building up the strength of Islam in Madinah. The culmination came within only two years of the Treaty of Ḥudaybiyyah: the Quraysh surrendered without even putting up a fight. There was no further barrier now to the Prophet's triumphant entry into Makkah. It was the deliberate imposition of a humiliating retreat from Makkah which had paved the way for a great victory.

People nowadays tend to resort to arms on the slightest provocation from their enemies. When the losses of meaningless war are pointed out to them, they justify themselves by saying that they were not the aggressors; the enemy had wickedly involved them in warfare. What they do not realize is that non-violence—does not mean remaining peaceful so long as no one is acting violently towards you; it is to refrain from violence even in face of violence—to refuse to be provoked even in face of provocation. Insidious plots should be met and defeated by quiet deliberations. Deeply-rooted though the antagonism of one's foes may be, one should not let their antagonism become either a stimulus or a vindication of one's actions.

To fight one's enemies is no way to succeed in life. Only by avoiding conflict can one consolidate one's strength. Then by awe alone will one be able to overpower one's foes. To fight at the slightest provocation, and ignore the need to quietly build up one's own strength, is to condemn oneself to destruction. Such conduct can never lead to success in this world of God. The Prophet achieved success by pursuing a policy of non-confrontation; how, then, can his followers succeed by pursuing a policy of confrontation? How can they be called his followers when they are blind to his example? How can they expect him to intercede for them on the Day of Judgement?

NOTES

1. Qur'ān, 33:21
2. Ḥadīth of Tirmidhī, Nasā'ī, Abū Dāwūd.
3. Ḥadīth of Ibn Hishām
4. Ibn Hishām, *Sīrah,* vol. 2, p. 29.
5. Qur'ān, 9:19-20.
6. Ibn Hishām, *Sīrah* vol. 3 and Ibn Kathīr, *Tafsīr*, vol. 1.
7. Ibn Hishām, *Sīrah* vol. 3, p. 7.
8. Ibn Hishām, *Sīrah* vol. 2, p. 29.
9. Ḥadīth reported by Abū Qatadah.
10. Ibn Hishām, *Sīrah* vol. 3, p. 357.
11. A minor pilgrimage which, unlike Ḥajj proper, need not be performed at a particular time of the year, and which entails fewer ceremonies.

6

The Path of the Prophet

EVOLUTION NOT REVOLUTION

The word "*sunnah*" in Arabic means a path. In the religious context it has come to refer to the manner of life pleasing to God, which has been revealed to man through His Prophets. The word is used in the Qur'ān for all the forms which divine law has taken throughout the ages.

When God created the world, He also ordained a path that it should follow. He enforced this divine course so strictly on the world of nature that there cannot be the slightest deviation from it. But God did not impose His will on humanity. He gave us freedom of thought and action: those who followed His path of their own free will were to be rewarded with paradise, while those who deviated from it would be punished in hell-fire.

> God wishes to make this known to you and to guide you along the path of those who have gone before you, and to turn to you in mercy. He is Wise, Knowing.[1]

God's prophets came to the world to make this chosen path plain to us. In their words and deeds, they showed us how to live in accordance with the will of God. It is this way of life which is known in Islam as the *sunnah*, or path, of the prophets. It covers every aspect of life, from personal matters to social reform and nation-building. Those who earnestly seek to be included amongst God's chosen servants must follow the path of the Prophet in all respects. In no walk of life should they consider themselves free to tread another course.

The most important practice of the Prophet's personal life was preaching the word of God. A study of his life shows that his greatest concern was to bring people to the path of the Lord. That his concern had turned to anguish is clear from this verse of the Qur'ān:

> You will perhaps fret yourself to death on account of their unbelief.[2]

The Prophet said that one who disregarded his *sunnah* was not one of his community. Just as this remark applies to the marriage contract and other such social obligations, so does it equally apply to the duty of calling people to the path of God. Only those have the right to be called true followers of the Prophet, who, along with other obligations enjoined by him, adopt this all-important practice of the Prophet as well.

One aspect of the Prophet's public mission was a realistic, step-by-step approach to everything he did. In the application of theoretical standards, he always made allowances for practical realities. He was always careful to introduce social reforms gradually. In modern jargon, his approach can be called evolutionary rather than revolutionary.

'Ā'ishah, the Prophet's wife, has explained this principle very clearly:

> The first chapters of the Qur'ān to be revealed were short ones making mention of heaven and hell. Then, when people became conditioned to accept Islamic teachings, verses dealing with what is lawful and unlawful were revealed. And if injunctions like: "Do not drink wine," and "Do not commit adultery," had been revealed first of all, people would have refused to abandon these practices.[3]

With the conquest of Makkah in the year A.H. 8, the Prophet assumed full control over the Arabian capital. Yet he did not seek immediate implementation of Islamic laws in the House of God in Makkah; whatever was to be done, he did gradually. Islamic rule had been established in the holy city when the pilgrimage of A.H. 8 took place, but it was performed according to ancient, pre-Islamic custom. Next year, the second pilgrimage of the Islamic era was performed with the idolaters following their own customs, and the Muslims theirs. It was only in the third year that the Prophet announced that the pilgrimage would be performed entirely according to Islamic tenets. This pilgrimage is known as Ḥajjat al-Widā' in Islamic history—the farewell pilgrimage of the Prophet.

It was instinctively abhorrent to the Prophet that the idolaters should come to the Sacred Mosque and perform the rites of pilgrimage according to their idolatrous customs. Yet, despite the power that he wielded, he did not hurry to implement the Islamic system. Rather, he himself refrained from going to Makkah on a pilgrimage for two years after the conquest. "I would not like to go on a pilgrimage while the idolaters are coming there and performing the rites of pilgrimage naked," he would say when the Hajj season arrived.

Some Muslims went on Hajj in the year after the conquest of Makkah (A.H. 8), but the Prophet was not among them. The next year in A.H. 9, the Muslim party of pilgrims was led by Abū Bakr. It was after this that the idolaters were banned from making the pilgrimage. The prohibition came in this verse of the Qur'ān:

> Believers, know that the idolaters are unclean. Let them not approach the Sacred Mosque after this year is ended.[4]

The Prophet then sent his cousin 'Alī to Makkah, with orders that he should mingle amongst the gathering of pilgrims, and proclaim that after this year no idolator would be allowed to come on Hajj, and *ṭawāf* (circumambulation of the House of God) in a naked state would not be permitted. Then, in the third year, following the gradual elimination of polytheism, the Prophet undertook what was to be his final pilgrimage to the Sacred Mosque.

This shows how the Prophet was careful to introduce reforms gradually. Even when he wielded power, he did not attempt to hurry Islamic legislation; he allowed matters to take their natural course, proceeding stage by stage until the desired conclusion was reached; he would hold himself back from introducing the desired measures, but he would not seek to hold the polytheists back from their activities until the time came when they themselves were ready to refrain from them.

There are many sides of the Prophet which have not generally been acknowledged as being important: for one thing, his realistic and gradual approach to everything he did has never been hailed as being of special significance. For instance, the Prophet lived in Makkah for thirteen years after the commencement of his prophetic mission, but not once during this time did he remonstrate against the continual desecration of the Kab'ah. Even after conquering the city, he was in no hurry to abolish vain and frivolous customs. He waited for two years, despite the fact that he had the power to take immediate action. Only in the third year did he introduce the reforms that he had in mind.

A gradual approach reaps several advantages which cannot be accrued from any other method. It guarantees success in attaining one's objectives. One who adopts this approach does not advance further until he is quite sure that he has consolidated his previous position. He does not let himself be carried away by his own zeal, rather, taking external factors into account, he proceeds in step with the times. There can be no doubt that one who is so cautious in his progress, will ultimately reach his goal.

Moreover, there is less risk of incurring unnecessary losses or liabilities. Those who seek to achieve too much too soon, find, inevitably, that they have to surmount enormous obstacles before they are really in a position to do so. Such attempts can result in incalculable loss of life and widespread damage to property. Making amends for such imprudence could take centuries.

UNSWERVING OBEDIENCE

Towards the end of the Prophet's life the fertile regions bordering pre-Islamic Arabia were controlled by the two great imperial powers of the day—the Sassanians and the Byzantines. To the north lay the emirates of Basra and Ghasasina, and the Roman province of Petraea, ruled through Arab chieftains. Roman influence there had led most of the inhabitants to embrace Christianity. To the south and north-east were the emirates of Baḥrayn, Yamāmah, Yemen and Oman, the last being known as the Mazun province. These states were under the Persian (Sassanian) Empire, and the religion of their Persian masters—Zoroastrianism—had spread among their peoples.

In the year A.H. 6 (A.D. 628), the Prophet had made a ten-year truce with the Quraysh at Ḥudaybiyyah. With peace on the home front, he sent letters to the rulers of territories surrounding Arabia, inviting them to accept Islam. One such letter was taken by the Prophet's envoy, Shujā' ibn Wahb al-Asadī, to al-Ḥārith ibn Abū Shimr of Ghasasina. The words in the letter, "have faith in God, you will retain your sovereignty" incensed the Arab chieftain. He threw the letter aside, saying: "Who can take away my kingdom?"

The ruler of Baṣra, Shuraḥbil ibn 'Amr Ghassānī, proved even more contemptuous. The Prophet sent Ḥārith ibn 'Umayr with a letter to this Roman governor. He entered the town of Mu'tah, on the Syrian border, and was killed there by an Arab, acting at the behest of the governor.

This act amounted to aggression by one state on another, according to international conventions. There were also signs that the Roman army based in Syria was planning to advance on Madinah: Byzantium could not tolerate the emergence and development of an independent power on Arab soil.

When news of Ḥārith ibn ‘Umayr's murder reached Madinah, the Prophet decided that military action would have to be taken against the perpetrators of such cold-blooded aggression. He gave orders that the Muslims should gather—with their weapons—at a place called Harq. A force of three thousand, under the leadership of Zayd ibn Ḥārithah, was assembled. After delivering some parting advice, the Prophet sent them on their way to Syria.

When the Muslim army arrived at Ma‘ān, in Syria, they pitched camp. The governor of Baṣrā had already prepared for battle, and he was further encouraged by the news that the Roman emperor, Heraclius, had arrived in nearby Ma'āb with a force of 100,000. The local Christian tribes, Lakhm, Juzām, Qayn, Bahrā and Ballī also rose in support of their Byzantine co-religionists, and agreed to fight under the leadership of the Banū Ballī chieftain, Mālik ibn Zafilah. This Roman force of over 100,000, then, was amassed on the Syrian front, to meet a Muslim army of only 3,000 men.

Zayd ibn Ḥārithah was slain in battle, and two subsequent leaders—Ja‘far ibn Abī Ṭālib and ‘Abdullah ibn Rawaḥah, were also martyred after him. The collapse of the standard led to disarray in the Muslims ranks. Then a soldier by the name of Thābit ibn Aqram came forward, lifted up the standard, and cried out to his fellow Muslims: "Agree on one leader!" "We have agreed on you," they shouted back.

Thābit, however, declined to accept the command, and asked for it to be confered instead on Khālid ibn al-Walīd. The Muslims shouted their agreement. Hearing this, Khālid ibn al-Walīd came forward, held aloft the standard, and advanced on the Roman lines. The Byzantine forces were then forced to retreat.

The outcome of this battle was indecisive, however, and there always remained the possibility that the Arabs of Petraea, with Roman help, would advance on Madinah and seek to stamp out the nascent power of Islam. That threat had been felt as early as A.H. 5, when 'Umar ibn al-Khaṭṭāb, on being asked by another companion if he had heard any news, replied: "What? Have the Ghasasina arrived?"

The Prophet was fully aware of this threat, and he made sure in his last days that full preparation had been made for a force to combat the Petraean wing of the Roman army. The force which was recruited included leading companions such as Abū Bakr and 'Umar, but the Prophet did not put them in command. Instead he wisely appointed Usāmah ibn Zayd, who, besides being a courageous young warrior, was also spurred on by the fact that his father, Zayd ibn Ḥārithah, had been killed by the Romans in the Battle of Muta. This army, however, was unable to advance during the lifetime of the Prophet. With his death in A.H. 10, Abū Bakr was appointed as the first Caliph, and it was he who finally gave the order to march on Syria.

After the death of the Prophet, news had started pouring into Madinah of mass apostasy among Arab tribes. Most of the Arab tribes that embraced Islam after the conquest of

Makkah in A.H. 8, had converted, impressed by the political dominance of Islam, rather than from having undergone any profound intellectual transformation or from having attained any such conviction as had the earlier followers of the Prophet. They had been accustomed to a free and easy life, and some of the Islamic injunctions—especially *zakāt*[5]—were more than they could tolerate. Some months before the death of the Prophet, demagogues had arisen in Yemen and Najd who exploited this situation putting forward a new brand of Islam, according to which there was no need to pay *zakāt*. To give their words more weight, these demagogues—notably Aswad and Musaylamah—laid claim to prophethood, for only then could they throw down a challenge to the *zakāt* system.

Zakāt was part of the religion revealed to the Prophet Muḥammad; they themselves would have to pretend to prophethood in order to speak with the same authority. Their "prophethood" became very popular among the tribes who looked upon *zakāt* as a burden, and they flocked to these false prophets' support. Their morale received a boost with the death of the Prophet in A.H. 10, and apostasy started spreading like wildfire, the only places remaining immune being Makkah, Madinah and Ṭā'if. There were reports, too, that these rebels were preparing to attack Madinah.

Much as the first Caliph, Abū Bakr, wanted the army to advance, most of the companions were against this. "These Arab tribes are in the throes of revolt," they said. "Madinah is liable to be attacked at any time. The army should stay to defend Madinah, rather than be sent to a distant land."

The other reservation they had were about Usāmah's leadership, for he was only seventeen years of age and, worse, was the son of a slave. How, they thought, could great companions of the Prophet serve under him, a mere stripling? An older and more experienced general in war than Usamah be appointed to lead that army.

'Umar, who had been with Usāmah's army, returned to Madinah to convey their message to Abū Bakr. The Caliph listened to what he had to say about the first matter, and replied: "Even if I am the only one remaining in Madinah after the departure of the army, and I am left to be devoured by wild beasts, still I cannot recall an army that the Prophet himself has despatched." He dismissed the matter of Usāmah's youth and rank with these words: "What, are the Muslims still proud and arrogant, as in the time of ignorance?" Saying this, he himself went on foot to send the army on its way under Usāmah's command. With Usāmah aloft on his mount, the Caliph of the Muslims walked alongside, speaking with him on matters concerning the military campaign. He wanted to put an end to the Muslims' misgivings about Usāmah's leadership, and this was the most practical and effective way of doing it. Their reservations vanished on seeing the Caliph walking alongside Usāmah's mount.

As news of the advance of Usāmah's army spread around Arabia, opponents saw in it a sign of the Muslims' confidence. They presumed that the Prophet's followers must have considerable reserves of strength to be able to send an army so far from Madinah at such a critical time. They decided to await the outcome of the Syrian campaign before attacking the city: if the Muslims met defeat, then they would be sufficiently weakened for an offensive against their capital to be feasible.

Usāmah ibn Zayd's army was eminently successful against the Romans. The campaign, which lasted forty days, also proved that Usāmah was the most suitable person for this expedition for, his father having been martyred fighting the Roman army at Muta, he was keen for revenge. A large number of captives and great quantities of booty went back with the Muslims to Madinah. The rebels lost heart on seeing this, and their revolt was quelled with comparative ease. So it was that the Muslims achieved success on both fronts, simply by having done as the Prophet said.

They thus provided a great lesson for subsequent generations of Muslims: that the place for Muslims to test their strength was the outside world, not among themselves. But successive generations of Muslims have failed to learn this lesson, and in the present age the situation has deteriorated to the point where the Muslim world is locked in battle with itself on every front.

No one is ready to face any challenge outside the Muslim world, but all are willing to fight against their own Muslim brethren. Undoubtedly the greatest challenge facing the Muslims today is the dissemination of Islam in the outside world; but since they are so busy fighting among themselves, it is not surprising that they have no time or energy for this all-important task.

There was another important reason for the Prophet's insistence on the despatch of the army. The Arab tribes had been fighting among themselves from time immemorial, and would start fighting again if not confronted with some external foe on whom to test their strength. Towards the end of his life, the Prophet averted this danger by pitting them against the might of the Roman army. The Arabs now had an eminently suitable arena in which to display their valour. They no longer had time for the fratricide and plundering which had hitherto been their way; instead, they turned their attention to distant horizons, blazing their way—within just one hundred years—to conquests that spanned three continents.

NOTES

1. Qur'ān, 4:26.
2. Qur'ān, 26:3.
3. Ḥadīth, *Ṣaḥīḥ*, Al-Bukhārī.
4. Qur'ān, 9:28.
5. A portion of property, bestowed in alms.

PART TWO

7

The Revolution of the Prophet

It is the will of God that His religion should reign supreme on earth. He wishes it to enjoy an intellectual dominance over other systems of thought. But for this to happen, certain conditions must prevail. The coming of the Prophet Muḥammad was the culmination of a lengthy process, extending over thousands of years, during which time the ground was fully prepared for his work. Conditions were created which would facilitate the accomplishment of his mission. What the Prophet had to do was understand these conditions, and make wise use of them. This he did, giving Islam a position of intellectual ascendancy in the world.

Now, once again, a process has been continuing over the last one thousand years, in which God has created conditions conducive to Islamic revival. If they are exploited to the full, Islam can once again come to dominate world thought, just as it did in the past.

But if these opportunities are to yield the maximum benefit, it will require an intense struggle, which only those with profound knowledge of contemporary conditions will be able to undertake. It will be those who rise above reactionary psychology and concentrate on positive action, who will be fit for this task; people who can sacrifice every other consideration, and devote themselves wholeheartedly to one overriding goal—the ascendancy of Islam; those who steer clear of the confusions of human thought, and are guided by divine wisdom in their course of action. Such noble spirits will not be inspired by thoughts of national glory or material grandeur; it will be the greatness of God alone that they seek to establish. It was people such as these who made Islam great in the past—who gave Islam its position of intellectual dominance—and it is people such as these who can do so once again. If, on the other hand, we are lured by superficial slogans, and distracted by every petty issue that arises, all we shall accomplish is the destruction of the opportunities God has created for us. We shall never then be able to convert possibilities into realities.

A COMPARISON

The Islamic revolution that occurred in the time of the Prophet was achieved at the cost of only 1018 lives. During the 23 years in which this revolution was completed, 80 military expeditions took place. The Prophet, however, only participated in some 27 of them, and an even smaller number of expeditions actually involved any fighting. 259 Muslims and 759 non-Muslims died in these battles—a total of 1018 dead. This is an extraordinarily small number of casualties to have been inflicted during such a great revolution—one which changed the entire course of human history. The Islamic revolution of the Prophet can, to all intents and purposes, be called a bloodless revolution.

Contemporary Muslim writers and speakers are wrongly eulogistic in their comparison of the Prophet's revolution with modern non-Islamic revolutions. They point with pride to the fact that only a thousand people died in the Islamic revolution, while in the Russian revolution of 1917 alone, 13 million people lost their lives. The democratic revolution in France also took a heavy toll which ran into thousands.

The Muslims like this comparison, because it gratifies their pride. But there is another comparison to be made here which they have never even considered. Perhaps their failure to give thought to this second comparison is simply a way of avoiding admonishment, for no one ever likes being admonished.

It would mean taking the number of dead in the initial Islamic missionary drive, and comparing it with the toll that modern-day Islamic movements have exacted; in other words seeing how many people died in the original Islamic revolution, and how many have died in Muslim revolutionary attempts of modern times. The 20th century has seen grand Islamic revolutionary movements, great "holy crusades", in the Muslim world. Just as Muslims compare the Prophet's Islamic revolution with modern, non-Islamic, secular revolutions, so also should they look at their own movements in the light of the revolution of the Prophet, and see how they stand up to the comparison.

Were the Muslims to take this comparison, they would be startled to find that their own movements are, in relation to that of the Prophet, no better than revolutionary movements in the non-Muslim world. Just as non-Muslim revolutions have been highly expensive in human terms, so the death toll in Muslims' revolutionary struggles has been incredibly high: two and half million dead in the Algerian war of independence; 500,000 Muslim martyrs in the Indian freedom struggle; 10 million lives lost in the formation of the Muslim state of Pakistan. The number of people who have given their lives for Islam in Syria, Iraq, Iran, Egypt, Palestine and various other countries, runs into millions. And for all that, these sacrifices have amounted to nothing. The effects of the Prophet's revolution were felt the world over, yet it was accomplished at the cost of only 1000 lives. Islamic movements of modern times, on the other hand, have involved millions of human lives, yet, despite this, one cannot point to even a small area in which Islamic revolution has been truly successful and effective.

The matter does not end there. Far from being successful, our recent struggle have produced a totally adverse effect. These words of the Bible ring exactly true with regard to our efforts of modern times:

> Ye shall sow your seed in vain, for your enemies shall eat it. They that hate you shall reign over you. And your strength shall be spent in vain: for your land shall not yield her increase, neither shall the trees of the land yield their fruits.[1]

Such has been the story of modern Muslim history. With great gusto we conducted the Caliphate and pan-Islamic movements, and made untold sacrifices for these causes, only to see the Muslim world split up under numerous national governments. We struggled for our country's independence, but, when it came, other parties took hold of the reins of government. We suffered great losses in forming the Islamic state of Pakistan, but, when it came into existence, secular leaders took control. We gave our utmost to establish Islamic rule in Egypt, but finally power fell into the hands—not of religious groups—but of military dictators. For nearly forty years we have been crusading for the end of the state of Israel, making enormous human and monetary sacrifices in the process, but all that has actually happened has been the expansion and consolidation of the Jewish state. And now, after the indescribable tribulations of the people of Iran, it will not be long before we hear that the Islamic republic was only a stepping stone for rule by unislamic forces.

These are the hard realities of our times. We can pull the wool over our eyes if we so please, but we cannot expect future historians to do likewise. True, they will be forced to say, the Russian revolution took a vast toll of human lives, but it also brought about great changes in world thought. It caused the collapse of Tsarist, or monarchical rule, and replaced it by a republican form of government; it established the ascendancy of the socialist economic system over capitalism. As for Islamic revolutionary efforts, they have been even more costly in human terms, but they have left no stamp on the pattern of world thought.

The revolution of the Prophet's time shows us that if just a thousand people are ready to give everything they have for the Islamic cause, then God does not let their sacrifices go unrewarded; He establishes the supremacy of Islam on earth. In modern times millions of Muslims have shown themselves willing to make sacrifices, but God has not taken up our cause. Despite all our sacrifices, our efforts have been frustrated. This shows that our efforts have been misdirected. If we had been following the straight path that God laid down for us, He would surely have made us successful, as promised in this verse of the Qur'ān:

> We have given you a glorious victory, so that God may forgive your past and future sins, and perfect His favour to you; that He may guide you to the right path and bestow on you His mighty help.[2]

A farmer who sows wheat will reap wheat. He is not telling the truth if he claims to have sown wheat, only for brambles to spring up in its place. It just does not happen that a wheat seed should yield a crop of brambles. Things do not work that way in this world of God. So it is with our efforts in modern times. If we had truly been following in the path of the Prophet and his companions—if we had made sacrifices in the same spirit as they—without doubt our mammoth efforts would have yielded positive results. It is no use deluding oneself into thinking that one is struggling in the path of Islam, when one's efforts are not producing the results which true Islamic struggle ought to ensure. One may live in a fool's paradise in this world, true paradise in the next world is for those who base their lives not on illusion and fantasy, but on reality.

DIVINE SUCCOUR

Addressing the faithful, God says in the Qur'ān, "Believers if you help God He will help you and make you strong."[3] Here the words "helping God" mean fitting in with His scheme. God has set a certain pattern for making things happen in this world; He has created favourable circumstances which, if properly exploited, will yield favourable results. We can fit in with His scheme by coordinating our own efforts with this pattern. God strengthens those who help Him in this way.

Here is an example of what happens when one fails to do so. There was a priest, who wanted to see a lush tree standing in front of his house. "If I plant a seed," he thought, "it will take at least ten years to grow into a full tree."

So what he did was to uproot a large tree and, hiring several labourers to transport it from where it had stood, he installed it in front of his house. "Good," he thought, "I have achieved ten years work in the space of a single day." How shocked he was, then, when next day he woke up to see the leaves of the tree withering away. By evening its branches were hanging limp, and within a few days the leaves had died and fallen to the ground; all that remained in front of his house was a stump of dry wood. A few days later the priest was visited by a friend, who found him walking restlessly in his garden. "What's wrong?" he enquired. "Why are you so upset today?" "I am in a hurry, but God isn't," the priest answered, and went on to tell the whole story of the tree. In whatever happens in the world, there is a part played by God and a part played by man. It's like a machine, which functions when two cog-wheels revolve in unison: one of the wheels is God's and the other man's. Man's success can only come from his keeping to God's pace. If he tries to proceed at his own, he will break, because God's wheel is stronger than his.

Over the millenia God has made certain provision for the growth of trees and plants: He has laid a layer of fertile soil on the surface of the earth; He has given them the heat that they need from the sun; He has provided them with water, and assisted their growth with alternation of the seasons; then He has created billions of bacteria which provide the roots with nitrogen. These arrangements are, so to speak, God's cog-wheel. What we have to do is attach our own wheel to God's, for only then will we be able to use these opportunities to form a tree. Once our own wheel is attached to God's, we have only to take a seed and plant it in the ground. Nature's machine will then set to work, and production will ensue. If, on the other hand, we plant our tree on a rock, or sow a plastic imitation seed in the ground, or do as the priest did and transplant a full-grown tree, then we have not set our own wheel at work with God's; we have not fitted in with God's scheme. We cannot expect, then, to see a lush tree growing in our garden.

So it is with Islamic revolution. It likewise comes from recognizing the opportunities that God has created, and using them well. True Islamic revolution does not emerge from haphazard action. The initial Islamic revolution was achieved by a few of God's servants fitting their own wheel in with God's. Our sacrifices of modern times, on the other hand, have all gone amiss because we have not followed God's scheme. We have trodden the path of our own desires, seeking to achieve by futile and irrelevant protests what can only come from wise use of the opportunities that God has afforded us.

The generations following Adam, the first man on earth, all worshipped one God. Mankind, as the Qur'ān says, "were one community."[4] So the situation continued for a few centuries, but soon worship of worldly phenomena, or polytheism, became prevalent. People found it difficult to focus their attention on an invisible God, so they focused it elsewhere, on visible objects, and in so doing reduced belief in God to the lowly and unimportant status of an abstract creed. It was at this time that the sun, moon and stars became objects of worship, and the mountains and oceans came to be thought of as gods. Divinity was even ascribed to those mortals who stood out among their fellows. So it was that, after a period of about 1000 years on earth, people saw the end of the conceptual dominance of monotheism, and their intellect became clouded with polytheistic thought.[5]

It was after the decline of other initial, monotheistic religion that God started sending prophets to the world. These prophets, however, never achieved enough popularity to eradicate polytheism and reassert the dominance of monotheism. At that time prophets came to every part of the inhabited world—according to one *ḥadīth* there were 124,000 thousands of them—but each and every one of them was scorned and laughed at.

When an individual rejects the truth, he or she does so for a reason; they do so because there is something which occupies such an important place in their lives that they cannot forsake it, even for the truth. The Qur'ān tells us the nature of the attachment that alienates individuals from the true message of the prophets:

> When their apostles brought them clear signs they exulted in such knowledge as they had; but (soon) the scourge at which they scoffed encompassed them.[6]

What is meant by knowledge here is the corrupted form of religion which people have been adhering to for so long that they have come to think of it as sacred. Religion which has been passed on from one generation to the next in this manner becomes lodged in people's minds. When they think of it, they think of the saints whose names are associated with it. It becomes a part of the establishment, the very foundation of a people's national infrastructure. Enshrined in elaborate tradition, it assumes a position of dominance in society.

When prophets visit such people as adhere to established polytheistic religion, their teaching of monotheism is a lone voice in that environment. They assert the truth of their teachings, but their claim is one which has yet to receive the ratification of history. They can only reason with their people, trying to persuade them to see the light. With the clamour of established religion on all sides, such quiet reasoning falls on deaf ears; the prophets appear insignificant compared to the grandeur surrounding the faith of their people's forefathers. Take the case of Jesus Christ, homeless and sleeping under a tree, while the chief priest of the Jews resided in the lavish splendour of the palace of Haykal.[7] How could people accept someone who slept under a tree as the bearer of truth rather than the occupant of the grand palace of Haykal? That is why people poured scorn on their prophets. They held established figures in reverence: why, then, should they forsake them for an insignificant creature without status? True, prophets of the past were also objects of their esteem, but these prophets had become more national heroes than preachers of truth in the eyes of their admirers.

It is one thing to attach oneself to a message, and quite another to attach oneself to an institution. There is nothing more difficult than service carried out in accordance with a message, and nothing easier than service in the name of an institution. All that a message has in support of it is its conceptual truth, while institutions are backed up by all sorts of material grandeur. It is those who extend their support to a message when it is backed up by nothing but simple truth who will find honour and rank in the sight of God. When it gains the status of an institution, then support of it will earn one no credit with God. Commitment to Islam as a message is an act carried out for God. Commitment to Islam as an institution, however, is all too often entered into for the material benefits that accrue from it.

EXALTATION OF THE WORD OF GOD

Just as traffic lights are erected at crossroads to guide and control traffic, so prophets have been sent by God to stand on the roads of life and show travellers the road leading to heaven, and warn them to steer clear of that which leads to hell. The Qur'ān has put this in the following words:

> Thus We have made of you a people justly balanced, that you may be witnesses over the nations, and the Prophet a witness over yourselves.[8]

It was for this purpose that, when polytheism first displaced monotheism as the predominant religion of mankind, prophets came to the world. Bestowing on them knowledge of truth, God sent them to guide people along the right path, and warn them to steer clear of evil. All of the prophets fully discharged this responsibility. Their teaching of truth was both understandable and reasonable. They left no stone unturned in their communication of truth: those who believed in them became worthy of paradise, while those who rejected them made themselves fit only for hell.

Yet God wanted more than mere proclamation of truth on earth; He wanted it to be exalted once again. Proclamation of truth necessitates its complete exposition before us. It is to make truth absolutely clear to all listeners, to enlighten them, using the "wise and mild exhortation," that the Qur'ān prescribes for preachers of truth.[9] When this is done, people are left with no excuse for not accepting the truth. They can no longer say that they were left in ignorance. The only defence that people who fail to follow the truth can offer is lack of awareness; where they have been shown every proof, there remains no pretext for denial.

Exaltation of the word of God is something more than

this. It means religious thought assuming ascendancy over all other systems of thought. The word of God does not become exalted on earth by any legislative or political programme; it can only come from a struggle on an intellectual level. It is when truth is engraved in people's minds that the word of God becomes truly exalted, not when it is written in statute books. In this day and age modern knowledge has stolen the limelight from ancient forms of knowledge: empirical science has taken over from analogical philosophy as the dominant mode of thought; socialism is a more prominent intellectual force than capitalism; democracy is a more forceful political theory than monarchy. These are all examples of conceptual ascendancy, the dominance of one system of thought over another. It is this nature of conceptual ascendancy of truth over falsehood that must be achieved for the word of God to become exalted.

God is able to do all things. It would have been easy for Him to make truth lord over all else, just as He has made the sun supreme over all other forms of light. But, since we are being tested in this world, God causes things to happen within the bounds of cause and effect. If events were to occur miraculously, we would have no choice but to see the hand of God in them: there would be no test involved. It was within the bounds of cause and effect, then, that God set about establishing the dominance of His word on earth. He created all the necessary circumstances for the achievement of this end, and then sent a prophet charged with the special task of bringing it to fruition. The Prophet's task, therefore, was not only to proclaim the truth, but also to make the truth a predominant force on earth, thus completing God's favour to mankind and allowing us to avail of the divine succour of which their waywardness had deprived us:

> They seek to extinguish the light of God with their mouths; but God will perfect His light, much as the unbelievers may dislike it. It is He who has sent His apostle with guidance and the Faith of Truth, so that He may exalt it above all religions, much as the pagans may dislike it.[10]

A NEW NATION IS BORN

The Prophet Muḥammad once said: "I am the prayer of Abraham." The prayer he was referring to was that offered by Abraham when he was building the Holy Ka'bah in Makkah:

> Lord, send forth to them an apostle of their own people (the Children of Ishmael) who shall declare to them your revelations and instruct them in the Book and in wisdom and purify them from sin. You are the Mighty, the Wise One.[11]

Yet, approximately two and a half thousand years elapsed between Abraham's prayer and the birth of the Prophet Muḥammad. The Prophet Zakariyyā (Zachariah) prayed for a prophet-son,[12] and within a single year his wife bore him Yaḥyā (John the Baptist). Why was it, then, that Abraham's prayer, which was of a similar nature, took so long to be answered?

The reason for this was that John the Baptist had an immediate mission to carry out. He was to expose the religious pretence of the Jews, by being martyred at their hands, so that they would no longer be fit to be bearers of the divine scriptures; another nation would have to come to replace them. The Prophet Muḥammad, on the other hand, had to reestablish the dominance of monotheism over polytheism. This could not be effected without the necessary antecedents: conditions conducive to this had to be created in the world; a nation upright enough to aid the Prophet in its accomplishment of this task had to come into existence. All this took two and a half thousand years to come about, in order that the event could take place within the bounds of cause and effect, as is the way of God.

In accordance with this scheme, Abraham was commanded to leave the civilized territory of Iraq for the dry, barren reaches of Arabia, where he was to settle along with his wife Hagar and son Ishmael.[13] This was an uncultivable area, cut off from the rest of the world. Here, far from the trappings of civilization, in the lap of nature, a community could be raised up in which all the natural abilities were fully preserved. Abraham had prayed for the emergence of a people submissive to God, and this was a land ideally suited for the development of such a people:

> Lord, make us submissive to You; make of our descendants a nation that will submit to You.[14]

A nation of unprecedented dynamism would be required to establish the dominance of true religion on earth. Earlier generations, which had grown up in the artificial environment of human civilization, had lacked the dynamism and vitality needed to perform this task. This was the reason the previous prophets failed to elicit a positive response. A new nation would have to grow up, nurtured under conditions specially suited to the cultivation of these qualities. This would involve a long process of human reproduction, extending over several generations. This accounts for the 2500 year gap between Abraham's prayer and its fulfillment: when the stage was fully set, the prophet that he had prayed for was born to Āminah, the daughter of Wahāb ibn 'Abd Manāf of the Banū Hāshim in Makkah.

Nothing but dry land and inhospitable rubble awaited Abraham in Makkah when he arrived there with his wife and infant son. Soon the water in their flask finished and Ishmael started thrashing with his hands and feet because of his great thirst. It was then that the spring of Zamzam gushed forth, a sign that although God had indeed made them face a stiff test, He would not leave them to face it alone: they were engaged in God's own work and He would always be there at crucial moments to grant them succour. When Ishmael grew into adolescence, Abraham dreamt that he was slaughtering his child. He interpreted it as God's commandment, and readied himself to carry it out. Then, as he held the knife poised over Ishmael's throat, a voice came from heaven telling him to stop, and sacrifice a lamb intead. This was a sign from God that Abraham would have to prepare himself for enormous sacrifices: but he was not in reality required to make them; it was the *will* to sacrifice that was desired. Once he had shown that he could pass this test, he would be spared the actual deed. After all, God intended to use Abraham and his family in the enactment of a great scheme; far from letting them pointlessly lay down their lives, He would protect them.

Ishmael grew up and married a girl of the Jurham tribe, which had settled in Makkah after the water of Zamzam had sprung up. Abraham was in Syria at the time. One day he came on horseback when Ishmael was not at home; only his wife was there and she did not recognize her father-in-law. "Where has Ishmael gone?" Abraham asked. "Hunting," she replied. "How is life treating you?" Abraham went on, and Ishamel's wife complained to him about the poverty and hardship they had to endure. Abraham, as he was leaving, told her to convey his greetings to Ishmael and tell him to "alter his threshold." When Ishmael returned, she told him the whole story. Ishmael realized that the visitor had been his father, who had come to see how things were going. By "altering his threshold," Ishmael knew what his father had meant: he was to marry a new wife, for this one was not suitable for the creation of the progeny that God had in mind. So he divorced that wife and married someone else. After a period of time Abraham made another appearance on horseback. Again Ishmael was not at home. Abraham asked his new daughter-in-law the same questions as he had put to the previous one. This time, however, Ishmael's wife was all praise for her husband and said that everything was fine with them; they had much to be thankful for. Abraham set off, and told her to convey his greetings to Ishmael, and to tell him to "keep his threshold." This wife was ideally suited to the task in hand; Ishmael should keep her in wedlock.[15]

So it was that, in the solitude of the Arabian desert, the seeds of the progeny that was to be known as the Children of Ishmael were sown. These were the initial states of preparation of a people who, 2500 years later, were to provide the Final Prophet with the support he needed in performing history's most mammoth task.

The qualities of the nation that grew up in the barren expanses of the desert around Makkah can be summed up in one word—*al-muru'ah* (manliness). This was the word of highest esteem that Arabs used to describe essential human qualities in a person. As an ancient Arab poet has written:

If a person fails to achieve manliness when young, then he will find it hard to do so when he grows old.

This is how the eminent Arab historian, Professor Philip K. Hitti, sums up the qualities of the people that developed over hundreds of years in the Arabian desert:

> Courage, endurance in time of trouble (*ṣabr*), observance of the rights and obligations of neighbourliness (*jiwār*), manliness (*muru'ah*), generosity and hospitality, regard for women and fulfilment of solemn promises.[16]

THE BEST NATION

The nation that emerged from this 2500 year development process was the nation most richly endowed in human qualities that mankind had seen:

> You are the best nation that has ever been raised up for mankind.[17]

Commenting on this verse, 'Abdullah ibn al-'Abbās says that it refers to those who emigrated from Makkah to Madinah along with the Prophet. In fact that small group of Muhajirs was representative of all those Arabians who made up the group known as the Companions of the Prophet.

Prophets of every age have confronted one major obstacle: the adherence of their people to an ancestral religion which enjoyed unrivalled material grandeur. They themselves, on the other hand, were standing on the abstract ground of truth and reason. This nation that had grown up in the Arabian desert was endowed with the unique ability to recognize truth on an abstract level—before it had gained any external lustre. They had been reared under open skies, in the wilderness of the vast desert, and had developed an extraordinary capacity for recognizing plain, unvarnished truth. They were prepared to give up everything for the sake of truth when it was a solitary force, and one that appeared to have nothing to offer them in return. 'Abdullah ibn Mas'ūd summed up these qualities of the Companions in the following words:

> They were the cream of the Muslim community—the most warm-hearted, the most knowledgeable, and the least formal. They were the ones that God chose to accompany His prophet, and to establish his religion.

What polytheism had deprived man of more than anything was the ability to see truth on an abstract level. It had made him want to see a thing and feel it before he would believe it. The prophets who came to the world spoke of a truth which was an abstract force. This was something that their peoples could not appreciate; hence the scorn and ridicule to which prophets have been subjected to in every age.

The polytheists had not denied the existence of God. What they had done was mould Him in the image of insensate objects. Finding it difficult to fathom a God that could not be seen, they depicted Him in material or human forms, and made these visible objects the focus of their attention. The objects that they chose to revere were invariably things that appeared great to them, so that when the prophets came they failed to achieve public recognition, for they appeared in the guise of ordinary people. At the time of their coming to the world, no historical greatness was attached to them. It was only much later that they came to be thought of as national heroes.

Part of Abraham's prayer when he commenced the construction of the Ka'bah in Makkah went like this:

> And remember when Abraham said: "Lord, make this town one of peace. Preserve me and my descendants from serving idols. Lord, they have led many men astray. He that follows me shall surely belong to me, but if anyone turns against me, You are surely Forgiving, Merciful. Lord, I have settled some of my offspring in a barren valley near Your Sacred House, so that they may observe the prayer..."[18]

Polytheism had reached its zenith in Abraham's time. Wherever one turned, great monuments glorifying idols were to be found. It appeared impossible for the human intellect to rid itself of the shackles of polytheistic thought.

It was at this time that Abraham was commanded to settle in Makkah, and to start a new line of descent. God's purpose was to raise a people in a land which had not been exposed to polytheistic influence, so that a nation with minds elevated enough to shun externals and think in terms of profound realities could develop. The Qur'ān characterizes the final product of this human progeny in the following words:

> God had endeared the Faith to you, and beautified it in your hearts, making unbelief, wrongdoing and disobedience abhorrent to you. Such are the rightly guided.[19]

We can only understand this verse if we think of the situation that prevailed one and a half thousand years ago, when the Companions adopted the Faith. It was surrounded by a host of visible "gods" that they took an invisible God as their own; from out of a multitude of worldly greats, they recognized and believed in a prophet who commanded no worldly stature. Islam at that time was a religion strange to the world, but it was this outlandish religion that the Companions grew to love so much that they were willing to renounce everything for it. In short, they saw truth when it was still an abstract force, before it was backed up by the ratification of history, before it had become a symbol of national pride. One had to be ready to give everything for it, and to expect nothing in return.

One outstanding example of the selflessness involved in the act of faith at that time was the event known as *bay'at 'aqbah thāniyah* (The Second Oath of Allegiance), which was made before the Prophet emigrated to Madinah. Just when persecution of Muslims in Makkah had reached intolerable levels, some of them started spreading the message of Islam in Madinah, and soon it reached every home there. At that time some of the people of Madinah resolved to go to Makkah, swear allegiance to the Prophet, and invite him to emigrate to Madinah. Jābir al-Anṣārī later recalled how, when Islam had spread to every house of Madinah, they held consultations among themselves. "How long can we let the Prophet wander around the hills of Makkah, fearful and distressed?" They said to one another. To those who judged from appearances alone the very fact that the Prophet was alone, with few supporters, was proof of his not being in the right: how could he be God's prophet, and be left in such an abject state? But the people of Madinah looked at the matter on a more profound level. They had realized the truth of his prophethood, and saw that by helping him they would earn God's grace and good favour.

Seventy representatives of the people of Madinah took this oath of allegiance. We can tell under what precarious conditions they did so from the account of one of their number, Ka'b ibn Mālik. He tells of how they surreptitiously joined a normal party of pilgrims belonging to their tribe, pretending that they too were going on a pilgrimage. Near Makkah, when the others put up camp, the Muslims also pretended to have fallen asleep. When a third of the night had elapsed, however, they rose quietly from their beds in order to keep their appointment with the Prophet, proceeding to the place of rendezvous "like birds, creeping silently in the undergrowth."[20]

What an extraordinary time it must have been when, with the Prophet rejected by the world, a few individuals arose, eager to follow him. At that time the Prophet had no place in his own home town; he had been chased out of Ṭā'if with a volley of stone-throwing and abuse; no tribe was willing to grant him protection. Yet, under such adverse conditions, the people of Madinah recognized the truth of his prophethood, and responded to his call. When the Anṣār[21] went forward to swear allegiance, one of them rose and asked: "Do you know what your oath of allegiance will entail? It will entail the destruction of your properties and homes." "We know," they replied, "and it is an oath entailing the destruction of our properties and homes that we are entering into." They then asked the Prophet: "What will be our reward if we are faithful till the end?" "Paradise," the Prophet replied. "Give us your hand," they said to the Prophet, "so that we can swear allegiance to you."

The Anṣār, en-masse, were giving their lives for a truth which was still disputed, for a reality which had found no place for itself in the world of humanity. It was an act which no community, before them or after them, has ever emulated.

AVOIDING EXTRANEOUS ISSUES

It is generally the issues that are called nationalistic in modern terminology that capture the imagination of a people's intelligentsia, and lead to the establishment of popular movements. Issues of this nature faced the Prophet Muḥammad also, but he scrupulously avoided them. The success of his mission depended upon his conforming to the scheme of God, which had been evolving over the last two and a half thousand years. If he had become involved in irrelevant side issues, all the opportunities which had been created could have been ruined.

The Arab border territory of Yemen had come under Ethiopian rule in A.D. 525, and Abrahah was appointed governor. This audacious individual launched an attack on the Holy Ka'bah, aiming to demolish it and put an end to the central position it enjoyed by virtue of its being a place of pilgrimage. The year of his attack on the Ka'bah, with an army of elephants, was also the year of the Prophet's birth (A.D. 571): it was also the year of the Sassanians' attack on Yemen and its assimilation into the Persian empire. Bāzān became the new governor. When the Prophet Muḥammad commenced his mission, the Persian emperor heard about him, and issued Bāzān with instructions to order the new prophet to desist from his claims; "Otherwise," the emperor said, "bring me his head."[22]

This shows how great the problems posed by foreign domination on the borders of Arabia had become at the time the Prophet Muḥammad commenced his mission. The Prophet could have incited his people to rise up against the foreign invaders, and drive them out of Arabian territory. But to have done so would have been contrary to God's scheme. It was His will that the Prophet should not clash with others over peripheral issues, but should concentrate on the central theme of his mission, which was to spread the word of God. The consequence was, as history bears witness, that Bāzān, as well as most of the Christians residing in Yemen, accepted Islam. What a leader in his place taking up national issues would have attempted to solve unscrupulously through political activities, the Prophet successfully solved by communicating to others the ideas of Islam.

After the death of Abū Ṭālib, Abū Lahab became leader of the Banū Hāshim tribe. Since the new chieftain refused protection to the Prophet, the latter was forced to seek the patronage of some other tribe. For this purpose he visited many tribes, among them the frontier-based Banū Shaybān ibn Tha'labah. The chief of this tribe, Musannā ibn Ḥārithah, explained to the Prophet that his people lived close to the Persian border, a territory which the Sassanian Emperor had allowed them to occupy only on receiving assurance that they would not preach any new doctrine, or give refuge to anyone who did so. "Perhaps rulers would disapprove of your teachings," the chieftain added.[23]

This shows how foreign rule on the borders of Arabia constituted more than a political and territorial encroachment on Arab sovereignty; it obstructed the Prophet's missionary work as well. The Prophet could have used this as a pretext for starting active resistance to foreign powers, saying that no missionary work could be accomplished until all external obstructions had been eliminated. But to have done so in the initial stages of his mission would have constituted a deviation from God's scheme, which was for the empires of Rome and Persia to become weak by fighting with each other for twenty years. When the time finally came for them to be conquered, it was they who had to shoulder the blame for the initiation of hostilities. It was, furthermore, relatively easy for the Muslims to subdue them, paving the way for the unprecedented conquests of the post-prophetic era. If the Muslims had confronted Rome and Persia prematurely, when these empires were strong, and they themselves weak, the outcome would have been the opposite.

FITTING IN WITH GOD'S SCHEME

If a farmer is to grow crops, he must fit his own cog-wheel in with God's. Providence has created unique opportunities for crop cultivation on earth, but in order to avail of them there are certain things that a farmer must do. On the surface of the earth, for instance, lies a layer of fertile soil which is quite unique in the entire universe. But this soil, despite its innate fertility, will not yield a crop unless it is moist: the barrenness of the arid regions of the earth is due to a lack of such moisture. Now there is nothing in the universe which will broadcast this fact to farmers; they must find it out for themselves by reading the silent signs of nature and then acting upon them. What a discerning farmer will do, then, is wait until the ground is moistened by rain before planting. If there is no rain, he will irrigate his land. So will the great disseminator of truth. He will wait for, or create, the right conditions to plant the seeds of truth in the hearts of mankind. This was the method followed by the Prophet Muḥammad. The spiritual ground of the Arabia to which he came was moist and fertile, ready to produce great fruits. Still, the Prophet had to employ the correct methods for his mission to advance; to achieve success, he had to fit in with God's scheme. There was no other way for him to utilize the opportunities that had been provided.

The basic principle of the Prophet's teaching mission was that emphasis should be laid entirely on matters pertaining to eternity. Under no circumstances was his teaching to dwell on worldly issues. The true issue confronting man is that of his eternal fate. All other issues are transitory and superfluous. Worldly success and failure have no meaning, for they are bound to end. It is on the next world, where success and failure will be abiding, that man should focus his attention.

Furthermore, it was the Prophet's aim to build a society of upright individuals, and such a society can only be formed if each separate individual behave with moral rectitude. True and consistent morality can come only from a profound belief in the hereafter. Belief in the hereafter means that we are is not free to act as we please but that we will expect to be taken to task for our actions by God. It rids one of wayward attitudes and makes one into a disciplined and responsible human being. If one reads the Qur'ān and Traditions of the Prophet with an open mind, one will find that it is the life after death which receives most attention. Other matters are mentioned, but only incidentally. The fundamental purpose of the Prophet's mission was to concentrate people's attention on the hereafter.

The Prophet's second principle was to scrupulously avoid any material conflict coming between himself—the teacher—and those to whom he was addressing his teachings. No matter what price had to be paid, he would let no worldly rivalry come in between himself and his congregation. One outstanding example of this policy was the Treaty of Ḥudaybiyyah. By constantly waging war against the Muslims, the Quraysh had made Muslims and non-Muslims into two separate parties eternally at loggerheads with one another. Both sides were spending all their time preparing for and engaging in warfare. In this treaty the Prophet accepted all the Quraysh's demands in return for a ten-year truce. The terms of the treaty were so one-sided that many Muslims considered it a humiliation; but, in reality, it paved the way for what the Qur'ān called a "clear victory."[24] This treaty put an end to the atmosphere of confrontation which had developed between Muslims and non-Muslims. Muslims could now freely communicate the teachings of their faith to non-Muslims, who in turn were free to accept them. No worldly rivalry or prejudice now stood in the way of dissemination of the faith. After this treaty, and the conciliatory effect it had on non-Muslims, the message of Islam spread rapidly throughout Arabia. In just two years, the number of Muslims increased tenfold. There had seemed no way that Makkah could ever be conquered by force of arms, yet it succumbed two years later to the force of Islamic teachings.

One important aspect of the Prophet's method was compassion towards his foes, even when they were wholly at his mercy. The reason for this was that he did not look upon anyone as an enemy; he saw all men and women as potential recipients of Islamic teachings, and was keen to give them every possible chance to accept the faith. One outstanding example of this magnanimity, which the Prophet displayed throughout his life, can be found in his treatment of the Quraysh after Makkah had been conquered. The very people who had been relentlessly persecuting the Prophet and his followers for the previous twenty years, were now at the Prophet's mercy. But, rather than punish them for past crimes, he forgave them all. When the Quraysh were brought before him in chains he simply said to them, "Be on your way: you are all free men." He pronounced suspended death-sentences on some, but these too were freed when they appealed for clemency, either personally or through representatives. In all, seventeen people were sentenced to death, but of these only five—those who made no appeal—were actually executed. In the Battle of Uḥud the Prophet's uncle, Ḥamzah, had been slain by Waḥshī ibn Ḥarb, after which Hind bint 'Utbah had mutilated Ḥamzah's corpse. When the Prophet learnt of this he said, in the heat of the movement, "If God makes me triumph over them, then I will mutilate three of them."[25]

Waḥshī and Ḥind were both among the seventeen whom the Prophet condemned to death. But when they appealed to him for clemency, he forgave them both. It was God's will that His Prophet should be lenient and forgiving towards his enemies, for this policy harmonized with God's scheme for the furtherance of the Islamic cause.

This principle is based on a profound insight into the nature of human society. Human society is a composite body of live, sensitive individuals, in whom an urge for vengeance is kindled when one of their number is harmed.

Human beings are not like pieces of stone, which show no reaction when another stone is broken. To suppress one individual is to invite rebellion from those associated with him, which means that the time which could be profitably spent on building up society is frittered away in containing discontent. By forgiving all his past enemies after the conquest of Makkah, the Prophet ensured that at no future date would insurrection rear its head. In fact, most of those he forgave accepted Islam and became a source of strength to it, one instance being that of 'Ikrimah, the son of Abū Jahl, formerly an implacable adversary of the Prophet and his followers.

Once the Prophet's authority had been established, there were certain social reforms which had to be undertaken. The Prophet was careful to proceed gradually in introducing such reform; he never hastened to impose measures when people were not ready to accept them.

The people of Makkah were heirs to the religion of Abraham, but they had distorted the true religion of Abraham and taken up various kinds of innovatory practices. For instance, in the time of Abraham, Ḥajj (Pilgrimage) used to be performed in the lunar month of Dhu'l-Ḥijjah. Since a year, according to the lunar calendar, is eleven days shorter than a solar year, its months do not revolve with the seasons. Hajj, then, sometimes fell in one season and sometimes in another. This went against the Quraysh's commercial interests. They wanted Hajj to fall in the summer each year, and for this purpose they adopted a method known as *nasi*'. This consisted of adding eleven days on to the lunar calendar every year. After this intercalation they maintained the names of the lunar months, but in effect their calendar was a solar one. This meant that for thirty-three years all dates were removed from their real place in the lunar calendar; every thirty-three years, when their annual addition of eleven days to the calendar had run the course of a complete year, Hajj would be performed on its proper date according to the lunar calendar. One of the tasks entrusted to the Prophet was to put an end to all the Quraysh's innovations and have Hajj performed according to Abraham's original system. The conquest of Makkah occurred in the month of Ramaḍān, A.H. 8. The Prophet was now ruler of the whole of Arabia. He could have put an immediate end to all the Quraysh's innovations. But instead he bided his time. There were just two years remaining until the completion of the full thirty-three year course of *nasi'*. The Prophet waited for these two years and although he was the conqueror of Makkah, he did not perform Hajj during that time. Only in the third year after the conquest of Makkah (A.H. 10), did he participate in the pilgrimage. That was the year when Hajj was performed on the correct date of Dhu'l-Ḥijjah, in accordance with the system established by Abraham. This was the Prophet's farewell pilgrimage, and during it he announced that, in future, Hajj would be conducted in the same way as in that year. Thus he put an end to the manipulation of the lunar calendar for all time. "Time has run its full course," he announced. "It is now in the same position as it was when God created the heavens and the earth. And there are twelve months to a year in the sight of God."[26]

There was a profound reason for the Prophet's delay in introducing this reform. When people have adhered to a certain religious practice for a number of years, they come to think of it as sacred and find extreme difficulty in changing their thinking. In two years time, Hajj would fall on the day desired by the Prophet, so he avoided taking any premature initiatives which would have made an issue of the matter. When the time came for Hajj to fall naturally on its proper day, then he announced that this was the right day of the year for Hajj to be performed, and it would in future continue to be performed on the same day.

From these examples, we can see how the Prophet's entire policy was moulded by the wisdom with which he had been endowed by God. One can say that he fitted his own cog-wheel in with God's; his every move was designed to be in accordance with the pattern set by God. It was for this reason that all his efforts produced highly fruitful results.

NOTES

1. Bible, Leviticus, Chapter 26.
2. Qur'ān, 48:1-3.
3. Qur'ān, 47:7.
4. Qur'ān, 2:213.
5. Qur'ān, 36:30.
6. Qur'ān, 40:83.
7. Solomon's temple in Jerusalem.
8. Qur'ān, 2:143.
9. Qur'ān, 16:25.
10. Qur'ān, 61:8-9.

11. Qur'ān, 2:129.
12. Qur'ān, 3:30.
13. Qur'ān, 14:37.
14. Qur'ān, 2:128
15. Ibn Kathīr, *Tafsīr*.
16. Philip K. Hitti, *History of the Arabs*, p. 253.
17. Qur'ān, 3:110.
18. Qur'ān, 14:35-37.
19. Qur'ān, 49:7.
20. Ibn Hishām, *Sīrah,* vol. 2, p. 49.
21. The people of Madinah who helped the Prophet.
22. Ibn Hishām, *Sīrah*.
23. Ibn Kathīr, *Sīrah*.
24. Qur'ān, 48:1.
25. Ibn Kathīr, *Tafsīr*, vol. 2, p. 352.
26. Ḥadīth, Ibn Jarīr, Ibn Marduiyah.

8

Rising above Events

The Arabian peninsula, in the period immediately preceding the coming of the Prophet Muḥammad, was confronted with immense political problems. The two super powers of the day—the empires of Rome and Persia-lay to the west and east of the Arabian peninsula, and both had turned the land of the Arabs into their political playground. The most fertile regions of the peninsula were under the direct control of one or the other of these two powers. Iraq had been annexed by the Persians, while Syria, Jordan, Palestine and Lebanon had become part of the Byzantine Empire. Despite the natural protective boundaries of the Red Sea to the west and the Persian Gulf to the east, the lands which bordered these seas were not immune from intrusions by their powerful neighbours. Persian warships had no difficulty in crossing the Gulf of Oman and entering Arab territory. The Red Sea also posed no barrier to interference in Arab affairs from Egypt and Ethiopia, both under the control of the Byzantine Empire.

Tribal chieftains had set up states in the inner regions of the Arabian peninsula, but they too enjoyed no real independence. The overall dominance of Rome and Persia meant that the only way these chieftains could preserve some measure of autonomy was by ruling as vassals for these imperial powers. On the borders of Syria lay the state of Ghasasina Arabiya subject to the Roman empire was ruled by Ḥārith ibn Abī Shimr Ghassānī at the time of the Prophet Muḥammad's mission. Then there was Buṣra which, besides being under the political control of the Romans, had also been subjected to Roman cultural influence, with many of its inhabitants accepting Christianity.

On the Iraq border lay the state of Ḥīrah 'Arabiyah which was subject to Iran. There were also several states bordering the Persian Gulf, in which the influence of their Persian neighbour was strongly felt. Foremost among them was Bahrayn, ruled by Mundhir ibn Sawa, where many of the inhabitants had accepted the Zoroastrian religion. Two other states to have come under Persian influence in this way were 'Ammān, ruled by the two sons of Jālandī—Jaifar and 'Abd—and Yamāmah, ruled by Hauzah ibn 'Alī al-Ḥanafī. Rivalry between the Persian and Roman empires was intense, and their respective vassals in Arabia would participate in the wars fought between them. Ghasasina, for instance, would side with the Romans and Ḥīrah with the Persians. So it was that Arab blood would flow in pursuit of the super powers' aims.

In those times Yemen was far larger than it is today. It contained several small tribal governments, the largest of which had its capital at Ṣan'ā'. It was there that Najrān was situated. Foreign rule in Yemen had commenced around A.D. 343, when the Romans sent Christian missionaries to the region. These missionaries met with great success in Najrān, and most of the country's inhabitants converted to Christianity.

Though this was a religious event, the Romans' rivals in Persia perceived it as a political threat. It seemed to them as if the Roman empire was seeking to establish a foothold in the southern region of Arabia. The Persians allied with the Jewish tribes who had settled in Yemen after being expelled from Syria by the Romans in A.D. 70. Yūsuf Dhū Nūwās was an Arab by birth, but had accepted Judaism. With Persian help he set up a semi-autonomous government in Ṣan'ā', under the sponsorship of the Sasanians. He then set about exterminating the Christians of Najrān, many of whom were burnt alive in A.D. 534.

The Romans now took steps to preserve their hold on the region. Ostensibly seeking to protect the Yemenese Christians, they chose the Ethiopian king Najāshī, a Christian, and loyal to the Romans, for fulfilment of their ends, and incited him to rise up against Yūsuf Dhū Nūwās. Najāshī then sent an army to the Yemen under the Ethiopian chieftain Aryāṭ. A short battle ensued, which ended with Ṣan'ā' being captured by the Ethiopian force and Dhū Nūwās drowning himself in the sea. Before long, however, Abrahah—a soldier in Aryāṭ's army—killed his commander and, having gained Najāshī's consent, set up his own government in Ṣan'ā'. It was he who, in A.D. 571, set out to attack the Holy Ka'bah in Makkah. He was succeeded by his sons, first Yaksūm and then Masrūq.

A member of the former royal family of the Yemen, named Sayf ibn Dhī-Yazan, was then filled with an urge to expel foreigners from his country and re-establish his ancestors' dynasty. He started a freedom movement, but when local support proved insufficient for the achievement of his aims, he went to the Iranian king Nawshyrwān in search of military support. Nawshyrwān was quick to seize this golden opportunity: while an Iranian army under Dahraz was being prepared to advance on the Yemen, Sayf ibn Dhī-Yazan died, but his son Ma'dī Karb completed the arrangement for bringing the Iranian force to his country. Crossing the Gulf of Oman, they landed at Ḥadhramawt, and from there proceeded to Ṣan'ā'. The alliance between Ma'dī Karb and Dahraz was successful in expelling the Ethiopians from the Yemen. Ma'dī Karb became king of Ṣan'ā', but an Iranian military presence was retained, in effect turning the Yemen into a transoceanic Iranian province. There was an Iranian governor there at the time of the advent of Islam. His name was Bazan and, after initial opposition, he later accepted Islam.

All this goes to show how far Arabian territory had become a prey to the expansionist designs of Rome and Persia at the time of the Prophet Muḥammad's mission. In such a situation two paths were open to a reformer such as the Prophet. He could have allowed himself to be carried by the tide of current events, and initiated political agitation against the colonial powers that were threatening his land. Or he could have concentrated on building up his people's internal strength to such a degree that, with a slight effort on their part, the imperial edifice would crumble to the ground.

The Prophet chose the second rather than the first course. Abraha's attack on the Holy Ka'bah is mentioned in the two chapters (105 and 106) of the Qur'ān entitled *al-Fīl* and *Quraysh.* The Qur'ān explicitly states that such threats should be countered by "worship." This is the Islamic way. When a political threat is perceived, a solution should be sought—not on a political level—but on a spiritual level, on a level of worship.

9

The Prophetic Method

STRENGTHENING ONESELF INWARDLY

The story of Islam began in A.D. 610, when the Prophet Muḥammad received his first revelation. At that time he was the only Muslim, the only believer, in the whole world. In A.D. 622 the Prophet emigrated from Makkah to Madinah. There he established an Islamic state, but its boundaries were extremely limited. They extended only to a few parts of the small town of Madinah, the larger portion remaining under the control of Jewish tribes and Arabs who had not yet converted to Islam. The Prophet died eleven years later. By the time of his death the frontiers of Islam had spread throughout the Arabian peninsula and reached southern Palestine. An Islamic empire covering 1 million square miles had come into existence. In just under one century Islam had advanced through north Africa to Spain on the western front, and from Spain to the frontiers of China in the east. There are still signs of Islamic influence in such far off places as Budapest, where a Muslim shrine,

"Gul Baba," still stands on the banks of the river Danube, and France where many church steeples contain stones with Arabic engravings—a remnant of the 8th century A.H., when southern France was a European province of the Caliph in Damascus. Two hundred years before, the people of Arabia had been driving camels; now they were leading the world. Baghdad had become the centre of the civilized world, taking over from Seleucia, Persepolis, Babylon and Rome as the major international seat of learning.

These outstanding triumphs were the result of an extraordinarily simple programme, which the Qur'ān explains in these words:

> You who are wrapped up in your vestment, arise and give warning. Magnify your Lord, cleanse your garments, and keep away from all pollution. Bestow no favours expecting gain. Be patient for your Lord's sake.[1]

When summarized, this programme can be divided into three stages:

1. Personal reform, so that one worships God alone, corrects one's moral standards and avoids all forms of sin and wrongdoing.

2. Impressing on others the reality of their existence and final destiny — that they are God's servants and will return to Him after death.

3. Remaining steadfast in the face of difficulties which afflict one in one's attempt to reform both oneself and society.

INWARD STRENGTH

The Islamic struggle is essentially a personal one, motivated by an overpowering urge for salvation in the next world, a longing that God should forgive us when we come before Him. When Islam penetrates into the depths of our consciousness, we become concerned with one thing alone: how to earn God's favour and forgiveness. We immediately seek to mould our faith, ideas, character, actions and all we do in life in accordance with our overriding concern to avoid displeasing God. It is on the hereafter that we focus all our attention. We call others to Islam, making sure that we are first good Muslims ourselves:

> Say: "I was commanded to be the first to submit to Him."[2]

As far as its motivation is concerned, becoming the "first to submit to God" is an entirely individual affair. But in its consequences this act has far-reaching implications for the whole of society. A volcanic eruption starts within a mountain, invisible from the eyes of humankind. But when the eruption takes place, it illuminates the whole surrounding area with its glow. So it is with those who first submit to God. The transformation that occurs within them has repercussions on their entire environment. The same sequence can be found in the revelation of the Qur'ān. The first verse to be revealed were those dealing with personal reform. Later came the chapters dealing with improvement of society at large. Comparing this sequence with the method adopted by the Prophet of Islam, Muḥammad

Marmaduke Pickthall, in the introduction to his translation of the Qur'ān, writes:

> The inspiration of the Prophet progressed from inward things to outward things.[3]

Generally people consider assaults on the outside world to be the most worthwhile task in life. But the lesson of the Prophet's life is that one should work to strengthen oneself inwardly. Individuals who have consolidated themselves from within become an irresistable force when they break out into the open. How is it that a person becomes strengthened inwardly? The Qur'ān does not give us any magical prescription for achievement of this purpose. It can only be attained by faith, righteous actions and steadfast perseverance. Firstly, divine truths should be embedded in the depths of our hearts and minds. We should make every effort to fix our thoughts on the next world, the world of eternal realities. The attitude that we should cultivate is that we have no rights in life, only responsibilities. Difficulties are bound to arise as we pursue the divine path. Rather than seek to lay the blame for them on others, we should bear them in a spirit of quiet and humble acceptance. These are the qualities that consolidate inward strength. The Prophet Muḥammad provided us with a perfect example of how to cultivate these qualities. He developed them to such a degree that no one was able to withstand the force of his character. When the Prophet exploded on the outside world, almost all of the known world capitulated before him. People succumbed before his inspired character, for the strength of his personality came from within.

In his article entitled "Bravery," the renowned Hindi writer, Sardar Pooran Singh (1882-1932), called the Prophet Muḥammad the bravest man in history. He had to be to bring about such a great revolution in the Arabian peninsula. His greatness can be judged from the fact that anyone who came in contact with him accepted him as his master. What kind of bravery is this which makes one so powerful? In the words of Pooran Singh:

> To strive every moment, every hour, towards making oneself greater and greater is bravery. It is the cowards who say, "Go ahead." While the brave say "Step back" (move backwards). Cowards say "raise the sword," while the brave say "bring your head forward! The policy of the brave is to gather and increase strength from all quarters. The brave build up their inner reserves, marching ahead within themselves. As they can move the entire world by moving the hearts of the people. Bravery does not consist of becoming emotionally overwrought and then cooling off like a piece of tin which heats up and cools off in no time. The fire may keep burning for centuries yet will not heat up the brave while centuries of snow may not be enough to dampen chill even the tip of the brave. People say, "Act, act, work, work" but all such talks seem futile. First create and gather the strength for work. It is futile to shout, Act, act, act!, without first creating and gathering the strength for work. One must grow and root oneself deep like a tree within oneself. The world does not stand on a heap of garbage where any cock can win fame and acclaim by mere crowing. The world, is rather borne aloft by the eternal principles of religious and spiritual truths.

> Whosoever fully associates with these truths emerges victorious.[4]

The secret of this bravery does not lie in magical prescriptions or spiritual exercises undertaken in seclusion. Exercises in the occult can delude in the world of matter, but they are of no use to people grappling with the day-to-day problems which confront them. Real strength is that which leads us to overcome the problems of life.

People really develop inner strength when they become free of all selfish ties; when they attain a level of thinking in which all superficial considerations are cast aside and, as the Prophet put it, "this see things as they are." Their thoughts and actions are not then guided by prejudice, anger, greed, hate, the lust for power, vanity, self-interest or any such base urge. This is what makes for strength of character. It is an irresistable force in life, one which enables a person to face every test. The initiatives of those endowed with inward strength are inevitably seen through to their conclusion. They make allowances for all eventualities, both probable and possible, in their decision-making. The more people oppose them, the more they adhere to their position of truth and righteousness.

An example of the manner in which the Prophet Muḥammad's inner strength provided solutions to all the problems that faced him can be found in the situation that developed after the conquest of Makkah. His strength of spirit manifested itself in different ways as the need arose. Sometimes it took the form of forgiveness, sometimes supreme courage, sometimes trust in God. Sometimes his success was due to farsightedness. Sometimes he showed how one who disavows self-interest becomes an invincible force, who gains all by forsaking everything.

After the Prophet Muḥammad, on whom be peace, had captured Makkah in A.H. 8, some of the Quraysh fled to the tribes of Hawāzin and Thaqīf, and incited them to start a new war against the Muslims. The tribes responded by mobilizing all their manpower, and amassed a force of 20,000 men. They met the Muslims on the field of Ḥunayn. The archers of Hawāzin had concealed themselves in a ravine and, when they rained their arrows down on the Muslims, about 11,000 of the 12,000 strong army turned and fled. Yet, despite this initial setback, the Muslims finally won an extraordinary victory. The reason for their recovery was the inner strength of their leader, the Prophet Muḥammad who, at this critical juncture, showed no signs of panic, but was the epitome of "tranquility"[5] and remained full of trust in God. Once his inner strength came out into the open, he immediately altered the course of battle. Standing up in the very midst of the enemy, he called out to his panicking followers:

> I am the Prophet, and I do not lie:
> I am the grandson of 'Abdul Muṭṭalib.

"To me, servants of God!" the Prophet called. His cousin Ibn 'Abbās, had a loud voice. The Prophet asked him to issue this appeal to the fleeing soldiers: "You who swore allegiance to the Prophet in the shadow of the Riḍwān tree: you swore that you would give your lives for the Faith! Where are you now?" When the Muslims saw that their leader was standing firm in face of the enemy, they realized that God's help was with him. Their flagging spirits were rekindled, and they returned with new determination to the field of battle. So unbounded was their new-found enthusiasm that they would not even wait for their floundering camels to turn around: they jumped off the backs of their mounts and ran back to the field of battle on foot. Suddenly the course of battle changed. Now it was the enemy's turn to take flight. The Muslims won the day, along with booty amounting to 24,000 camels, 40,000 goats and 40,000 ounces of silver. They also took some 6,000 prisoners.

Despite this victory, the situation continued to deteriorate. The Thaqīf were the second most prominent tribe in the whole of Arabia. They also owned the only fortified town in the peninsula. They were now besieged in Ṭā'if, but during the three weeks siege they inflicted more losses on the Muslims than they themselves had received at Ḥunayn. Their opposition to Islam was so deep-rooted that when one of their number, 'Urwah ibn Mas'ūd Thaqafi—who was reputed to be "dearer to his people than sweet maidens"—came to the Prophet and accepted Islam, they forgot their previous affection for him, and cruelly riddled him with arrows.

Once again the Prophet's inner strength came to his rescue. As the siege was tightened, 'Umar asked the Prophet to pray for the destruction of the people of Ṭā'if; but instead the Prophet prayed for their guidance. He was entirely free of anger and prejudice in this treatment of them. After besieging the town for three weeks, he ordered his army to retreat. On his return from Ṭā'if, the Prophet reached

Ji'rānah, where the spoils of the Battle of Ḥunayn had been stored. Here the Prophet had an opportunity to take reprisals against the Thaqīf's ally, Hawāzin. But he did quite the opposite, accepting an appeal from a delegation of that tribe for the release of all their six thousand prisoners. His magnanimous treatment of them—he not only set them free, but also gave them clothes and provisions for their journey—was bound to make an impression on them. And it did: the whole of the Hawāzin tribe, won over by the Prophet's unbounded generosity, accepted Islam.

The effects of this event were also felt in Ṭā'if. The Hawāzin and the Thaqīf were two branches of one large tribe. The Thaqīf felt much more threatened by the Hawāzin's conversion to Islam than they had been by the siege of their city. The severance of the Hawāzin from their alliance was a mortal wound which they knew would render them incapable of doing battle with the Muslims:

> The Thaqīf consulted among themselves. They saw that they would not now be able to fight against all the Arabs around them who had sworn allegiance to the Prophet, and accepted his Faith.[6]

In the year A.H. 9 (A.D. 630) a delegation from Ṭā'if arrived in Madinah. They expressed their willingness to accept Islam, but only under certain quite unusual conditions. They denied right of passage to the Muslims' army through their territory; they refused to pay land tax; they declined to participate in *jihād*; they also said that they would not pray, or recognize any ruler who was not from their tribe. The Prophet accepted all their conditions, but made it clear that there was no good in a religion which did not include bowing down to God. The Companions were amazed that the Prophet should accept their Islam, along with all these reservations. But the Prophet was looking further into the future, and put their minds at rest with these words:

> Once they have submitted to God, they will, after a while, give alms and strive in the path of God.[7]

Imām Aḥmad has related, on the authority of Anas ibn Mālik, that the Prophet used to grant any request that people made before they accepted Islam. One person who came to the Prophet was given a herd of goats so large that they stretched from one mountain to another. He then returned to his people and urged them to accept Islam, "for Muḥammad gives in such abundance that one need never go wanting again." But, as Ibn Kathīr has pointed out, even if a person came to the Prophet seeking only the world, before a day had passed he would undergo a transformation: the Prophet's Faith would become dearer to him than all the world has to offer.

Once the matter of the Thaqīf and the Hawāzin had been settled, another even more serious problem reared its head. The Muslims had accumulated a massive stock of booty in the victory over the Hawāzin. With great generosity, the Prophet distributed these spoils among the new Makkan converts. Some of the Anṣār—the people who had helped the Prophet when he emigrated to their town—found this hard to bear. It seemed to them that, now that the Prophet was re-established in his home town, he had adopted a chauvinistic attitude and was showering his own people with riches just to please them. There is no doubt that the Prophet was above such base motivations, but the resentment that the Anṣār felt at being left out was real enough, and posed serious problems for Muslim unity. The Prophet's sincerity of purpose, however, showed in the emphatic manner in which he removed their doubts.

The Prophet called all the Anṣār together in a courtyard, and addressed them in the following manner: "What is this that I am hearing about you? Is it not a fact you were lost, and God guided you, through me, to the right path. Whatever you were in need of He granted you in abundance—again through me. You were at war with one another and God brought you together as one people around me?" Everyone shouted out their agreement. Then the Prophet continued:

> You have every right to say that we Muhājirs came to you as refugees, expelled from our own land, and that you gave us shelter; we were in need and you looked after us; we were terrorized and you made us secure, friendless and you gave us company. Tell me, helpers, are you resentful just because I have given some new converts a trivial gift in order to raise their spirits, and make them secure in the Faith, while entrusting you with the great gift that God has bestowed upon you—that is Islam? Company of Helpers, are you not happy to see people take camels and goats home with them, while you return home with the Messenger of God?[8]

On hearing this speech, everyone broke down and wept. "We are happy with the Messenger of God!" they cried in unison. It was in this way that the Prophet's inner strength broke down every barrier, opened every door and surmounted every obstacle. It was his key to success in every situation in life.

THE EXTERNAL TARGET: MISSIONARY ACTIVITY

When the Prophet Muḥammad started his active struggle, he was not motivated by any urge to revenge himself on an outside world that had mistreated him. Usually popular movements are sparked off by some sort of instinct for revenge, but the Prophet's struggle was based on positive concepts of its own; it was not a negative reaction to event, or to the way he had been treated by others. Certainly, all the circumstances which usually cause political, social and economic reactions, leading to the establishment of popular movements, were present in full force when the Prophet was sent to the world. But it was not these points that the Prophet dwelt on in his communication of the Faith. He pursued his aims unremittingly, according to the programme mentioned at the beginning of this chapter, but he did so without clashing with anyone on political, social or economic issues.

When the Prophet commenced his mission, the land of the Arabs had become a prime target for attacks by the imperial powers of the day, who had been especially swift in annexing the comparatively fertile and prosperous parts of the country. The whole of Syria, in the north of the peninsula, was under Roman rule, governed by Arab chieftains who owed allegiance to Caesar. In the southern territory of the Yemen, the Persians held sway, being ruled in the time of the Prophet by a governor named Bazān. The only regions to have retained their independence were Ḥijāz, Tahāmah and Najd. Besides these, there were only rocky deserts, with the occasional oasis standing out in the wilderness. The Caesars and the Khusraus considered Arabia their property: that was why, when the Prophet wrote to the Emperor of Persia inviting him to accept Islam, that proud monarch tore up his letter and said indignantly:

> He writes to me—and he is my slave!

Abrahah's attack on the Ka'bah in the year of the Prophet's birth (A.D. 570), was part of this encroachment of foreign powers on Arab territory. Before the advent of Islam, the Ka'bah had been a centre of idol-worship for the whole of Arabia: every tribe had erected its own idol there, and considered its precincts sacred. All through the year people would flock to Makkah from far and wide to pay their respects to the Holy Ka'bah and make offerings to the idols that were lodged there. The economy of Makkah benefited greatly from this constant influx of pilgrims, and Abrahah desired to divert this great source of wealth towards his own land—the Yemen, which lay south east of Makkah. He had shown his willingness to resort to any means for the achievement of his ends by killing the previous Yemenese governor, taking over the country, and forcing the king of Abyssinia to recognize his authority in the province. A Christian by faith, Abrahah had built a huge church in the town of Ṣan'ā', after which he launched an intensive propaganda campaign to induce people to go on pilgrimages to it. In this way he hoped to divert the lucrative pilgrim trade from Makkah to Ṣan'ā'. It is recorded in Arab history that when all his efforts failed, he set out to destroy the Ka'bah, so that people would have nowhere left to make their pilgrimage to, save the church that he had built in Ṣan'ā'. For this purpose he took an army of elephants, which gained him the name of "Lord of the Elephants." Even the names of some of the people who built his church are known. The Arabs called the road that he passed along "The Road of the Elephants." The spring from which they drank, the gate through which they entered Makkah and the year of their attack were also similarly named.

What most leaders would have done under such adverse conditions was raise a popular movement against the political threat posed by foreign, imperial powers. They would have sought to rid their land of the yoke of foreign domination and revived the nationalistic instincts of their people. But the Prophet of Islam refrained completely from instigating any nationalistic freedom struggle of this nature.

There were also critical economic problems facing Arabia when the Prophet came to the world. Arabia was an almost entirely arid land: in an agrarian age it had no agricultural foundation on which to base its economy. This was a problem that affected every individual in the land, and could easily have provided the incentive for a popular revolutionary movement. But the Prophet did not capitalize on the economic problems of his people in any way. On one occasion the Makkan gentry gathered in front of the Ka'bah after sunset and summoned the Prophet. When he laid the basic teachings of Islam before them this is how they reacted to his message:

> Muḥammad, you know well that there is no country poorer or drier than ours. You know how hard it is for us to make a living. So pray to your Lord on our behalf that He should remove these dry mountains that have made life so difficult for us; that He should make our land fertile and make rivers, like those of Syria and Iraq, flow in its valleys.[9]

In order to understand what made the leaders of the Quraysh speak to the Prophet in this manner, one has to understand the geographical situation of Arabia. A chain of mountains that stretched along the coastline of Ḥijāz as far as Najd prevented sea winds from penetrating inland, with the result that rainfall in the Arabian peninsula, in contrast to that of Iraq and Syria, was minimal. This geographical situation was at the root of Arabia's economic problems. Any budding leader could instantly have attracted people's attention by exploiting these problems. The Prophet, however, did not choose this path. In fact, he did not pay any direct attention to problems of this nature and devoted his efforts entirely towards preaching the oneness of God. History shows that the Prophet's struggle in the field of missionary activity had far-reaching effects, opening up new opportunities for the Arabs in political and economic fields also. But it is important to realize that these advantages were an indirect result of the Prophet's struggle: it was not towards political and economic gain that he himself directed his efforts.

The Prophet's whole life shows that the matter to which

he attached basic importance was preaching of the faith. As soon as he started his active mission he laid all other matter aside and concentrated solely on propagating the message of Islam. First of all he was determined to inform his kinsfolk that he had been chosen to communicate the word of God to humanity. For this purpose he called all his relatives—about forty were invited of whom at least thirty attended—to a dinner. After dinner, he addressed his guests, but he met with little success. "Banū Muṭṭalib," he said, "I have been sent to you in particular, then to mankind as a whole. Who then will fulfill on my behalf my debts and my promises? Who will look after my family while I am away? Whoever does so will be my companion in paradise." The Prophet repeated his words, but only 'Alī, who was a young boy at the time, responded positively. "I will, Prophet of God," he said. "You, 'Alī, you, 'Alī!" came the Prophet's reply.[10]

One day Abū Jahl threw a stone at the Prophet, drawing blood from his face. The Prophet's uncle, 'Abbās, heard about this. Though at that time 'Abbās had not accepted Islam, family pride moved him to go and smite Abū Jahl in return. Then he came back to the Prophet, "Nephew," he said triumphantly, "I have taken your revenge." "It would make me happier if you were to accept Islam," The Prophet replied.

Once the leaders of the Quraysh came to Abū Ṭālib, another of the Prophet's uncles. "Abū Ṭālib," they said, "your nephew enters into our arenas and our gatherings, and says things which upset us. Please, if you can manage it, stop him from doing so." Abū Ṭālib sent his own son,

Aqīl, to fetch the Prophet. When he had told his nephew what the Quraysh had said, the Prophet raised his eyes up to heaven. "By God," he said, "is anyone among you able to light a fire from a flame of the sun? Well, I am no more capable of forsaking the message that God Himself has entrusted to me." Having said this, the Prophet broke down weeping.

The Banū Hāshim, to which tribe the Prophet belonged, were the cream of Arab society. Since his tribe was already in a dominant position in Arabia, some people thought that perhaps the Prophet wanted to consolidate his own authority and be crowned king. But the Prophet's actions showed that he was interested in only one thing, and that was to convey to people the importance of preparing themselves for the next world. So persistently would he emphasise this matter that sometimes the leaders of the Quraysh would plead with him in almost desperate terms to leave them alone. "Muḥammad," Abū Jahl once said to him, "will you stop insulting our gods? If you just want us to bear witness that you have communicated your message, then all right: we bear witness, you certainly have communicated it."

The Prophet, however, was undeterred and went on delivering his message. This infuriated the Quraysh still further, and, they decided to ostracize the whole of the Banū Hāshim family. An interdict stopped inter-marriage and commercial relations. On learning of this the Banū Hāshim moved to the place known as Shi'b Abī Ṭālib. While this interdict was in force, preaching was confined to those affected by it, and the Prophet took full advantage of this. These restrictions, however, came to an end temporarily in the sacred months. The Prophet's family used to benefit from this period of respite in that they could conduct transactions. Then, gathering together the meat of sacrifice, they would dry it for use during the rest of the year. But the Prophet would use this time in a different manner: he would go to tents where various tribes were staying, and communicate to them the message of Islam.

Imagine how precarious the Prophet's situation must have been when he was emigrating from Makkah to Madinah. Yet even during this journey he did not miss a single opportunity to preach Islam to those he came into contact with. When he reached Ghamīm, for instance, he communicated the message of Islam to Barīdah ibn Ḥaṣīb, who then—along with eighty members of his family—accepted Islam. On reaching the mountain pass of Rakūbah he met two men whom he told about Islam, and who accepted the Faith. When the Prophet asked them their names, they said that they belonged to the tribe of Aslam, and were bandits. For this reason, they explained, they were called "Muhānān," or "The Two Despicable Ones." "No," the Prophet told them, "you are two honourable ones."[11]

The Prophet Muḥammad inculcated in his companions the same attitude. It was not to be their aim to conquer territory or accumulate spoils of war. Rather they were to become a source of wealth—the wealth of true faith—for others. When the Prophet entrusted 'Alī with the Muslim standard in the field of Khaybar, he told his cousin to proceed softly: "And when you reach their fields, call them to Islam and tell them what their responsibilities to God are. By God, if the Lord guides just one of them through you to Islam, then that will be better for you than a herd of red camels."

Missionary activity was such a prominent part of the Prophet's life, that if one were to put his whole struggle under one heading, this would surely be the one. He did not concentrate on political, economic and social issues, as leaders usually do; rather he devoted his entire time and energy to preaching the word of God. At first it may have seemed that his single-mindedness was unjustified. But from the outcome of his efforts, it became apparent that if we set our sights on the next world—as the Prophet did—then worldly goals are automatically achieved.

PATIENCE AND STEADFASTNESS

The third part of the Prophet's mission, mentioned at the beginning of this chapter, was a steadfast forbearance in face of the difficulties encountered on the divine path. The Arabic word for patience is *ṣabr*. One of the words derived from the same root is *ṣabbārah*, meaning hard, unfertile ground, which does not accept any seed. Likewise a patient person, one endowed with *ṣabr* is one who does not let events affect him, who never loses heart but pursues his goal with unflagging resolution. Courageous people are also called *ṣabūr*, for they do not bend to pressure; they stand firm and uncompromising, no matter how adverse the circumstances may be.

Patience is the most lofty virtue that one who has

adopted Islam as a cause can have. When Islam has become a vital part of our life, it imbues us with an undying spirit which enables us "never to lose heart on account of what befalls (us) in the path of God"—never to weaken or cringe abjectly.[12] To believe in God is to trust in Him absolutely, and one who trusts in God is the possessor of great strength: there is nothing that can weaken his or her resolve.

Without patience, preachers of God's word cannot continue their work for long. When they embark on their mission, they find that they are alone in a company of strangers. They are restricted by God's commandments, while others feel themselves free to do as they like. Everything that they do is geared towards success and salvation in the next world, while all the avenues towards worldly success are open before their adversaries. All their efforts are concentrated on spiritual ends, while the political and economic expertise of others makes them strong in the eyes of men. They maintain strict ethical standards, while others' actions are free of all restrictions. The preachers of God's word can easily be affected by such matters. They may even be tempted to follow the madding crowd, and give up their task. It may occur to them that if what they are doing is so ineffectual, they may as well spare themselves the trouble. This is where *ṣabr* comes to their rescue, preventing them from giving up just because their words seem to be having no effect on others:

> Therefore, have patience. God's promise is true. Let not those who have no certainty make you impatient.[13]

Sometimes, *ṣabr* takes on another form, and that is

steadfastness and forbearance in the face of persecution from others. This was the method adopted by all the prophets of God: They used to say to their adversaries:

> ...We will endure your persecution patiently. In God let all the faithful put their trust.[14]

The afflictions which beset preachers of God's word are in fact an integral part of their mission. Those they address are bound to show some reaction to their words, and sometimes it is going to be violent and uncompromising. If they start bemoaning their treatment by others, the very seriousness of their efforts to bring them over to the true faith is cast into doubt. Those who are really working for God's sake will not be affected by the reactions of others to what they are doing. The difficulties we encounter in pursuit of God's good pleasure, then, are really a test of our sincerity. Unless we have proved our sincerity, we cannot expect our words to have an effect on others.

When faced with enemy onslaughts people usually take retaliatory measures of their own: People are generally used to retaliate when they face any unpleasant treatment by others. *Ṣabr*, on the other hand, means to bear patiently whatever is meted out by the enemy. For instance, if Muslims in a certain country find themselves up against the economic bias of their non-Muslim compatriots, the way of *ṣabr* is not to start demanding equal treatment, but is rather to make extra efforts oneself to excel over others. Prejudice can only have an adverse effect when people of equal ability are competing for one job. If one of the contestants clearly excels the others in ability, then not even prejudice can deny him his rightful place.

When the Muslims were economically isolated in Makkah in the time of the Prophet, some of them emigrated to Abyssinia, thus consolidating their own position. The people of Makkah had made it impossible for the Prophet's followers to carry on with their trading. What the Muslims did was to move to a neighbouring country and pursue their livelihood there. So hard-working and honest were they in their dealings that Najāshī, the king of Abyssinia, proclaimed that anyone who wronged a Muslim would have to pay the wronged party 8 dirhams compensation. This was just one of the ways in which God helped the Muslims re-establish themselves, considering their patience in the face of persecution by others.

Patience may appear to be a negative virtue, but, as far as its results are concerned, it is a highly positive one. Once we have realized the value of *ṣabr*, we do not take immediate retaliatory measures against our oppressors; rather we look further into the future and sets in motion a series of events which lead to final success. Feelings run high when we have just been wronged. If we take immediate action, we may not be able to consider rationally what we should do: rather, we may act on the basis of our emotions at the time. Patience, on the other hand, leads us coolly and objectively to consider all the possibilities open to us, and the real nature of the situation we have to deal with. We are then in a position to pursue a sound and solid policy. Impatience precipitates immediate action, to contain the other party, while patience inclines us to wait for the eternal laws of nature devised by God to start working against our adversaries.

When we combat our enemy with impatience, we are spurred on by superficial motives and base emotions. We are bound to make mistakes and errors of judgement which only serve to weaken our case. When one is patient, on the other hand, a divine strength—intelligence—is born within us. Our intellect is a most extraordinary source of strength. It is able to look ahead, beyond temporary obstacles and barriers, and plan for the future. Intelligence frees one from negative impulses and enables one to think on a profound level, penetrating to the very depths of a situation. There we discover secrets which enable us to gain control of our rival from all angles. He becomes like the quarry caught in the huntsman's net: movement only enmeshes him further and serves to tighten the huntsman's hold on him.

The emigration from Makkah to Madinah was an example of the Prophet's patience. When the Quraysh had decided to kill the Prophet, the latter had two options before him: either he could take up his sword in self-defence, or he could leave Makkah for some safer abode. The Prophet adopted the second course of action. He coolly thought the situation over and decided on emigration to Madinah, where he would be able to continue the same work, only in a different place. According to 'Ā'ishah, the Prophet used to come to their house every day in the period prior to the emigration. There he would hold consultations with her father, Abū Bakr. Preparations were made, in the utmost secrecy, over a period of six months. Everything went according to plan, and finally the Prophet set out for Madinah, taking a dependable guide with him. From the point of view of a zealous Muslim political leader of the modern age, the emigration would appear as a flight, for what he would advocate in a similar situation would be a fight to the death; he would be looking no further ahead than making a martyr of himself. But if one looks at the results of the emigration of the Prophet, one can see that it was clearly the greatest watershed in Islamic history.

Patience also enables us to refrain from taking action, and permits things to take their natural course. Human nature is an unchangeable reality that always exerts a strong influence on the course of human life. Deep down, people always have a soft spot for one who bears abuse quietly, for one who refuses to be provoked even in face of the utmost provocation. The human conscience naturally tends to favour the oppressed rather than the oppressor. Great opportunities open out in the world of nature for those who are denied them in the world of men: then, when they stand firm in face of persecution, they prove themselves to be in the right. The boycott that was imposed on the Prophet and his family in the seventh year of the prophetic mission was just such an example. As a result of this boycott the whole of the Banū Hāshim clan, with the exception of Abū Lahab, were besieged in a mountain ravine, called Shi'b Abī Ṭālib. The manner in which these people quietly endured all this cruel oppression was bound to have an effect on the conscience of others. And it did. Within three years, people like Abū'l-Bakhtarī, Hishām ibn 'Amr, Zubayr ibn

Umayyah, Zam'ah ibn al-Aswad and Muṭ'am ibn 'Adī broke away from the ranks of the enemy, openly challenging the propriety of the pact by which this boycott had been imposed on the Banū Hāshim. The pact collapsed, and the Banū Hāshim were rescued from their terrible plight.

The most important thing about patience is that it qualifies one for divine succour. Patient perseverance in pursuit of a worthy cause means putting one's own affairs in the hands of the Lord of the Universe. It is inconceivable that those who trust in Almighty God, for the sake of a just cause, should find themselves forsaken.

There are various ways in which this divine succour manifests itself. The human mind can neither understand nor fathom them. Some of the forms which divine succour takes, however, have been mentioned in the Qur'ān. When Muslims confront non-Muslims in the field of battle, for instance, divine succour compensates for their inferior resources: calmness and confidence enter the hearts of the believers, while fear weakens their opponents:

> Believers, remember God's goodness to you when there came against you hosts. We unleashed against them a wind and soldiers you could not see. God saw all that you were doing.[15]

This verse deals with the Battle of the Trench (A.D. 627) when God sent two things—wind and an army of angels—in support of the believers. There is nothing extraordinary about wind. There is nowhere that it does not blow. But at a special time, and in a special place, it was made to blow faster, thus assisting the believers. This shows that when God decides to help anyone, he makes normal physical happenings assume a certain intensity which ensures success.

As for the army of angels, they did not come and wield their swords alongside the Muslims. They provided psychological rather than military support. What they did, as on several other occasions, was "give courage to the believers, and cast terror into the hearts of the infidels."[16] They made the enemy appear as a "small band," while the Muslims were made to appear as a "great army" in the eyes of their enemies.[17]

During the reign of the second Caliph, 'Umar (A.D. 634-644), the Muslim army landed at Qādsiyyah, on the threshold of Iran under the leadership of Sa'd ibn Abī Waqqāṣ. They had to stay there longer than expected, and it was not long before their provisions ran out. Sa'd then sent a few men to look for some cattle which they could eat. They met an Iranian, whom they asked whether there were any goats or cows around. Although the Iranian was a shepherd himself, he denied all knowledge of there being any animals in the vicinity. He had hidden his own flock in a dense jungle nearby on hearing of the presence of the Muslim army. But then an ox called out: "The shepherd is lying. We are here, in this undergrowth." On hearing the cry the Muslims entered the wood, seized of a few of the beasts, and took them before Sa'd. When the rest of the army heard the story they were very happy and interpreted it as a sign that God's succour was with them.

But, as the historian Ibn al-Ṭaqṭaqī has written, one should not be under the impression that the ox actually called out, "We are here," in Arabic. It lowed as oxen usually do, and from its sound the Muslims realized that cattle were hidden in the undergrowth.

TRUSTING IN GOD

The Qur'ān sums up the Islamic method in the following words:

> And if they incline to peace, incline you also to it, and put your trust in God. Surely He is the Hearing, the Knowing. Should they seek to deceive you, God is All-sufficient for you.[18]

This shows that the true Islamic method is to pursue our aims peacefully. Even when there is a fear that our opponents may deceive us, Muslims should still put their trust in God, and be ready to make peace.

What this means is that we should concentrate our efforts in that field of action where—without any confrontation with others—there are opportunities for us to advance. As for other fields, those in which no opportunities present themselves—one should let the forces of nature go to work. If we reserve our efforts for those areas in which we are able to operate effectively, God will help us in others where we can do nothing. If we leave the arena of action that has been allotted to us, and seek to operate in some other where we have been afforded no opportunities, it is as if we have tried to function not from our own arena, but from God's. To try to usurp God in His work can only lead to His displeasure; it cannot earn us His succour.

NOTES

1. Qur'ān, 74:1-7.
2. Qur'ān, 6:15.
3. Muḥammad Marmaduke Pickthall, *The Glorious Qur'ān*, London, 1938.
4. Sardar Pooran Singh, Article "Bravery."
5. Qur'ān, 9:26.
6. Ibn Hishām, *Tahzīb Sīrah*, vol. 2, p. 107.
7. Ḥadīth of Abū Dāwūd.
9. Ḥadīth of Aḥmad, on the authority of Ibn Isḥāq.
9. *Tahzīb Sīrat Ibn Hishām*, vol. 1, p. 67.
10. Ḥadīth related by Al-Bazār.
11. Ḥadīth of Aḥmad, on the authority of Ibn Sa'd.
12. Qur'ān, 3:146.
13. Qur'ān, 30:60.
14. Qur'ān, 14:12.
15. Qur'ān, 33:19.
16. Qur'ān, 8:12.
17. Qur'ān, 8:44.
18. Qur'ān, 8:61-62.

10

The Prophet in Makkah

There are two main periods of the Prophet Muḥammad's life: the Makkan and the Madinan, these names being derived from the towns of Makkah and Madinah. Place names tend to assume historical significance over and above their literal meaning, and Makkah and Madinah are no exceptions. They may originally have been just place names, but now they have become symbolic of the two faces of the Islamic coin—two aspects of the process by which Islam has come to the world. On the one hand, Makkah is symbolic of "*da'wah*," or calling people to the faith, while, on the other hand, Madinah is symbolic of revolution. One can put this another way and say that Makkah was the place where the "*da'wah* power" of Islam was first activated, while Madinah was the place where this power actually achieved supremacy. This verse of the Qur'ān tells the whole story of both Makkan and Madinan Islam:

> Muḥammad is God's Messenger. Those who are with him are hard on the unbelievers but merciful to one another. You see them bow and prostrate

> themselves, seeking the grace of God and His good will. Their marks are on their faces, the traces of their prostrations. Thus they are described in the Torah and in the Gospel: (they are) like the seed which puts forth its shoot and strengthens it, so that it rises stout and firm upon its stalk, delighting the sowers. Through them God seeks to enrage the unbelievers. God has promised those of them who will believe and do good work forgiveness and a rich reward.[1]

The reference to the Torah in this verse is made with regard to the individual qualities of the companions of the Prophet. The reference to the Bible shows their qualities when they came together as a group. Their individual qualities developed in Makkah, whereas their qualities as a community emerged in Madinah.

Biographies of the Prophet usually treat their subject as if he were a person endowed with great magical powers, one who by mysterious means brought the whole of Arabia under his wing. These books read like fairy stories; even events which have no miraculous content have been given a fanciful miraculous interpretation. Take the case of Ṣuhayb ibn Sanān's migration from Makkah to Madinah. When some Quraysh youths blocked his path, Ṣuhayb pleaded with them: "If I let you have all my property, will you let me go?" They said that they would. Ṣuhayb had a few ounces of silver with him. He gave it all to them and carried on to Madinah. According to a tradition in Bayhaqī, Ṣuhayb said that when the Prophet saw him in Madinah he told Ṣuhayb that his trading, that is, his handing over of his property to the Quraysh, had been very profitable. Ṣuhayb, according to the tradition, was astounded, for no one had arrived in Madinah before him who could have brought the news. "It must have been Gabriel who told you," he said to the Prophet.

But the same event has been related by Ibn Marduyah and Ibn Sa'd. According to them, Ṣuhayb told his own story in these words:

> I carried on until I reached Madinah. When the Prophet heard about my handing over my property to the Quraysh he said: "Ṣuhayb has profited! Ṣuhayb has profited!"[2]

The fact that the Prophet led such a simple life means that it is simple for others to follow his example. He was a human being like any other, but his life was a perfect pattern for others. According to al-Bukhārī, he used to stumble on the road like anyone else. Indeed, the reason his congregation refused to believe that he was the receiver of divine revelation was the very fact that, to all appearances, the Prophet appeared just like any normal human being:

> You make transactions in the town. You seek a livelihood just as we do.[3]

The truth is that the greatness of the Prophet's life lies in its being a human event rather than a far-fetched tale of inimitable miraculous actions. The Prophet was God's humble and very human servant, and, having been chosen by God to spread His message, he was helped by Him at every critical hour. In this sense his success was miraculous, but the Prophet himself was in no way endowed with miraculous powers. It is rather the human aspect of his life which emerges from a study of the Qur'ān.

THE BEGINNING OF THE PROPHET'S PUBLIC MISSION

When, at the age of forty, the Prophet Muḥammad received his first revelation, he reacted as any normal human being would in such a situation. He was meditating in the Cave of Ḥirā' at the time. Petrified, he returned home, where his wife Khadījah was waiting for him. Being an impartial judge, she was in a position to view the situation objectively. She was able to see that the Prophet's experience, far from being a bad dream, must have been a sign that he had been chosen by God. "It cannot be," she said, "God will surely never humiliate you. You are kind to your relatives; you always give the weak a helping hand; you help those who are out of work to stand on their own feet again; you honour guests. When people are in trouble you give them assistance."[4]

The Prophet went about his task in a manner befitting one who was to preach a new message in a society attached to traditional beliefs and customs. He proceeded cautiously, following an entirely natural sequence. At first he had to work in secret. This is how the historian Ibn Kathīr describes an incident that occurred at the beginning of the Prophet's mission:

> 'Alī, son of Abū Ṭālib and cousin of the Prophet, came into the Prophet's house while he and Khadījah were praying. He asked his cousin what they were about. The Prophet told him that this was God's religion, the path that God had chosen Himself. It was to call people to this path that He had sent His

prophets to the world. "Believe in One God," the Prophet said. "He has no partner. Worship Him alone. Forsake the idols Lāt and 'Uzzā.' "I have heard nothing of this nature before today," 'Alī replied. "I cannot make a decision until I have talked the matter over with my father, Abū Ṭālib." But the Prophet did not want anyone to know about his secret until the time had come for it to be made public. "'Alī," he said. "If you are not ready to become a Muslim, keep the matter to yourself." 'Alī waited for one night, then God made his heart incline towards Islam. He went back to the Prophet early in the morning. "What was it that you were telling me yesterday?" He asked. Bear witness that there is none worthy of being served save God. He is One. He has no partner. Forsake Lāt and 'Uzzā, and disown all those who are set up as equals with God." 'Alī did this and became a Muslim. Then, in fear of Abū Ṭālib, he used to come and see the Prophet secretly. 'Alī kept his Islam a secret; he did not tell anyone about it."[5]

Even later, when the first Muslims among the tribes of Aws and Khazraj returned to Madinah, they followed the same policy. According to the historian Ṭabarānī, "They returned to their people and invited them, secretly, to embrace Islam."

Throughout his entire public mission, the Prophet was very careful not to take any initiative until he was quite sure that he possessed the necessary resources. 'Ā'ishah, wife of the Prophet and daughter of Abū Bakr, tells how, when the Prophet had gathered 38 followers around him, Abū Bakr urged him to publicize his mission. Abū Bakr was of the opinion that the prophet and his companions should go out into the open, and publicly preach Islam. But the Prophet said to him: "No, Abū Bakr, we are too few." The same thing happened in the sixth year of the Prophet's mission, when 'Umar accepted Islam. He protested to the Prophet: "Why should we keep our Islam a secret, when we are right. And why should others be allowed to publicize their faith, when they are in the wrong?" The Prophet gave 'Umar the same reply that he had given Abū Bakr several years earlier: "We are too few, 'Umar." As long as the Prophet remained in Mecca, he continued this cautious posture. Until after the emigration, with the consolidation of Muslim ranks, when the armed Quraysh advanced on Madinah to extirpate the Islam and Muslims then permission was given to Muslims to counter the Quraysh. The first battle fought between the Muslims and their antagonists was the Battle of Badr. "Whoever is successful on this day," the Prophet said as the battle began, "will be successful in times to come." The meaning of the Prophet's remark was that the time for Muslims to take positive initiatives was only when they were in a position to fashion a new future for Islam. If their actions were not likely to produce such results, it was better for them to be patient.

One thing is quite clear from biographies of the Prophet. When the task of public preaching devolved upon him, he became very conscious of the greatness of this task, realizing that it would require his complete and single-minded attention. He hoped that his family would look after him financially so that, freed from having to look for a livelihood, he would be able to concentrate on his preaching work. He called 'Abd al-Muṭṭalib's family together in his own house. There were about thirty family members at that time. The Prophet told them what his true mission in life now was. He asked for their support, so that he would be free to discharge his prophetic duties. This is how Imām Aḥmad describes the incident, on the authority of 'Ā'ishah:

> "Banū Muṭṭalib," the Prophet said, "I have been sent to you in particular, and to the whole of mankind in general. Who will swear allegiance to me and become my brother and companion? Who will fulfil my debts and my promises on my behalf? Who will look after my family affairs for me? He will be with me in heaven." Someone spoke up: "Muḥammad, you are an ocean. Who can come forward and accept such responsibility?"[6]

The Prophet's own family were not ready to accept responsibility for him. 'Abbās ibn 'Abd al-Muṭṭalib, the Prophet's uncle, was financially in a position to look after his nephew. Yet even he remained silent, for fear that this responsibility would devour his wealth. God, however, helped His Prophet, first through the Prophet's wife, Khadījah bint Khuwaylid, and later on through Abū Bakr, whose wealth saw the Prophet through the years in Madinah.

The Prophet displayed boyish enthusiasm in his efforts to communicate the faith to others. The historian Ibn Jarir tells, on the authority of 'Abdullah ibn al-'Abbās, how the nobles of the Quraysh had gathered around the Ka'bah one day, and called for the Prophet. He came quickly, thinking that they might be feeling some leanings towards Islam. He was always eager that his people should accept the guidance of Islam. The thought of their being doomed was a great distress to him. It transpired, however, that they had just wanted to pick a quarrel. Acceptance of Islam was the last thing on their minds. The Prophet talked to them at length, then went away in distress. Ibn Hisham takes up the story:

> The Prophet returned to his home sad and disillusioned, for the hopes that he had for his people when they called him had been dashed. He had seen how far people were from accepting his message.[7]

When the Prophet's uncle, Abū Ṭālib, lay dying, people came to him and asked him to settle matters between his nephew and themselves before he died. "Take an undertaking from him on our behalf, and one from us on his behalf, so that he should have nothing to do with us, nor us with him," they said. Abū Ṭālib called his nephew, and asked him what he wanted of the people. The Prophet replied that he just wanted them to testify that there was none worthy of being served save God, and forsake all other objects of worship. His people, however, were unwilling to accept this. When everyone went away, Abū Ṭālib said to his nephew: "You know, I don't think it was anything very difficult that you asked of them." On hearing his uncle's words, the Prophet's hopes soared, for now perhaps he would accept Islam. "Uncle," he said, "then why don't you testify to the oneness of God, so that I may be able to intercede for you on the Day of Judgement?"[8] The Prophet was sorely disappointed that his uncle never accepted Islam.

The dedication with which the Prophet applied himself to his task was total, all his mental and physical energy being channelled into it. Not only his time, but also his property went into the furtherance of the Islamic cause. Before the start of his mission, the Prophet had become quite rich by virtue of his marriage to the wealthy Khadījah. At the beginning of the Makkan period, the Quraysh sent 'Utbah ibn Rabī'ah to talk to the Prophet. As Ibn Kathīr explains, he soon found himself being won over; (an event which was unfortunately misinterpreted by his kinsmen as being due to the love of the Prophet's wealth):

> Afterwards 'Utbah stayed at home and did not go out to see anybody. "Fellow Quraysh," Abū Jahl said, "It seems to me that 'Utbah has become attracted towards Muḥammad. He must have been taken by the food that Muḥammad offered him. This can only be due to some need of his. Let's go and see him." So off they went. "Utbah," Abū Jahl said, "we have come to see you because we are sure that you have taken a liking to Muḥammad and his religion. Look, if you want we can accumulate enough money to ensure that you will not have to go to him to be fed." 'Utbah became angry, and swore that he would never speak to Muḥammad again![9]

Similarly, Walīd ibn Mughīrah once came to see the Prophet. When the latter recited some verses of the Qur'ān to him, Walīd was very impressed by the style of the Book of God. When Abū Jahl heard about this, he went to see Walīd, and told him that people would make a collection for him, because he was obviously in need of some money, and had gone to Muḥammad for this purpose. The Prophet, then, was financially very well placed when he commenced his mission. But when, after 13 years, he emigrated to Madinah, it was a very different story. He had nothing left, and had to borrow some money from Abū Bakr for the journey.

THE PROPHET'S CALL

Looked at from a logical point of view, the Islamic call consists of certain constant, recurrent factors. It is the same points—the oneness of God, the importance and inevitability of the life after death, the need for people to understand their position as God's servants, and live as such according to the prophetic pattern—which are stressed again and again. When these points come from the tongue of the preacher of God's word, however, they take on the hue of the preacher's own person; he adds an element of individuality to what are basically unvarying themes. This addition means that the message of Islam, far from being a repetition of set texts, is expressed with irresistable vitality and spontaneity. One in meaning, it becomes diverse in the forms it takes. Fixed though its topics are, it becomes impossible to compile a complete list of them. The heart of the preacher of God's word is full of fear of God; it is his ardent desire to bring his audience on to the path of right guidance. He knows that if he can bring God's servants close to God, God will be pleased with him. These factors spur him on in his task. They ensure that his words, far from being repetitive and monotonous, have an inspired air about them. Despite being one in theme, his message becomes varied in tone. The preacher of God's word thinks first and foremost of his congregation. More than anything, he wants them to find right guidance. This means that he makes allowances for the needs of every individual that he is addressing, and casts his words in a mould that will be understandable to them.

No one followed this pattern more completely than the Prophet of Islam. Night and day, he was busy preaching the word of God. But his preaching was far from a bland repetition of certain set speeches. He used to take into consideration the nature of his congregation in formulating his message.

On one occasion, in the early days in Makkah, the Prophet preached Islam to Abū Sufyān and his wife Hind. This is how he framed his address:

> Abū Sufyān ibn Ḥarb, Hind bint ‘Utbah. You are going to die, then you will be raised up. The good will then be admitted into heaven, and the wicked will enter hell. I am telling you the truth.[10]

The historian Ibn Khuzaymah has recorded the following conversation between a member of the Makkan nobility, Ḥaṣīn, and the Prophet Muḥammad, on whom be peace. "Tell me, Ḥaṣīn," the Prophet said, "how many gods do you worship?" "Seven on earth and one in heaven," Ḥaṣīn replied. "Whom do you call on when you are in trouble?" the Prophet asked. "The one in heaven," Ḥaṣīn answered. "And whom do you call on when you have suffered loss of wealth?" the Prophet asked again. "The one in heaven," came the same reply. "He alone answers your prayers," the Prophet said, "Then why do you set up others as His equals?"[11]

Imām Aḥmad has reported, on the authority of Abū Umāmah, that a man from a certain tribe came to the Prophet, and asked him what teachings he had brought from God. "That relationships should be strengthened and wrongful killing avoided. Roads should be left open. Idols should be broken. Only one God should be served; no others should be set up with Him as His equals," was the Prophet's reply.

After he had reached Madinah, however, when he sent a formal invitation to the people of Najrān, he presented his message in a different manner:

> I call you to serve God rather than men, and to acknowledge the sovereign power of God rather than that of men.[12]

The Qur'ān itself provided a constant and important basis of the Prophet's preaching work. Whenever the Prophet met anybody, he would recite a passage of the Qur'ān to him. Often phrases like, "He made mention of Islam, and read some of the Qur'ān to them," or "He presented the message of Islam before them, and recited to them a passage of the Qur'ān," recurred in traditions concerning the Prophet's preaching mission. The Qur'ān possessed extraordinary magnetism for the Arabs. Even some of the direst enemies of Islam used to steal up to the Prophet's house at night, put their ears to the wall, and listen to him reciting the Qur'ān. The sublime style of the Qur'ān used to have the most profound impact on the Prophet's people. Take the case of Walīd ibn Mughīrah who once came to the Prophet on behalf of the Quraysh. When the

Prophet read him a passage of the Qur'ān, Walīd was so impressed that he went back to the Quraysh and told them that the Qur'ān was a literary work of such unsurpassable excellence that it overshadowed everything else. Recitation of the Qur'ān was, in those days, a common method of preaching Islam. When Muṣ'ab ibn Zubayr was sent to Madinah as a preacher, he used to "talk to people, and recite a passage of the Qur'ān to them." That was why people came to know him as "al-Muqrī", the reciter of the Qur'ān.

During his time in Makkah the Prophet's preaching was always conducted on a refined intellectual level. It was dominated by the lofty literary standard set by the Qur'ān. The Prophet's opponents, on the other hand, could offer only abuse and opprobrium in reply. Sensible people in Makkah could not help but come to the conclusion that Muḥammad's opponents had nothing concrete to offer in support of their case. According to Ibn Jarīr, some of the nobles of the Quraysh planned to call a meeting and talk to the Prophet. Their intention was "to place themselves above reproach as far as he was concerned" that is, to assure him that they had nothing to do with the base tactics being followed by the Prophet's direst enemies.

THE APTITUDE OF THE ARABS

Now we come to the factors that produce the reaction that Islamic preaching evokes. However untiring the efforts of the preacher, and no matter how accurately he presents the true message of Islam, it is more the disposition of his audience that determines whether his call is accepted or not. The character of the Arabs was a valuable factor which contributed towards their acceptance of Islam. They were simple human beings, brought up in simple, natural surroundings. Despite their superficial ignorance and stubbornness, they retained the qualities of their environment. Thirty million square kilometres of desert, the hot, bare, hard country in which they lived, was an ideal breeding ground for the most lofty human values. An average Arab had just one source of income—his camel. But if he had guests he would sacrifice this invaluable beast in order to provide them with food. If a victim of oppression took refuge with an Arab in his tent, he knew he had a friend who would give his own life in defence of the wronged. Even plunderers did their looting in a chivalrous manner. If they wanted to snatch clothes and jewellery off a tribe's womenfolk, they would not allow themselves to snatch them off the womens' bodies with their own hands: instead, they would tell the women to hand over their valuables, and they themselves would look in the opposite direction, so that they did not catch sight of them while they were taking off their clothes.

It would be misleading to think of the desert Arabs as pure simpletons who knew nothing. They were a highly intelligent, alert people, quick to penetrate to the depths of a matter.

Seven Muslim converts came to the Prophet from a certain tribe. They told him that they had learnt five things during the time of ignorance that preceded Islam. They would adhere to these principles, they said, unless the Prophet gave them other instructions. The Prophet then asked them what these characteristics that they had inherited from the time of ignorance were. "Thankfulness in times of affluence," they answered, "and patience in times of difficulty. Steadfastness on the field of battle and resignation to fate. We learnt not to rejoice over another's setbacks, even if it was one's own enemy that was afflicted." "These people are intellectuals, men of letters," the Prophet said when he heard this. "They are cast in the mould of prophets. How wonderful their words."[13]

Ḍamād, a practising exorcist belonging to the tribe of Banū Azdashanūah once came to Makkah. People there told him about the Prophet. "He is possessed by an evil spirit," they said. Ḍamād went to see the Prophet, thinking that he might be able to cure him. But when he heard the Prophet's words, his attitude changed. "I have heard soothsayers and conjurors," he said. "I have seen the works of poets. But I have never come across anything of this nature. Give me your hand," he said to the Prophet. "Let me swear allegiance to you." As was his custom, the Prophet did not give a long talk on this occasion. Actually this was all he said:

> Praise be to God. We praise Him and seek help from Him. One whom God guides, no one can send astray, and one whom God sends astray, no one can guide. I bear witness that there is none worthy of being served save God. He has no equal.[14]

In these few words Ḍamād found a wealth of meaning. "Say that again," he requested the Prophet. "Your words are as deep as the ocean."[15]

For an Arab there was no question of any discrepancy between words and deeds. He himself was true to his word, and expected others to be the same. As soon as he comprehended the truth of a matter, he accepted it. According to the Prophet's biographer, Ibn Isḥāq, the Banū Sa'd tribe sent Ḍamām ibn Tha'labah to the Prophet on their behalf. He arrived in Madinah, sat his camel down near the gate of the mosque and tied it up. Then he went inside. The Prophet was sitting there with his companions. Ḍamām was a brave and intelligent man. He stood in front of the gathering and asked: "Who among you is the son of 'Abdul Muṭṭalib?" "I am," the Prophet replied. "Muḥammad," Ḍamām said, "I am going to ask you a few questions, and am going to be quite severe in my questioning. I hope you won't mind." "Not at all," the Prophet replied. "You can ask what you like." "Will you swear to me by the name of your God and the God of those before you, and the God of those who will come after you, that God has sent you as His Prophet?" "By God, yes," the Prophet replied. "Will you swear to me," Ḍamām continued, "by the name of your God, and the God of those before you, and the God of those who will come after you, that God has told you to exhort us to worship Him alone and ascribe no partners to Him; that He has commanded you to tell us to forsake idol worship, and all the things that our forefathers used to worship?" "By God, yes," the Prophet replied. "I ask you to swear to me," Ḍamām said once again, "by the name of your God and the God of those before you, and the God of those who will come after you that has God commanded that we should pray five times a day." Ḍamām then asked about *zakāt* (alms), fasting, Ḥajj (pilgrimage) and all the other injunctions of Islam, framing each question in the same manner. When he had finished his questioning, and the Prophet had given him the same simple answer to every question, Ḍamām spoke these words:

> I bear witness that there is none worthy of being served save God, and Muḥammad is the Prophet of God. I shall discharge these obligations, and I shall avoid the things you have prohibited. I shall do no more and no less.[16]

He then mounted his camel and rode away. When he reached his people, he told them what had happened. Before the day was out, all the men and women who had been awaiting his homecoming, had accepted Islam.

There was not a trace of hypocrisy in these people. They knew only acceptance or denial—nothing in between. When they made a promise, they fulfilled it, come what may. No threat of loss of life or property could prevent them from converting their words into actions. Such was the nature of the Arab temperament. Historians have described the speeches of both the Aws and the Khazraj—the two tribes of Madinah—on the occasion of the Second Oath of Allegiance. They have all the lustre which distinguished their race. 'Abbās ibn 'Ubaydah had this to say: "People of Khazraj, do you know what you are committing yourselves to, swearing allegiance to this man? You are committing yourselves to war with men of all races. Think about this. If, when you incur loss of life and property, you are going to send him back to his people, then it is better that you do so now. If you do so later on, it will mean humiliation for you in both this world and the next. But if you think you will be able to keep your promises, however much loss you incur, and however many of your leaders are killed, then take him with you to Madinah. This will be better for you in both this world and the next."

Everyone said in unison that they would take the Prophet with them, no matter what loss of life and property they incurred. "What will we have in return if we keep our word?" They asked the Prophet. "Paradise," he replied. "Hold out your hand to us," they cried out. He extended his hand and accepted their allegiance.[17]

These were not mere words on the part of the Ansar; they were words borne out by actions. Even when the Muslims became dominant, they did not demand any political compensation for the sacrifices they had made. They were quite willing to let the Caliphate remain in the hands of the Makkans. They did not seek reward in this world, but were content to leave this world to others and, to look forward to their reward in the next world from God.

THE ALL-PERVASIVENESS OF THE PROPHET'S MESSAGE

The Prophet's biographer, Ibn Ishāq, tells how the Quraysh nobility once gathered at the house of Abū Ṭālib, the Prophet's uncle. Among those present were 'Utbah ibn Rabī'ah, Shaybah ibn Rabī'ah, Abū Jahl ibn Hishām, Umayyah ibn Khalf and Abū Sufyān ibn Ḥarb, all outstanding leaders of the Quraysh. Through Abū Ṭālib, they asked the Prophet what it was he wanted to them. "Just one thing," the Prophet replied. "If you accept it, you will become lords over the Arabs. Even the people of Asia will capitulate to you."[18]

Monotheism is more than just a doctrine. It is the secret of all forms of human success. To believe in one God is to give true expression to human nature. That is why this faith lodges itself in the depths of the human psyche. It even finds a place in the hearts of one's enemies. Khālid ibn al-Walīd became a Muslim just before the conquest of Makkah, but he had been conscious for quite some time before that of the truth of the message of Islam. Later on, he told of his early conviction that Muḥammad, not the Quraysh, was in the right, and that he should join forces with the Prophet of Islam. "I participated in every battle against Muḥammad," he said. "But there was not one battle from which I did not go away with the feeling that I was fighting on the wrong side."[19]

Many people are reported to have had inclinations towards Islam long before they accepted the faith. Some even had dreams about Islam. One such person was Khālid ibn Sa'īd ibn al-'Āṣ. He saw himself in a dream standing on the edge of an enormous pit of fire. Someone was trying to push him in. Then the Prophet Muḥammad came and rescued him from the pit of doom.

Difficult though it may be to see the economic connection in missionary work, there is an indirect link of the utmost significance. When a person becomes Muslim, all his resources are automatically put at the disposal of the Islamic cause. First it was Khadījah, the Prophet's wife, who provided the Islamic movement with financial assistance. Then Abū Bakr, who had accumulated

40,000 dirhams from his trading, put all his capital into the service of Islam. When he and the Prophet emigrated from Makkah to Madinah, he took 6000 dirhams with him—enough to finance the entire expenses of the journey. 'Uthmān donated 10,000 dinars towards the expedition to Tabūk in A.H. 9. On one occasion alone, 'Abd al-Raḥmān ibn 'Awf gave 500 horses, to be used in the service of the Islamic cause. So it was with others who accepted Islam. Just as they themselves entered the Islamic fold, so their properties became part of the Islamic treasury.

Belief in one God is the only creed which does not allow for any social distinction or racial prejudice. For this reason the masses flock to join any movement which rises on the basis of this creed. They realize that under the banner of monotheism all people become equal in the real sense. As humble servants of one great God, they all become true human beings with a right to human dignity. By finding their true place in the world, they achieve the greatest position that man can aspire to. When Mughīrah ibn Shu'bah entered the court of the Iranian warrior, Rustam, he made a speech to the courtiers gathered there. As Ibn Jarīr explains, his words had a devastating effect on all who heard them:

> The lower classes said: "By God, this Arabian has spoken the truth." As for the upper classes: they said, "By God, he has attacked us with words which our slaves will find irresistable. God damn our predecessors. How stupid they were to think lightly of this community.[20]

When, in the thirteenth year of the Prophet's mission, he and Abū Bakr arrived in Madinah, about 500 people came to meet him. They greeted the newcomers with these words:

> Welcome! You are both safe with us. We accept you as our leaders.[21]

It was the Prophet's preaching alone which had made him leader of the people of Madinah. The first inhabitant of Madinah to whom the Prophet had preached Islam was probably Suwayd ibn Ṣāmit al-Khazrajī. When the Prophet had given him an outline of the teachings of Islam, Suwayd said: "It seems that your message is the same as mine." "What's your message?" The Prophet asked. "The wisdom of Luqmān," Suwayd replied. When the Prophet asked him to explain the wisdom of Luqmān, Suwayd recited a few poems. "I have the Qur'ān," the Prophet said, "which is far superior to this." He then recited a few verses of the Qur'ān, and Suwayd immediately accepted Islam. He went back to Madinah and preached the message of Islam to his own tribe, but they killed him.[22]

After this, a chieftain of Madinah, Abu'l Ḥaysar Anas ibn Rāfi', came to Makkah. With him was a group of youths of the Banū 'Abd al-Ashhal tribe. They had come to Makkah to make an alliance with the Quraysh on behalf of the Khazraj, one of the main tribes of Madinah who were embroiled in a conflict with the other main tribe, the Aws. The Prophet heard that they were in Makkah. He went to see them and said: "Shall I tell you about something even better than what you have come for?" He then went on to explain to them the meaning of belief in One God. There was a youth among them called Ayās ibn Mu'ādh, who told his people that what the Prophet had told them was much better than what they had come for. The delegation, however, did not agree. "Leave us alone," they said, "We are here on other business." They returned to Madinah. Soon afterwards there was waged the vicious and devastating battle between the Aws and Khazraj known as Bu'āth.

According to Khubayb ibn 'Abd al-Raḥmān, two people from Madinah, Sa'd ibn Zarārah and Zakwān ibn Qays, came to Makkah and stayed with 'Utbah ibn Rabī'ah. When they heard about the Prophet, they went to see him. The Prophet called on them both to accept Islam and recited to them a passage of the Qur'ān. They accepted the Prophet's invitation, and became Muslim. Rather than return to the house of their host, 'Utbah, they went straight back to Madinah after seeing the Prophet. They were the first to communicate the message of Islam to the people of Madinah. This was in the tenth year of the Prophet's mission, three years before the emigration to Madinah.

In the following year, six people from the Khazraj tribe came to Makkah for Hajj. They became Muslim, swore allegiance to the Prophet, and then returned to Madinah to propagate Islam there. Then, in the twelfth year of the Prophet's mission, twelve people came to swear allegiance to the Prophet. The oath that they took, at 'Aqabah near Makkah, is famous in Islamic history as the First Oath of 'Aqabah. There followed another pact, in the same place, the next year, in which 75 people participated.

Contrary to what happened in Makkah, the outstanding personalities of the city of Madinah accepted Islam at the very outset. According to tribal custom, people in those days used to follow the religion of their leaders. Islam, then, spread quickly in Madinah. Soon there was not a single home into which Islam had not entered. It was only natural that, as the Muslims achieved a majority in Madinah, they should become the dominant force in the city's affairs. And so it was that, as Ṭabarānī has reported, "the Muslims were the most influential people in the city."

FACTORS WORKING IN FAVOUR OF PREACHING WORK

There are always some who resist the corruption of the world they live in, and remain attached to their own true, primordial, natures. This is true of every day and age, but it was especially true of the Arabs when the Prophet commenced his mission. Besides the simple way of life to which they were accustomed, there was the legacy of the religion of Abraham, which made many inclined to seek out the truth, and turn away from idol-worship. Such people were commonly known as *ḥanīf*, or upright. Quss ibn Sā'idah and Waraqah ibn Nawfal were among these *ḥunafā'*. So was Jandub ibn 'Amr al-Dawsī. During the period of ignorance that preceded Islam, he was known to have said:

> I know that there must be a Creator of all this creation, but I do not know who He is.[23]

When he heard about the Prophet, he came with 75 of his fellow tribesmen and accepted Islam. Abū Dharr al-Ghifārī was another such person. As soon as he heard about the Prophet, he sent his brother to Makkah to find out more about him. One sentence of the account that Abū Dharr's brother later gave him ran as follows:

> I saw a man whom people call irreligious. I have never seen anyone who more resembles you.[24]

People such as these had no trouble in understanding the truth of the Prophet's message.

The preacher of God's word is like a planter who goes out to sow seeds. If sometimes his seeds fall on barren ground, there are other times when they fall in places which produce a good yield, without the planter even knowing it.

Certain people took a considerable time to accept Islam. This does not mean that the truth of Islam finally dawned on them all of a sudden. The Prophet lived a life of the highest moral calibre. Moreover, he spent his whole time preaching the word of God. Even the opposition to the Prophet proved to be a factor in his favour: it meant that his personality and his message were topics of conversation. All these things had contributed to planting the seed of Islam in the minds of many Arabs. Adherence to tribal tradition, and ancestor worship were still extant, and this sometimes made it appear that there was stiff opposition to Islam, but all the while, in people's hearts the seed of Islam was silently growing. It is generally thought that 'Umar's acceptance of Islam, for instance, came all of a sudden, under the influence of a certain event. It would be more accurate, however, to say that it was this event which put the final seal on his faith, which had been developing for some time within his soul.

Well before 'Umar had accepted Islam, when he appeared to be in the forefront of the opposition to the Prophet's mission, some Muslims emigrated to Abyssinia. Umm 'Abdullah bint Abī Ḥathmah was one of them. She tells her own story in these words:

> We were setting off for Abyssinia. My husband, 'Āmir, had gone to collect some of his belongings. All of a sudden, 'Umar ibn al-Khaṭṭāb, a man who had subjected us to untold suffering and torment, came and stood next to me. He had not up to that point accepted Islam." 'Umm 'Abdullah," he said to me, "are you going away somewhere?" "We are," I replied, "for you people inflict such suffering upon us, and torment us so, that we must go and seek a place for ourselves in God's land. We will keep going until God releases us from our affliction." "May God go with you," 'Umar said, and tears were running down his face as he was talking. I had never seen him act like this before. Then he went on his way, and he was certainly very sad to see us leave Makkah.[25]

In every day and age some ideas take root in the popular psyche. Before these ideas are banished, no new message, however rational it may be, can become acceptable. The opposition which the Arabs first presented to the message of Islam was not just the result of stubbornness or expediency on their part. Rather, it was genuinely difficult for them to understand how any religion which differed from that of the patrons of the Holy Ka'bah could be the true religion. Arab tribes living in the vicinity of Jewish areas were generally free of such restrictive creeds. They had often heard from the Jews that it was written in their scriptures that a Prophet would come among the Arabs. As the historian Ṭabarānī explains, that was why it was easier for the people of Madinah to see the truth of Islam:

> When the Anṣār heard the teachings of the Prophet, they remained silent. Their hearts were satisfied that what he preached was true. They had heard from the People of the Book what the Final Prophet would be like. They recognized the truth of his message. They confirmed his teachings, and believed in him.[26]

When the Prophet went to the fair of 'Ukāz and, entering the tent of the Banū Kandah, explained his teachings, this is what one youth had to say in reply:

> My people, let us hurry and be the first to follow this man, for by God, the People of the Book used to tell us that a Prophet would arise from the Sacred Territory, and that his time has drawn nigh.[27]

The Aws and Khazraj had become intellectually prepared, then, for the coming of an Arab Prophet. When he came, it was comparatively easy for them to accept him. As far as the people of Makkah were concerned, however, and most of their compatriots along with them, truth could only be seen in terms of who controlled the Ka'bah. In ancient Arab tradition, the Ka'bah was thought of as a king's crown. In fact, its symbolism was of a higher order even than that of a crown, for the latter brings with it only political power, whereas one who held sway over the Ka'bah was heir to a wealth of spiritual tradition as well. As the following conversation between Dhū'l Jawshan al-Ḍubbā'ī and the Prophet shows, Arabs, in their simplicity, could think of truth only in terms of who was in control of the House of God, the Ka'bah in Makkah:

> "Why don't you accept Islam," the Prophet said to Dhū'l Jawshan, "so that you may be counted among the first to have done so?" Dhū'l Jawshan said that he would not. The Prophet asked why. "I have heard that your people are after your blood," Dhū'l Jawshan said. "Have you not heard about their defeat at Badr?" the Prophet asked. Dhū'l Jawshan said that he had. "We are only showing you the path of guidance," the Prophet said. Dhū'l Jawshan said that he would not accept Islam, until he (the Prophet) had conquered Makkah, and won control of the Ka'bah. "If you live, you will see this happen," the Prophet said. Dhū'l Jawshan says that later he was with his family in Ghawr when a rider came up. Dhū'l Jawshan asked him what was afoot. "Muḥammad has conquered Makkah and taken control of the Sacred Territory," he said. "Woe betide me," Dhū'l Jawshan said. "If only I had accepted Islam on that day: if I had asked Muḥammad for an emerald he would have given it to me.[28]

REACTION TO THE MESSAGE OF ISLAM

When the Prophet of Islam commenced his preaching mission, he met with exactly the reaction one would expect from a society hearing a new message. People were at a loss to grasp the meaning of his teachings. Once the Quraysh nobility sent ‘Utbah ibn Rabī‘ah as their representative to the Prophet. He made a long denunciation of the Prophet and his teachings. When he had had his say, the Prophet asked him: “Have you finished?” ‘Utbah said that he had. “In the Name of God, the Beneficent, the Merciful,” the Prophet began, and then went on to recite the first thirteen verses of the chapter of the Qur’ān entitled *Ḥā Mīm al-Sajdah*. “Don’t you have anything else to say?” ‘Utbah asked indignantly. The Prophet said that he did not. When he returned to the Quraysh, they asked him what had happened, “I said whatever you would have wanted me to say,” replied ‘Utbah. They asked whether Muḥammad had given any answer. ‘Utbah said that he had, but that the proofs he offered were incomprehensible. All that he had gathered was that he was warning them of a thunderbolt like that which had overtaken Thamūd and Ād. “What has become of you?” the Quraysh asked. “How is it that a person speaks to you in Arabic, and you do not understand what he says?” “Really, I didn’t understand anything,” ‘Utbah insisted. “All I gathered was that he mentioned a thunderbolt.”[29]

Some people were only familiar with religion in a particular, conventional form. To them, the message of Islam just appeared to be an indictment of their elders. Ḍamād once came to Makkah to perform ‘Umrah. He had occasion to sit in a gathering along with Abū Jahl, ‘Utbah ibn Rabī‘ah and Umayyah ibn Khalf. “He (Muḥammad) has caused a split in our community,” Abū Jahl declared.

"He thinks we are all fools, and considers our ancestors woefully astray. He insults our idols." "He is insane, without doubt," Umayyah added.[30]

When 'Amr ibn Murrah al-Juhanī preached Islam among his own tribe, the Juhaynah, one of them spoke up: "May God make you taste the bitterness of life, 'Amr. Do you want us to forsake our idols, disunite our people, and contradict the religion of our righteous ancestors? The religion that this Quraysh from Tahāmah preaches has no affection, no graciousness to it."

He then went on to recite three verses, the last of which went like this:

> He seeks to prove that our forefathers were fools.
> One who acts thus can never prosper.[31]

Some people were prevented by jealousy from accepting the message of Islam. The Prophet made no secret of the fact that he was sent by God; he proclaimed the fact to all and sundry. But people always find it very difficult to accept the fact that someone else has been given a knowledge of reality that they themselves have been denied. Bayhaqī has related, on the authority of Mughīrah ibn Shu'bah, how Abū Jahl once took the Prophet aside and said to him, "By God, I know full well that what you say is true, but one thing stops me from believing. The Banū Qusayy say that they are the gate keepers of the Ka'bah, and I agree with them. They say that it is their job to bear water for pilgrims, and again I agree. They claim a place in the Dār al-Nadwah, and I agree that they have every right to it. They say that it is their responsibility to carry the standard in battle, and again I agree. Now they say that there is a Prophet among them. This I cannot accept."[32]

For some people it was the threat of financial loss which prevented them from accepting the message of Islam. The House of God at Makkah had been turned into a house of idol worship before the coming of the Prophet. People of every religion had placed their idols there. There were even statues of Jesus and Mary within the walls of the Ka'bah, which had thus become a place of pilgrimage for people of all denominations. This was why four months had been made sacred—so that people would be free to visit the Ka'bah during that time, without fear of being harmed or attacked on the way. During the four months that people used to flock to Makkah, Makkan traders did exceptionally good business. Were the idols to be removed from the Ka'bah, people would stop visiting the city, and its inhabitants would suffer immense losses. So there were many people with a vested interest in the continuance of polytheistic practices. They feared that if monotheism were to spread in the land, Makkah would suffer drastically; the area would be reduced to the uncultivable valley that it basically was.

Added to this, the Quraysh, due to their position as patrons of the Ka'bah, had come to lord over tribes far and wide. Their caravans used to travel east and west, far beyond the boundaries of the peninsula. In accordance with long-standing pacts, they used to do business with tribes as far afield as Persia, Abyssinia and the Byzantine Empire. The Quraysh thought that their accepting Muḥammad as a prophet could only result in neighbouring tribes—in fact all the polytheists of Arabia—breaking off the commercial agreements they had made with the Quraysh. That would also be the end of their hegemony over the Arabs. This is the meaning of the verse in the *sūrah* of the Qur'ān entitled, *al-Wāqi'ah* (The Event): "And have you made denial your means of livelihood."[33] The allusion is to the Quraysh's notion that, by denying the Prophet Muḥammad, and the monotheistic religion he taught, they were saving themselves from financial ruin.

Once the Prophet started to preach his message, his person became the subject of general curiosity. According to the historian Abū Ya'la, people who saw him used to ask one another: "Is this him?" He might be travelling amidst a host in a caravan, but people would single him out for mention. Anyone who came to Makkah would, among other things, take back news of the Prophet. "Muḥammad, the son of 'Abdullah, has laid claim to prophethood and the son of Abū Qahafah has followed him," they would say. The Quraysh used to call the Prophet "*muzammam*," meaning blameworthy, instead of Muḥammad, meaning praiseworthy. They used to accuse him of insulting their ancestors. Once, as the Prophet's biographer Ibn Hishām has related, when the Prophet noticed the litter which his fellow Quraysh had put in the street on which he was passing, he said in dismay: "What bad neighbours the Banū 'Abd al-Manāf are."[34]

While the Prophet's uncle, Abū Ṭālib, was alive, his enemies were unable to take any action against him for, according to tribal custom, aggression against the Prophet would have amounted to aggression against his whole tribe—the Banū Hāshim. Before he accepted Islam, 'Umar ibn Khaṭṭāb once set off with the intention of killing Muḥammad, on whom be peace. It was only sufficient for someone to say to him, "How are you going to live with the Banū Hāshim if you kill Muḥammad?" for 'Umar to change his mind. The same question faced anyone who sought to harm the Prophet. Persecution in Makkah was mostly directed against slaves who had become Muslim—people who had no tribe to protect them. According to the Prophet's close companion, 'Abdullah ibn Mas'ūd, in the early days in Makkah only seven men actually came out into the open about being Muslim: the Prophet himself, Abū Bakr, 'Ammār, Sa'īd, Suhayb, Bilāl and Miqdād. "As for the Prophet, God protected him through his uncle. As for Abū Bakr, his tribe looked after him. The rest would be seized by the idolators who would put coats of armour on them, and lay them out in the boiling sun."[35]

When the chief of the Banū Hāshim, the Prophet's uncle, Abū Ṭālib, died, an uncouth member of the Quraysh threw dirt at the Prophet and it stuck to him. When the latter reached home, one of his daughters, Fāṭimah, brushed the dirt off him. "The Quraysh did nothing nasty to me like this before," the Prophet commented. It was only after the death of Abū Ṭālib that they committed mean acts of aggression of this nature. As the Prophet's companion, Abū Hurayrah, has pointed out, "the Quraysh used to treat the Prophet very harshly after the death of his uncle." "Uncle, how quickly I have felt your loss," the Prophet once lamented.[36] The Quraysh even started planning to do away with the Prophet. It was during this period that Abū Jahl threw the intestines of an animal on to the Prophet's head, and 'Uqbah ibn Mu'īṭ tied a sheet around his neck and pulled it tight in an attempt to strangulate him. Fortunately, it was unsuccessful. Now that Abū Ṭālib was dead, it seemed as if there was nothing to stop vicious attacks on the Prophet's person. The only thing that held people back was that nothing of this nature had happened before in Arabia; for a member of the Banū Hāshim to be attacked and killed by his own fellow Quraysh would have been an action without precedent. Added to this, there were still people among the idolators whose consciences pricked them, who in their heart of hearts supported the Prophet. The first time that Abū Jahl made a murderous attack upon the Prophet, Abū'l Bakhtarī heard about it. He took a whip and went to the Ka'bah, where Abū Jahl was sitting triumphantly with his associates. Abū'l Bakhtarī first made sure that Abū Jahl had really attacked the Prophet in this way, and, when it turned out that he had, he took his whip and struck Abū Jahl so hard on the head that the latter roared with pain.

One can see from the history of various religions how, even as a creed, polytheism has always been super-sensitive to criticism. But in ancient times polytheism was more than just a creed; it provided the very foundation of the structure of social orders. There were political reasons too, then, for the people's fanatical attachment to polytheism. This was the situation in Makkah, and it was for this reason that the

Prophet's time there was such a supreme test of patience. Only a handful of people believed in him during the first three years of his mission. The town of Makkah was as devoid of supporters who would help the Prophet as it was of shade-giving trees. Only four people managed to remain close to him—'Alī, Zayd, Abū Bakr and Khadījah—five if one includes the first person who was born a Muslim, 'Ā'īshah the daughter of Abū Bakr.

So the situation remained for three full years. When the Prophet left his house, he was greeted with derisive jeers in the street, as if he were a madman. One day—on the instigation of Abū Jahl—a group of people were abusing the Prophet. A passer-by was unable to put up with the sight of a person from a noble Quraysh family being treated in this manner. He went straight to the Prophet's uncle, Ḥamzah. "Have you lost all sense of honour?" he said. "You are sitting back while people are disgracing your nephew." This was enough to ignite Ḥamzah's sense of Arab pride. He had an iron bow which he took with him and went to see Abū Jahl. Striking the Prophet's oppressor, he said: "I have adopted Muḥammad's religion as my own. If you have it in you, do something about it."[37]

Ḥamzah was famed as a fighter all over Arabia. After he took this action, people gained new courage and the number of Muslims went up to thirty. At this time there were two highly influential people in Makkah—'Umar ibn al-Khaṭṭāb and Abū Jahl ibn Hisham. The Prophet offered a prayer to God: "Lord, strengthen Islam by means of 'Umar ibn al-Khaṭṭāb or Abū Jahl ibn Hishām." This prayer was accepted in the former's case. In the sixth year of the Prophet's mission, 'Umar ibn al-Khaṭṭāb accepted Islam. Along with him, several other people converted, and the number of Muslims increased to forty. During this period the Muslims had a hideout in Dār al-Arqam. According to the historian, Ibn Kathīr, thirty-nine people used to gather there.

But such a small number could not combat the might of the conventional system, which in numbers and resources was far stronger. It was not long before oppression of the Muslims started again. The Prophet was subjected to every form of persecution, but all attempts to kill him failed. The tribal system was still protective to the Prophet. No one could dare to take his life, for to do so would have been to declare war on the whole of the Prophet's tribe. He was not the only prophet to be defended in this way. The Prophet Shu'ayb's people also refrained from killing him for the same reason, despite their desire to do so:

> They said: "O Shu'ayb, we do not understand much of what you say to us. And we see you weak among us. But for your tribe, we would have stoned you. You are not dear to us."[38]

The Quraysh once presented a demand to the chief of the Banū Hāshim, the Prophet's uncle, Abū Ṭālib, that he should expel his nephew from the tribe. Only then would they be able to slay the Prophet. Abū Ṭālib's honour prevented him from taking this step. When Abū Ṭālib, at the Quraysh's behest, asked his nephew to stop criticizing their gods, the Prophet became concerned that his uncle was going to hand him over to the Quraysh. But Abū Ṭālib immediately put his nephew's mind at rest. "By God, I will never hand you over to anyone," he told him.[39]

When all else failed, the Quraysh decided, in the seventh year of the Prophet's mission, to ostracize the Banū Hāshim. Abū Ṭālib took his nephew, and the whole of his family, out of Makkah, and they took up their abode in ravine known after Abū Ṭālib. Except for a few wild trees, there was nothing in this mountain pass. For three years Abū Ṭālib's family lived on the leaves and roots of these trees. Their only respite was during the four sacred months, when the Banū Hāshim used to come to Makkah. They would take back animals of sacrifice and live for a few months on the dried meat that they prepared.

After three years, in the tenth year of the Prophet's mission, the pact to ostracize him that the Quraysh had made among themselves came to an end. The Banū Hāshim were now able to return to Makkah. But the strain of the time in exile had been too much for Abū Tālib, and he died in the same year (A.D. 620). 'Abd al-'Uzzā, known as Abū Lahab, became chief of the Banu Hashim. He was an implacable opponent of the Prophet, and took the decision that Abū Ṭālib had held back from: he expelled the Prophet from his tribe.

EXPULSION

To expel an Arab from his tribe in those days was like putting him out among a pack of wolves. There was no government in those days, responsible for the safety of its citizens. There was only the tribal system, and one could only live under the protection of a tribe. In the pilgrims' tents in Minā the Prophet once preached his message to a certain tribe, but they refused to accept it. Still, one can tell from what one of their number, Maysirah ibn Masrūq al-'Abbasī, had to say, that the Prophet's words had made an impact on him. Ibn Kathīr explains how the Prophet's hopes were raised with regard to Maysirah. "How well you have spoken, and how enlightening your words are. But my tribe do not agree with me, and one cannot go against one's tribe."[40] That was how much a tribe meant to a person. What a grave matter it must have been, then, to be expelled from one's tribe. The Prophet now had nowhere to go in his own land. There was no other option but to seek the protection of some other tribe. His first attempt in this direction was his journey to Ṭā'if. Later on he explained the whole episode to his wife 'Ā'ishah, saying that he had "presented himself before Ibn 'Abd Yalīl." In the words of 'Urwah ibn Zubayr, "When Abū Ṭālib died, and the Prophet's affliction became more intense, he betook himself to the Thaqīf tribe in the hope that they would grant him asylum and support."[41] But one can tell what savage treatment the Prophet received at their hands from this prayer that he made on his return to Makkah:

> Lord, I complain to you of my weakness and helplessness. How vulnerable I am among men, most Merciful one![42]

After his return to Makkah, the Prophet commented that it was just as well that the people of Makkah had not heard about what had happened to him in Ṭā'if. If they had, it would have made them even more audacious.[43] The Prophet was unable to live within the city. He stayed outside, and sent messages to various people, asking them to take him under their personal protection so that he could return to the city. Eventually Muṭ'im ibn 'Adī agreed to extend protection to the Prophet, who, shielded by the swords of Muṭ'im's sons, once again entered the city walls.

Fairs, attended by tribes from all over Arabia, used to be held in various places in those days. The Prophet would go along and speak to different tribes, in the hope that one of them would agree to extend him protection. He explained his plight to his uncle 'Abbās. "I am not safe here with you and your relatives. Will you take me to the fair tomorrow, so that we can visit people in their tents and talk to them?" he said to him.[44]

The Prophet would then go into people's tents and, presenting himself before them, would enquire what protection they could afford him. He would tell them that his people had rejected him and expelled him from their midst. "Protect me and grant me refuge so that I can continue to preach the faith that God has revealed to me." Historians have mentioned the names of fifteen tribes that the Prophet approached individually, only to meet with one refusal after another. Although it was considered a shameful matter for someone to seek refuge of a tribe, and his request not be granted—in fact, this was the first notable example in Arab history of a person spending several years looking for a tribe to take him in—no one was prepared to shoulder this responsibility in the case of the Prophet. When a group from one tribe felt inclined to take pity upon the Prophet, one of their elders rebuked them: "His own tribe has expelled him and you intend to grant him protection.

What do you want to do? Wage war upon the whole of the Arab nation?"[45] He knew that to offer refuge to a person who had been disowned by his own tribe was to declare war against that tribe.

It was the Quraysh that had expelled him, and the Quraysh were masters of the entire Arab peninsula. To grant asylum to one expelled by them was to declare war on every Arab tribe—on everyone who looked up to the Quraysh as their leaders and guardians of the Holy Ka'bah. That was why, when the Ansar were swearing allegiance to the Prophet, Abū'l Haytham ibn al-Tayyihān warned them: "If you take him with you the whole Arab nation will descend upon you with one accord."[46]

Added to this there was the fact that Arab border tribes had made pacts with neighbouring foreign powers. These tribes were afraid of repercussions if they took a controversial personality like the Prophet with them. As Ibn Kathīr has explained in *Al-Bidāyah wa al-Nihāyah*, the Prophet once went into the tent of the Banū Shaybān ibn Tha'labah in Makkah, and talked with their elders. They were impressed by the Prophet's words but finally decided that their position, on the border of Persia, was too precarious for them to take responsibility for the Prophet. As their spokesman, Hānī ibn Qubaiṣah, put it, they had made pacts with the Persian emperor, and "it might be that kings will not take kindly to the message that you preach."[47]

The Prophet was desperate to find a tribe that would afford him protection, for there was no other way that he could continue his mission. Once he went to see a tribe which went by the name of Banū 'Abdullah. After the Prophet had, as usual, called them to Islam and presented himself to them, in the hope that they would grant him asylum, he said: "Banū 'Abdullah, what a beautiful name your forefather had." But they were untouched by his evident good will and rejected his proposals.[48]

The last three years of the Prophet's time in Makkah were spent among various tribes, looking for one which would grant him asylum. Yet despite his untiring efforts, not a single tribe was ready to take him in. Some of the people he approached used to taunt him, saying, "Isn't it high time that you despaired of us?" Eventually God gave the tribes of Aws and Khazraj, which hailed from Madinah, the courage to extend the Prophet their support. There was one special, psychological reason for their decision. In their vicinity dwelt Jewish tribes, notably the Jews of Khaybar, who had possession of the most fertile lands in the area as well as control of the region's commerce. Many of the Aws and Khazraj were given employment by them, but the work was so hard and the recompense so inadequate that it was more like slavery for them. (Mention is made of this by the Prophet when, after the emigration to Madinah, he had his companions built the Prophet's mosque with their own hands. According to Ibn Kathīr, the Prophet commented that "this is not the labour of Khaybar; this is much more worthwhile and honest work.") In a situation of economic domination by the Jews and their exploitation of the Madinan tribes, fighting often broke out between the Jews on the one side, and the Aws and Khazraj on the other.

The Jews used to deride these tribes, telling them that a Prophet would soon come among the Arabs, and that when he did, they would join forces with him and totally eliminate the Aws and Khazraj.

When the Aws and Khazraj heard the teachings of the Prophet Muḥammad, they recognized him as the prophet the Jews had taunted them with, and they made haste to accept him before the Jews could do so. There were, of course, other historical reasons for it being comparatively easier for the Aws and Khazraj to understand the message brought by the Prophet, and to believe in him personally then it was for the other tribes. They did not deliberate long, therefore, before swearing allegiance to him.

So the time which the Prophet had been awaiting for years finally came. He had found a place in which, under tribal protection, he would be able to continue his struggle effectively. The Muslims of Makkah and the surrounding territories would be gathered together with one centre. The fact that the majority of the people of Madinah accepted Islam made it easier for the Muslims' scattered resources to be brought together in one place, and used more effectively for the furtherance of the Islamic cause. When the Aws and the Khazraj swore allegiance, the Prophet quickly returned to his companions. "Praise God" he told them, "for today Rabī'ah's offspring have as good as overcome the Persians."[49] The Prophet saw how Islam had been strengthened by the Ansar taking the Muslims in. He realized that it would now only be a matter of time before the Muslims conquered mighty Persia.

The Prophet began to make preparations for emigration to Madinah. He was to take six months after the conversion of the Aws and Khazraj to do this. All this while he attempted to maintain the utmost secrecy, but still the idolators, the Quraysh, learnt of his plans to leave. They heard about the refuge that he had been granted in Madinah, and the protection that the Anṣār had extended to him. The fact that the Anṣār had accepted Islam also came to their notice, and they learned too that the Muslims were gathering in Madinah. Plotting against the Prophet, they decided to take him captive at the moment of his departure and then either kill him or keep him prisoner.[50] But their plans came to nothing. When all his arrangements were complete, he succeeded in slipping away quietly to his new abode.

NOTES

1. Qur'ān, 48:29.
2. Ḥadīth related by Ibn Marduyah and Ibn Sa'd.
3. *Al-Bidāyah wa al-Nihāyah*.
4. Ḥadīth of al-Bukhārī and Muslim.
5. *Al-Bidāyah wa al-Nihāyah*, vol. 3, p. 24.
6. Ḥadīth, Imām Aḥmad on the authority of 'Ā'ishah.
7. *Tahzīb Sīrat Ibn Hishām*, p. 68.
8. *Al-Bidāyah wa al-Nihāyah*.
9. *Ibid*.
10. Ḥadīth of Ibn 'Asākir.
11. *Al-Asabah*, vol. 1.
12. Ḥadīth of Imām Aḥmad on the authority of Abū Umamah.
13. Ḥadīth, *Kanz al-'Ummāl*, vol. 1, p. 69.
14. Ḥadīth of Muslim.
15. *Al-Bidāyah wa al-Nihāyah*, vol. 3, p. 36.

16. *Ibid.*, vol. 5.
17. *Ibid.*, vol. 3, p. 162.
18. *Ibid.*, vol. 11, p. 123.
19. *Ibid.*, vol. 4.
20. *Tārīkh al-Ṭabarī*, vol. 3, p. 36.
21. *Al-Bidāyah wa al-Nihāyah*, vol. 3.
22. *Tārīkh al-Ṭabarī*, p. 234.
23. Ibn 'Abd al-Barfī, *Al-Isti 'āb*, vol. 2.
24. Ḥadīth of Muslim, on the authority of 'Abdullah ibn al-Ṣāmit.
25. *Al-Bidāyah wa al-Nihāyah*, vol. 3, p. 79.
26. Related by al-Tabarānī.
27. Abū Na'īm, *al-Dala'il.*
28. Ḥadīth of Ṭabarānī.
29. Ḥadīth of Bayhaqī.
30. *Al-Asābah*, vol. 2, p. 210.
31. *Al-Bidāyah wa al-Nihāyah*, vol. 2.
32. *Ibid.*, vol. 3.
33. Qur'ān, 56:82.
34. *Tahzīb Sīrat Ibn Hishām,* p. 86.
35. Ḥadīth of Imām Aḥmad, on the authority of Ibn Mas'ūd.
36. Abū Na'īm, *al-Ḥilyah.*
37. Ḥadīth of Ṭabarānī.
38. Qur'ān, 11:91.
39. *Tahzīb Sīrat Ibn Hishām,* p. 60.
40. *Al-Bidāyah wa al-Nihāyah*, vol. 3.
41. Abū Na'īm, *Dala'il al-Nubuwah.*
42. *Al-Bidāyah wa al-Nihāyah*, vol. 3.
43. *Tahzīb Sīrat Ibn Hishām*, p. 60.
44. *Al-Bidāyah wa al-Nihāyah*, vol. 3.
45. Abū Na'īm, *Dala'il al-Nubuwah.*
46. Ḥadīth of al-Ṭabarānī.
47. *Al-Bidāyah wa al-Nihāyah*, vol. 3.
48. *Ibid.*
49. *Ibid.*, vol. 3, p. 145.
50. Ḥadīth of al-Ṭabarānī on the authority of 'Urwah.

11

Islam comes to Madinah

Before the coming of Islam, the city of Madinah was known as Yathrib. Besides the two main tribes of the Aws and Khazraj, some Jewish tribes lived in the area, who had established their dominance by pursuing a policy of divide and rule. Their prime concern had always been to keep their Arab neighbours weak and disunited. Just five years before the Prophet emigrated to Madinah, the Khazraj, at the instigation of the Jews, rose up against the Aws. An Aws chieftain by the name of Abū'l Ḥaysar Anas ibn Rāfi' went to Makkah along with a few of his fellows, in order to seek the help of the Quraysh. The Prophet, hearing about their arrival, went to see them, and invited them to accept Islam.

One of their company, a youth by the name of Ayās ibn Mu'ādh, was impressed by the Prophet's words. He told his companions that this was much better than what they had come for, but they did not agree. Abū'l Ḥaysar threw some earth in Ayās' face in disgust and told him to forget about what Muḥammad had said, for they had other, more pressing business of their own.

The Aus delegation returned without accepting Islam. Soon afterwards the Aws and Khazraj fought a war known as Bu'āth. The enmity between the two tribes had become so strong that each wished to obliterate the other. In this war the Khazraj first had the ascendancy. Then the Aws, under Abū Usayd, defeated the Khazraj. They inflicted heavy losses on one another, even burning houses and orchards. In this way the Arabs weakened themselves by their own internal warfare.

It was the Jews who benefited from this war, and their ascendancy in Madinah was further consolidated. When feelings cooled, responsible people of both the Aws and the Khazraj realized that they had made a grave mistake. They had played into the hands of their enemies. They had weakened themselves and strengthened the Jews. Many people in both tribes realized the need to rectify this situation. But this could be done only by both tribes agreeing to forgive and forget. The best way to achieve reconciliation would be by appointing a king to coordinate the peace-making process. 'Abdullah ibn Ubayy of the Khazraj tribe, a man of personality and gifted with qualities of leadership, was chosen for this task. At this very juncture some Khazrajis travelled to Makkah on a pilgrimage. There they met the Prophet Muḥammad. He told them that God had sent him with the true religion, and he called on them to believe in him. The Prophet's words rang a bell in their minds. They remembered that the Jews used to tell them that a Prophet who would reign supreme would soon be coming. The Jews used to rejoice in the promise of his coming, for they envisaged joining forces with him to vanquish the Arabs permanently. The people of Madinah realized that this was the Prophet the Jews had told them about. Here was a golden opportunity to accept him before the Jews could do so.

So, expressing their belief in the Prophet, they said to him: "We have left our people behind. No nation is torn by hostility and infighting as they are. Perhaps God will unite them through you. We will return to them and tell them about the religion we have accepted. If our people unite on this faith, then there will be no one more powerful than you in this land."[1]

After this, the people of Madinah accepted Islam in large numbers. They became known as the Anṣār, or helpers, of Islam. It was the selfless support they offered to Islam that enabled the Prophet's religion to gain supremacy in Arabia.

Five years before the Prophet's emigration to Madinah, the people of that city had thought nothing of his message, and had rejected it out of hand. Yet just five years later these same people accepted Islam. The reason for this was that when they first met the Prophet they were preoccupied by military considerations; they could think of nothing else but how to subdue their enemies. This meant that they had no time to give consideration to spiritual matters. God, and life after death, appeared to them to be extraneous issues, designed to divert them from their real aim.

The Aws and the Khazraj poured all their resources into the war of Bu'ath. All they received in return, however, was self-destruction. The very future of the two tribes was cast into doubt: it seemed as if the Jews would set them against one another until they were annihilated. These thoughts ushered in a change of attitude. They began to think in terms of peace instead of war, of unity instead of civil conflict. They started setting their relations with their neighbours in a wider context than that of the battlefield. They saw that the problem lay more between the Arab tribes of the Aws and Khazraj on one side, and the Jews on the other, than between the two Arab tribes themselves. If the Aws and Khazraj could unite on a single platform, they would be able to present a united front to the Jews. A unifying faith was just what they needed to heal the wounds of tribal conflict, and patch up the differences between the two tribes. And if they could find a leader acceptable to both sides, he would be able to see the process of reconciliation through to its completion. In the person of the Prophet Muḥammad, they found the leader and the faith they needed. They rushed to accept his religion.

It was Islam, then, that benefited indirectly from the war of Bu'āth, for it made the Aws and Khazraj realize the futility of war and seek peace among themselves. This peace they found in Islam, and they united with one another as helpers of the Prophet. "The war of Bu'āth," 'Ā'ishah once said, "was a war that God brought about to create support for his Prophet."

NOTE

1. *Tahzīb Sīrat Ibn Hishām*, vol. 2, p. 38.

12

Emigration—From Makkah to Madinah

The Prophet's emigration from Makkah to Madinah was the most important event of Islamic history. That is why the companions marked the beginning of the Islamic calendar with this event. But in order to understand the real significance of the emigration, it is necessary to remove the dust of legends and fairy tales that have, over the years, accumulated over the glass case of history.

One of these myths has grown up over the Prophet's stay in the Cave of Thawr, on his way from Makkah to Madinah. The Quraysh were hot on his heels, and to hide from them, he took refuge in the cave. The story goes that, after the Prophet entered, God commanded a spider to weave a web at the door of the cave. Then He commanded a dove to come and lay an egg on top of the web, thus—providentially—giving the impression that the cave was uninhabited. But as is usual with such events, the facts of the Prophet's emigration to Madinah have been exaggerated and distorted beyond recognition. This is clear from a perusal of the actual historical version of what happened.

As the historian Ibn Kathīr has pointed out, the most reliable account of events is that given by Imām Aḥmad on the authority of ʻAbdullah ibn ʻAbbās. This is how the account goes:

> They (the Quraysh) followed close on the heels of the Prophet, but when they reached the mountain, they lost trace of him. They then climbed the mountain, and passed by a cave. Noting a spider's web on the mouth of the cave, they said to one another, "If he had entered this cave, the spider's web would not have remained intact."[1]

It is not explicitly stated that the cave they saw was the cave of Thawr. Even if we accept that it was, then all that is clear from this account is that they saw a spider's web in the mouth of a cave. There is no mention of God commanding a spider to weave a web after the entry of the Prophet, or of His making a dove lay its egg on top of the web. Such additions are fanciful, and are the result of wishful thinking.

The greatest damage caused by such interpolations is that they divert one's attention to fantastic, far-fetched tales, and cause one to miss the real lesson which is to be derived from purely factual accounts.

THE EMIGRANTS ARE MADE AT HOME

The manner in which the tribes of Madinah aided the Prophet is one of the most extraordinary events of history. Because of their assistance, they came to be known as the Anṣār—the Helpers. Usually when people give something, it is in return for some favour, or it is in order to ingratiate themselves with someone. There are also those who give offerings to "holy men," because they think that to do so will cause blessings to descend on their families and properties. But the emigration of the Prophet is perhaps the sole example in the annals of history of people opening their doors to destitute and forlorn refugees when they themselves had nothing to gain, and probably a great deal to lose by doing so. The action of the Anṣār was based entirely on their dedicated commitment to the cause of Islam. Not only did they accommodate the emigrants in their homes; they treated them as brothers and sisters, and shared their possessions with them. And they did all this, fully conscious of the fact that their action involved much more than economic sacrifice. They knew full well that what they were doing would arouse the hostility of the most powerful factions in both Arabia and Persia. There are no words more fitting than those of 'Alī to describe them: "They were true to their word, steadfast in adversity."[2]

When the Muhājirūn forsook their own country for Madinah, every one of the Anṣār was eager to extend hospitality to them. They even drew lots among themselves for the privilege of being able to entertain such noble guests. They handed over the better part of their properties to the Muhājirūn. And all this despite the fact that, in the oath of allegiance they took, it was specifically laid down that others would be given priority over them. Though they had made the most extreme sacrifices for the sake of Islam, they did not show the slightest disapproval of this clause.[3]

Despite all the assistance that was afforded him, the

Prophet did not have an easy life in Madinah. Apprehensions that the whole of Arabia would unite against the Muslims proved only too true. This is how Ubayy ibn Ka'b, a companion of the Prophet, describes the situation:

> When the Prophet and his companions arrived in Madinah and the Anṣār gave them asylum, the Arabs united against them. The Muslims used to remain in their armour, night and day.[4]

The Quraysh declared economic sanctions against the people of Madinah. All Arab tribes, following the Quraysh's lead, severed links with the city. Internal resources ran far short of providing for the considerably increased population of Madinah, and the expense of defending the city pushed the economy to its very limit. 'Umar says that the Prophet was restless with hunger all day in Madinah. There were not even enough rejected dates for him to eat his fill. In later years someone asked 'Ā'ishah if they had a lantern. "If we had had oil to burn a lantern," she said, "we would have drunk it." The Muslims used to go out on expeditions with hardly any provisions. Abū Mūsā tells of one expedition he made with the Prophet. "There was only one camel between six of us. We used to take turns to ride on it. The skin began peeling off our feet from incessant walking, and we used to bind them with rags. That was why the expedition came to be known as *Dhāt al-Riqa'*, (*riqa'* meaning rags or patches)." Food rations used to run so low that people used to suck dates rather than eat them. Acacia leaves and locusts would make up the rest of their diet. Added to this the Muhājirūn had to contend with a drastic change of diet. In Makkah they had been used to a diet of meat and milk. In Madinah dates constituted the major portion of their diet. Tabarani has related an incident which occurred one day when the Prophet came to take the Friday congregational prayer. A Makkan Muslim called out to him: "Prophet of God, these dates have burnt our intestines."[5]

The emigration to Madinah was a watershed in Islamic history. From a practical point of view, Islam emerged from a purely missionary episode and entered a period of active confrontation. During the period when he was solely concerned with preaching, the Prophet used to work according to one hard-and-fast principle. He used to steer clear of all controversial issues and concentrate entirely on giving good news of the joys of paradise, and warnings of the punishment of hell. He would avoid any discussion of political, economic and tribal affairs. When he preached the message of Islam to the Banū 'Āmir ibn Ṣa'ṣa'ah tribe in the fair of 'Ukāz, he assured them at the same time that all he would do was pursue his preaching work in a peaceful manner; he would not raise any extraneous issue. "I am God's Prophet," he said. "If I come amongst you, will you protect me so that I can continue to communicate my message? I will not force you on any matter."[6]

In Madinah preaching work still remained the basic purpose of the Prophet's mission. But the spectrum had broadened, and now Islam had to take account of social issues as well. The policy adopted by the Prophet at this juncture was aimed at softening people's hearts towards

Islam, so that the purpose of his mission could be achieved without conflict. "I have been assisted by the feelings of awe which I inspire—this has been the equivalent of one month's journey," he once said. Usually his missions were carried through to success by sheer force of personality.

There were two complementary aspects to this method: one was based on overawing the opponents of Islam, while the other was aimed at planting in them the seed of love. The first meant accumulating strength awesome enough to convince the opponents of Islam that they could not beat it and that being so, they had best come to its fold.[7]

The second way was to offer gifts to the opponents of Islam for softening their heart towards Islam and Muslims.[8] The generosity that the Prophet showed to win people over to his cause was without peer. No one before or after him can lay claim to such boundless munificence. Safwān ibn Umayyah, a noble of Makkah, went and hid in a mountain ravine. After the Muslim conquest of Makkah the Prophet extended an amnesty to him, and asked to see him. After Hawāzin had been subdued, the Prophet was overseeing the distribution of spoils at Ji'ranah. Safwān ibn Umayyah was with him. As yet he had not accepted Islam. Standing on the side of a gully, he gazed in wonderment at the goats and camels swarming beneath him. "Abū Wahāb," the Prophet enquired on seeing him, "would you like all these cattle?" Safwān said that he would. "It's all yours," the Prophet told him. "No one but a Prophet could be so generous," Safwān replied. He immediately accepted Islam, and testified that there was no one worthy of being served save God, and that Muḥammad was His servant and Prophet.[9]

The Prophet's numerous marriages were also part of this policy. Prime importance was attached in the tribal system to relationships through marriage. This gives us an insight into the marriages entered into by the Prophet after his emigration to Madinah. Through them relationships were established with countless people, whose hearts then mellowed towards his mission. The Prophet's first marriage was with Khadījah, a widow almost twice his age. Except for that one marriage, his other marriages were entered into for the political and missionary advantages that accrued to Islam from them.

The year after the Peace of Ḥudaybiyyah (A.D. 628), the Prophet—along with 2000 Muslims—went on a pilgrimage to the Holy Ka'bah. During his three-day stay in Makkah, he married a widow by the name of Maymunah bint al-Ḥārith. She had eight sisters, all of whom were married into distinguished Makkan families. By marrying her, the Prophet became related to all these eight families. Khālid ibn al-Walīd was Maymunah's nephew, and she had brought him up as a son. So Khālid, the Quraysh's greatest warrior, became the Prophet's step-son. After this Khālid did not join in any hostilities against the Muslims, and before long he himself entered the fold of Islam. After his marriage to Maymunah the Prophet had arranged a wedding reception for the people of Makkah, but the Quraysh reminded him that—according to the terms of the Treaty of Ḥudaybiyyah—he was only allowed to remain in

Makkah for three days. His period was up and he would have to leave the city immediately. The wedding reception, which was aimed at attracting people to the faith, could not take place. But Khālid ibn al-Walīd and 'Amr ibn al-'Āṣ had become Muslim together. So that on their arrival in Madinah people exclaimed: "With these two in the bag, Makkah has been tamed."

Umm Ḥabībah, the daughter of Abū Sufyān, a prominent member of the Quraysh, and her husband ʿUbaydullah ibn Jaḥsh accepted Islam and emigrated to Abyssinia. There, however, the husband became a Christian. Not long after that he died. Hearing of this, the Prophet made arrangements to marry Umm Ḥabībah by proxy. After the death of Abū Jahl on the field of Badr, Abū Sufyān had become the most prominent leader of the Quraysh. The Prophet would now be his son-in-law. The marriage had to be completed by proxy, for it was feared that if Umm Ḥabībah returned to Makkah, her father would not allow the marriage. The ceremony was then conducted by Najāshī, king of Abyssinia, and the bride left immediately for Madinah. With this relationship now established, Abū Sufyān's enmity to the Prophet mellowed, and he converted to Islam one day before the conquest of Makkah.

The other aspect of this policy was that of "striking terror" into the hearts of the enemies of Islam. This consisted of mustering up enough strength and making such a show of it that there would be no need to use it. The defeat of the Muslims at Uhud (A.H. 3) could have turned into a rout if Abū Sufyān had followed up his victory with another attack, instead of turning back to Makkah. Indeed, when he reached Rūḥā, he realized his mistake, and made to turn once again on the Muslims' stronghold. But even at this time of utter disarray, the Prophet's information system was still working effectively. He heard about Abū Sufyān's intention, and decided to go out to meet him. Immediately he resembled his shaken army and set off towards Makkah. Contrary to his moral practice, which was to maintain a veil of the utmost secrecy over military manoevres, this expedition was given a fanfare of publicity. When the Muslims reached Ḥamrā al-Asad, eight miles from Madinah, Abū Sufyān heard of the pursuit. Thinking that fresh reinforcements must have arrived, he gave up his idea of attacking Madinah and returned to Makkah. The Prophet turned back to Madinah when he became sure of the withdrawal of Abū Sufyan's army.

One year after the Battle of Mu'tah, which occurred in the month of Jumada al-Awwal, A.H. 8, the Byzantine emperor started gathering his forces on the Syrian border. The Ghassanids, along with other Roman allies among Arab tribes in the region, followed the emperor's lead. In response, the Prophet advanced to Tabuk with an army of 30,000. The expedition to Tabuk was really a military manoevre, a pre-emptive strike. The aim was to strike fear into the enemy, so that they would lose heart and abandon their hostile intentions. When the Prophet reached Tabuk, he heard that Caesar was not advancing to meet the Muslims but, instead, was beginning to withdraw his forces from the frontier. There was now no question of a battle, and

Caesar's very withdrawal had assured the Prophet of a moral victory, which he decided to turn to his own political advantage. During his 20 day stay in Tabūk, he established contact with the neighbouring Arab tribes, who were at that time under Roman influence. The Christian chieftain of Daumat al Jandal, Ukayḍir ibn 'Abd al-Malik al-Kindī, Yūḥannah ibn Ruyah from Aylah, along with Christians of Maqnā, Jarba and Azrūḥ, agreed to pay *jizyah*, a tax levied on non-Muslims living under the protection of a Muslim government, which guarantees the safety of their lives and property, and free exercise of their religion.

The same reason lay behind the expedition under Usāmah, undertaken soon after the death of the Prophet. Except for the tribes of Madinah the whole of Arabia had risen in revolt when the Prophet died. Suddenly the Muslims found themselves at odds with all their Arab countrymen. It appeared expedient at the time to preserve all strength in Madinah, in order to counter the enemy within. But rather than do this, Abū Bakr acted on a decision taken by the Prophet. A force of 700 men was sent to the Roman front under Usāmah. Abū Hurayrah explains the impact that this expedition had on the rebellious Arab tribes:

> "When Usāmah's force passed those tribes by that were on the verge of apostasy, they would exclaim: "If the Muslims did not have great reserves of strength, they would never have despatched a force like this. Let us leave them to fight against the Romans.' The Muslims fought against the Romans and defeated them, returning safely after doing

> battle with them. Seeing this, those who had been thinking of apostasy became firm in Islam."[10]

When the Prophet reached Madinah, there were, besides a small minority of idolators, two main communities living there—the Jews and the Muslims. These two communities were split up into several small groups. Neither was able to present a united front. People were just waiting for someone who would organize and unite them. When the Prophet realized that this was what people wanted, he issued a decree in which Jews and Muslims were recognized as communities in their own right. "The Jews are a community along with the Muslims.... They shall have their religion and the Muslims theirs." No encroachment was made on the customary rights and responsibilities of either Jews or Muslims, and acceptable concessions were made to the sentiments of both communities. A clause was added, however, which read as follows:

> Whenever there is a disagreement about something, the matter should be referred to God Almighty and to Muḥammad.[11]

This decree amounted to a political initiative which, in the most tactful and ingenious manner, introduced Islamic constitutional government to the city of Madinah.

The Prophet's departure to Madinah, instead of appeasing the Quraysh, aroused their anger to new levels of intensity. They saw that the Muslims were all gathering in one place, and becoming stronger in the process. Only two years elapsed before the Prophet had to decide whether to meet the Quraysh army outside the city, or allow them to enter Madinah and cast the newly built nest of Islam into disarray. The Quraysh had 950 men in their army, while the Muslims numbered only 313. But the Prophet's insight told him that the Quraysh were moved by solely negative impulses. Hatred of the Muslims, and jealousy of the Prophet, lay behind their aggression. The Muslims, on the other hand, were moved by the most positive and noble instincts. They had faith in God to spur them on, as well as the certainty that they were fighting for a true cause. The Muslims, then, were immeasurably more strongly motivated than their foes. Besides this, Arab warfare was an individual affair. Every warrior sought to make a name for himself by exhibiting his own bravery. Faith in God had removed this weakness from the Muslims. The Prophet was the first person in Arab history to command his forces to pursue a united course of action, and fight in ranks. He stressed the importance of fighting, not as individuals, but as a unit. The believers were urged to destroy the Quraysh's individual strength with the strength of solidarity:

> God loves those who fight for His cause in ranks as if they were a solid cemented edifice.[12]

It was faith and the Muslims' ability to fight as one unit that brought about the first victory of Islamic history—the Battle of Badr.

VICTORY OF ISLAM

Defeat at Badr had the effect of further provoking the Quraysh, and several battles, notably those of Uhud (A.H.

3) and the Trench (A.H. 5), ensued within the space of a few years. The Muslims ran into severe difficulties during these campaigns. The 800 who participated in the Battle of the Trench had to suffer extreme cold, hunger and exhaustion. So much so that when the Prophet asked for someone to volunteer for a spying foray into the enemy camp, no one stood up. Eventually the Prophet personally delegated this task to Ḥuzayfah.

There were also recurrent problems with the Jews of Madinah who, in alliance with the Quraysh, were always conspiring against the Muslims. Madinah was beseiged for twenty days during the Battle of the Trench. Finally the Quraysh were forced by a violent sandstorm to make their way back to Makkah. Now that collaboration with the Quraysh had been exposed, the Prophet chose this time to solve this problem. There were three Jewish tribes in and around Madinah—the Banū Naḍīr, Banū Qaynuqah and Banū Qurayzah. Immediately after the Battle of the Trench, they were besieged and exiled applying on them their own Judaic law. The threat that they had posed to the Muslims in Madinah was thus permanently eliminated.

Then there was the problem of Khaybar. Six years after the Prophet's emigration, Madinah was an island of Islam between the Quraysh in Makkah, 400 kilometres to the south, and the Jews in Khaybar, 200 kilometres to the north. The Quraysh and the Jews were united in their enmity towards Islam but neither being strong enough to take the Muslims on alone, they had entered into negotiations aimed at setting out a plan of joint action against the Muslims. The latter, for their part, were not in a position either to take on both enemies at the same time.

It was against this background that the Prophet, acting under divine inspiration, set out for Makkah in the year A.H. 6 along with 1400 companions. He made it absolutely clear that the Muslims had no intention of fighting anybody, and were just going for ʿUmrah. The sacrificial camels which the Muslims took along with them provided further proof of their peaceful intentions. The camels were even given the sacrificial emblem, known as *qalādah*, so that the people of Makkah could be quite sure that they were meant for sacrifice. This journey was also aimed at allaying the fears of the Quraysh that the Muslims intended to destroy the Kaʿbah's religious and commercial status.

As expected, the Quraysh advanced to prevent the Muslims from entering Makkah. The two parties met at Ḥudaybiyyah, some eleven kilometres from Makkah. Anxious to avoid hostilities, the Prophet set up camp then and there. He then sent a message to the Quraysh, suggesting a peace treaty between the two sides. He impressed it upon his envoys that they had not come to fight anybody. "We have come as pilgrims. War has weakened and caused the Quraysh to suffer great losses. If they wish, I am willing to make a truce with them: they shall not come in between myself and the people during that time. If I emerge supreme, and they so wish, they can accept the religion which others have accepted. If I do not emerge supreme, they will have the right to do as they please. If the Quraysh refuse this offer, I will fight with them in support of my cause, even at the risk of losing my life. And what God wishes will come to pass."[13]

The theme of this message shows that the Prophet was appealing to a soft spot in the Quraysh's own psyche. When the Prophet first commenced his public mission in Makkah, 'Utbah ibn Rabī'ah came to him on behalf of the Quraysh. When he returned to his people, this is what he had to say to them:

> Leave this fellow to carry on with his work for, God knows, he is never going to give it up. Do not prevent him from preaching to the Arabs. If he wins them over, then his honour will be your own. If they prevail over him, then, thanks to others, you will be free of him.[14]

The Prophet thus appealed to the Quraysh in the very terms of which they themselves had been thinking; consequently, he was able to find supporters of his peace initiative within the enemy camp itself.

The Prophet sent the Quraysh this message, and at the same time initiated various procedures aimed at influencing them. One of the Banū Kinānah came from Makkah to Ḥudaybiyyah to ascertain the Muslims' intentions. When the Prophet heard about his impending arrival, he told his followers of the Banū Kinānah's reverence for sacrificial camels, and directed them to take the camels with them when they went out to meet him. They did so, chanting the prayer of pilgrimage—"We are here at your service, Lord..."—at the same time. The Quraysh's envoy was extremely impressed. On his return to Makkah he told the Quraysh that he was quite sure that the Muslims had come on a pilgrimage and for no other reason, and should be allowed to carry on.

The very spectacle of 1400 Muslims displaying their faith in God also made a deep impact on the Quraysh.

When one of their envoys came into the Muslim camp, the Muslims were all praying in ranks, lined up behind the Prophet. He was highly impressed by the organization and discipline of the worshippers. When he returned to the Quraysh, he told them that the Muslims worked as a unit: when Muḥammad made a move, all his followers did likewise. Another envoy saw that when the Prophet performed his ablutions, the Muslims rushed to catch the water he had used in their hands before it could touch the ground. He noticed the hush which descended upon them when the Prophet was speaking, the reverence which prevented from looking him straight in the eye. When this envoy reported back to the Quraysh, they were deeply impressed by his description of the Muslims' loyalty and affection for their leader. 'Urwah ibn Mas'ūd asked them: "Are you not as my fathers and sons?" The people told him that they were indeed. "Are you suspicious of me in any way?" he asked them. They said not. "Well," 'Urwah continued, "this man (Muḥammad) has made a fine proposal to you. Agree to it, and let me go to confer with him."[15]

The Prophet made clear his intention to accept any demand the Quraysh made, as long as it did not contradict the law of God. The Quraysh displayed all manner of bigotry while the treaty was being compiled. They removed the words, "Muḥammad, Messenger of God" from the draft and inserted "Muḥammad, son of 'Abdullah" instead. Taking offence at the words "In the Name of God, the Beneficent, the Merciful," they insisted on "In Your Name, Oh God," being written. They added a clause saying that any Quraysh who joined the Muslims would have to be returned. The Quraysh, on the other hand, would not have to do the same with any Muslim who came to them. They refused the Muslims permission to enter Makkah for their pilgrimage that year. These clauses were more than the Companions could bear. 'Urwah ibn Mas'ūd even commented that those whom the Prophet had gathered around himself were about to desert him. 'Urwah's remark was too much for the normally placid Abū Bakr, who sternly rebuked him and said, "So you think that we will leave the Prophet on his own?" But the Prophet himself refused to be provoked. He accepted all the Quraysh's demands, and completed a ten-year truce with them. As long as the truce lasted, the Quraysh were prevented—directly or indirectly—from participating in any hostilities against the Muslims.

This treaty weighed so heavily on the Muslims that, after it had been completed, no one responded to repeated calls by the Prophet for sacrifice of the camels they had brought with them. It was with heavy hearts that finally they rose to make the sacrifice. So much so that when they shaved their heads afterwards it seemed as if they were going to cut one another's throats, so deep was their sorrow. But this truce, the terms of which appeared so unfavourable to the Muslims, was destined to reap incalculable benefits for them later.

At the time of the truce two main enemies confronted the Muslims—the Jews of Khaybar and the Quraysh of Makkah. The Muslims were not yet strong enough to confront both simultaneously. To attack one would have been to provide the other with a golden opportunity to attack Madinah from the rear, thus demolishing the Muslims' stronghold. Now the Prophet, by accepting all the Quraysh's demands, had consolidated a ten-year truce with one of the two. No longer could they conduct forays against the Muslims. With the Quraysh out of his way, the Prophet was now able to turn his attention to the Jews of Khaybar. The attack on Khaybar (Muḥarram A.H. 7) followed in quick succession after the Treaty of Ḥudaybiyyah (Dhū'l-Qa'dah, A.H. 6) which finally solved the Jewish problem.

Twenty thousand armed men were holding out in the eight mighty fortresses of Khaybar. The fortresses were also equipped with highly sophisticated defences. The story of the sacking of this fortified city is a long one, in which methods of extraordinary military ingenuity were used. The gate of the city was broken with a massive tree trunk, wielded by about fifty men. A few strong blows were enough to break the gate, allowing the Muslims to enter amidst a hail of arrows and stones. Four fortresses were captured in this manner. The rest took fright, opened their gates, and put themselves at the mercy of the Muslim army.

There remained the Quraysh to be subdued. The Prophet's intuition told him to wait until they broke the treaty before entering into the field of battle with them. The Prophet knew the negative sentiments that spurred the Quraysh on in their fight against the Muslims. Since the former were motivated by feelings of jealousy, hate, greed and arrogance, the Prophet realized that they would stop short of no immoral and unreasonable action in pursuit of their aims. His estimate proved correct. In Sha'bān A.H. 8, fighting erupted between the tribes of Khuzā'ah and Banū Bakr. The Banū Bakr were allied to the Quraysh and the Khuzā'ah to the Muslims. In blatant contradiction of the terms of the Treaty of Ḥudaybiyyah, the Quraysh provided their allies with clandestine support, enabling them to attack the Khuzā'ah. This incident occurred just two years after the Treaty of Ḥudaybiyyah. During this time the number of people with the Prophet had risen from 1,500 to 10,000. Along with them, the Prophet secretly set out for Makkah. So wise and diplomatic was his strategy that Makkah was conquered with next to no bloodshed:

> God has promised you many gains which you will acquire, and thus He has given you this beforehand, and He has restrained the hands of men from you.[16]

When the Treaty of Ḥudaybiyyah was signed, the Prophet had been preaching for twenty years. The message of Islam had spread throughout the Arabian peninsula. There were people in every tribe in whose hearts the Prophet's religion had found a place. But they still looked up to the Quraysh as their leaders. Many who realized the truth of Islam were unable to proclaim their faith out of fear of the Quraysh. They knew that declaration of Islam amounted to a declaration of war against the mightiest tribe in Arabia. Now they heard that the Muslims and the Quraysh had agreed to curtail hostilities for ten years. The Quraysh would no longer be able to take reprisals against people becoming Muslims. There was now nothing to stop people accepting Islam. It was as if a large crowd had gathered at the gate of Islam. The gate was thrown open with the Treaty of Ḥudaybiyyah and the crowds flocked in. As Ibn Shahāb al-Zahrī and others have pointed out, the Muslims gained more from the Treaty of Ḥudaybiyyah than from any of their campaigns. The Prophet returned to Makkah two years later with 10,000 men, whereas previously the Muslims had numbered no more than 3,000. This was a direct result of the removal of the greatest obstacle to acceptance of Islam—the anger and irritation of the Quraysh which would result from such a move. Barā' was one of the Muslims present at Ḥudaybiyyah. Bukhārī has related how he used to say to later-day people, those who considered the Conquest of Makkah to be the great victory of Islam, that the Companions of the Prophet used to consider the Peace Treaty of Ḥudaybiyyah as the outstanding victory.

The economic blockade of Madinah was now lifted. Caravans from that city were now permitted to pass freely through Makkah. But Abū Jandal, Abū Baṣīr, and others who had accepted Islam, had to be returned to the Quraysh under the terms of the treaty. Before long, however, they escaped and took refuge in Dhū'l-Marwah. So many Muslim converts assembled in that place that it became a new, flourishing centre of Islam. From there they used to play havoc with the Quraysh's trading caravans. Finally the Quraysh were forced to abandon their insistence that anyone deserting the Quraysh for the Muslim camp would have to be returned to the Quraysh.

The great lesson of Ḥudaybiyyah is that one should avoid impatience and should not judge matters by appearances alone. The outwardly unfavourable Treaty of Ḥudaybiyyah held great opportunities for the Muslims, which only people of insight could perceive. Ibn 'Asākir has recorded some comments of Abū Bakr on the Treaty of Ḥudaybiyyah. "It was the greatest Islamic victory," he said, "though on that day people were too shortsighted to realize the secrets between Muḥammad and his Lord. People are impatient but God is not. He lets matters take their course, until they reach the stage that he intends." It is realism which brings success in this world; but people want instant success, and are unwilling to go through the lengthy stages it takes to achieve it.

After finishing with Khaybar, the Prophet began to make preparations for another campaign. The target he kept secret, not even telling Abū Bakr where they would be advancing. Only in Ramaḍān A.H. 8, when the Muslim army was actually directed to set out towards Makkah, did people realize where they were heading. So stealthy and discreet was their advance that they reached Marr'uz-Zahrān without the Quraysh knowing that the Muslims were upon them. The Prophet had prayed before he set out that "the spies and informers of the Quraysh" should be restrained until the Muslims entered the city of Makkah.

The Prophet went to amazing lengths to keep preparations for the advance on Makkah secret. He gave orders that Madinah should be cut off from the rest of Arabia: no one was to be allowed to enter or leave the city. A party under 'Alī was sent to guard the roads leading to Madinah. It was they who arrested Ḥāṭib ibn Abī Balta'ah's messenger, who was taking a letter to the people of Makkah warning them of the danger to their city. As Ṭabarānī reported on the authority of Ibn 'Abbās, "every tribe provided manpower and weaponry in full measure." No one was left behind. The army of 10,000 was divided into groups of several hundred men. Each division marched in ranks, led by a commander bearing a standard. The Prophet asked his uncle 'Abbās to let Abū Sufyān, an old opponent of the Prophet, witness the Muslims' march. Abū Sufyān watched from beside a narrow mountain pass as, row upon row, the Muslim army filed past. He could hardly believe his eyes. "Who has the power to confront this army?" he exclaimed. "I have never seen anything like it." The Prophet thus went to great lengths to impress Abū Sufyān. At the same time he announced that anyone entering Abū Sufyān's house would be safe. The result was that Abū Sufyān himself appealed to the people of Makkah to capitulate before Muḥammad, for no one was strong enough to fight him. Events which followed the conquest of the city prove conclusively that the extensive preparations were not aimed at causing bloodshed: they were aimed at frightening the Makkans into submission, so that the city could be captured for Islam without any need for fighting. As the Muslim army neared Makkah, one of its leaders, Sa'd ibn 'Ubādah, called out: "Today is the day of battle!" The Prophet told him that it was not; it was the day of mercy. Sa'd was then told to step down and the standard was handed over to his son instead.

There were some engagements after the Conquest of Makkah, bringing the total number of military expeditions that the Prophet conducted up to eighty. But now that the Muslims had gained control of the capital of Arabia, it entailed only minor skirmishes before all Arabia capitulated, and accepted the Prophet as their leader.

NOTES

1. Ḥadīth of Imām Aḥmad on the authority of 'Abdullah Ibn 'Abbās.
2. *Al-Bidāyah wa al-Nihāyah*, vol. 3.
3. Ibn Hishām, Tahzīb Sīrah, vol. 1, p. 111.
4. Kanz al-'Ummāl, vol. 1, p. 259.
5. Al-Tabarānī.
6. Abū Na'īm, *Dalā'il al-Nubuwwah*, p. 100.
7. Qur'ān, 8:60.
8. Qur'ān, 9:60.
9. *Kanz al-'Ummāl*, vol. 5, p. 294.
10. *Al-Bidāyah wa al-Nihāyah*, vol. 6, p. 305.
11. *Tahzīb Sīrat Ibn Hishām*, p. 129.
12. Qur'ān, 61:5.
13. Ḥadīth, *Ṣaḥīḥ*, al-Bukhārī.
14. *Al-Bidāyah wa al-Nihāyah*.
15. *Ibid.*
16. Qur'ān, 48:20.

13

Victory and after

Victors usually tend to be susceptible to two kinds of feeling—pride and vengeance. The Prophet of Islam, however, after his conquest of Makkah in A.H. 8, displayed neither of these traits. His victory was that of a Prophet of God. According to Ibn Isḥāq, when the Prophet entered Makkah, his head was bowed so low that people saw that his beard was touching the camel's saddle. Such was the humility of the Prophet, even in his hour of triumph. Standing at the door of the Ka'bah, the Prophet delivered an address, in the course of which he said,

> There is none worthy of being served save the One God. He has fulfilled His promise and offered succour to His slave. He alone has brought the hosts of enemies low.[1]

He did not, in other words, claim any credit for the victory: he attributed it entirely to God. Later on in the same speech, he had this to say to the Quraysh:

> "What do you think I am going to do with you now?" "We think you will treat us well." they replied, "for you are our noble brother, and the son

> of our noble brother." Then the Prophet said: "I say to you as Joseph said to his brothers: Let no reproach be upon you this day. Go, you are free."[2]

At the very outset, then, the Prophet put vengeance aside, thus eliminating all possibility of adverse reaction on the part of his new subjects. A nation defeated on the field of battle usually resorts to clandestine resistance. By granting a general amnesty the Prophet nipped resistance in the bud. Forces which might have sought to destroy the fortress of Islam were thus engaged in the building of it.

When the Prophet entered Makkah after the conquest of the city, he gave his commanders orders not to do battle with anyone unless they themselves were attacked. He forgave all those who had committed outrages against him. Only a few, who were to be killed "even if they took refuge beneath the curtain of the Ka'bah," were sentenced to death. Ibn Hishām, and other biographers of the Prophet, have mentioned them individually. Here are their names, and the nature of their cases:

1. 'Abdullah ibn Sa'd, who had become Muslim and been appointed as a scribe of revelation by the Prophet. He later reneged and joined the infidels. After the Conquest of Makkah, when he heard that the Prophet had ordered his execution, he took refuge with his milk-brother 'Uthmān. The latter gave him shelter, then took him to the Prophet with a request once again to accept his conversion to Islam. The Prophet remained silent. Then 'Uthmān asked a second time, whereupon the Prophet accepted 'Abdullah ibn Sa'd's oath of allegiance. The latter subsequently became governor of Egypt during the caliphate of 'Umar

and 'Uthmān, playing a major part in the conquest of Africa.

2. 'Abdullah ibn Khaṭal, who had previously accepted Islam and been sent by the Prophet to collect alms tax. A slave and one of the Ansar went along with him. Coming to a halt in their journey, 'Abdullah ibn Khaṭal told the slave to prepare a chicken for a meal, but the slave went to sleep instead, and was unable to prepare the food in time. 'Abdullah ibn Khaṭal became angry and killed the slave. Fearing that if he returned to Madinah, the Prophet would exact retribution for the slave's death, he reneged and joined the infidels. A poet, he used to recite verses abusing the Prophet. On the day Makkah was conquered, he wrapped himself up in the curtain of the Ka'bah. When the Prophet was told, he gave orders for 'Abdullah ibn Khaṭal to be killed in that very place. Abū Burzah and Sa'īd ibn Ḥārith executed him in between the Black Stone and the Place of Abraham.

3. Fartanā, who was 'Abdullah ibn Khaṭal's slave-girl. She also used to recite poems abusing the Prophet. Her dances were a regular feature of the Quraysh's wine-drinking orgies. She was also killed along with her master.

4. Quraybah who was also 'Abdullah ibn Khaṭal's slave, and pursued the same profession as Fartanā. Orders were given for her execution, but when she came to the Prophet and sought asylum, her request was granted. She then became Muslim.

5. Hūwayrith ibn Nafīdh ibn Wahab, another poet and who held Islam in very great contempt, who made his name

from heaping opprobrium upon the Prophet. While 'Abbās ibn 'Abdul Muṭṭalib and the Prophet's daughters Fāṭimah and Umm Kulthūm were on their way from Makkah to Madinah, Hūwayrith ibn Nafīdh followed them and stabbed their camel with a spear. The camel reared up and the Prophet's daughters fell to the ground. Orders were given for his execution, which was carried out by 'Alī.

6. Miqyas ibn Ṣubābah, Hishām ibn Ṣubābah's brother. In the Dhū Qarad campaign, an Anṣārī had killed Hishām by mistake. After this Miqyas came to Madinah and accepted Islam. He asked the Prophet for compensation for his brother's death, and his request was granted. He stayed in Madinah for a few days, then killed the person responsible for his brother's death, escaped to Makkah and reneged. The Prophet ordered that he be put to death, and Numaylah ibn 'Abdullah Laythī slew him.

7. Sārah, a slave-girl of 'Ikrimah ibn Abī Jahl, who revelled in pouring scorn upon the Prophet. Permission was given for her to be put to death, but she came to the Prophet and sought asylum, which was granted her, and she accepted Islam. She remained alive until the caliphate of 'Umar.

8-9. Ḥārith ibn Hishām and Zubayr ibn Abī Umayyah were also to be killed, but they took refuge in the house of their relative, Umm Hānī bint Abī Jahl. 'Alī followed them and swore that he would not let them live. Umm Hānī blocked 'Alī's path and, locking the two fugitives in her house, went to see the Prophet. She told him that 'Alī sought to kill two people to whom she had given refuge. "Whomsoever you have granted refuge, we have also granted refuge, and whomsoever you have taken into your asylum, we have also given asylum," the Prophet told her. 'Alī was ordered to let them go, and he did so.

10. 'Ikrimah ibn Abū Jahl who, following in his father's footsteps, was an uncompromising opponent of Islam. Seeing that he was sure to meet his end in Makkah, he fled to the Yemen. His wife, Umm Ḥakīm bint Ḥārith, who had accepted Islam, appealed to the Prophet for asylum on behalf of her husband. Her request was granted, and she went to the Yemen to collect 'Ikrimah. He returned with her and became Muslim at the hand of the Prophet. After his conversion, he made great personal and financial sacrifices for Islam, finally meeting his death at Ajnādīn while fighting against apostates during the caliphate of Abū Bakr.

11. Habbār ibn al-Aswad, who had been responsible for great persecution of the Muslims. When the Prophet's daughter Zaynab, wife of Abū'l 'Āṣ, was on her way from Makkah to Madinah, he stabbed her camel's side with a spear. The camel went into a frenzy and Zaynab fell down. She was with child at the time. Not only did she suffer a miscarriage, but the effects of the mishap remained with her for the rest of her life. Orders were given for him to be killed, but he came to the Prophet and pleaded for mercy. "Prophet of God," he said, "forgive my ignorance. Let me become a Muslim." The Prophet forgave him.

12. Waḥshī ibn Ḥarb, who had been responsible for the death of the Prophet's uncle Ḥamzah. Realizing that the Muslims would kill him if they laid their hands on him, he

fled from Makkah to Ṭā'if. Later on he came before the Prophet in Madinah, sought forgiveness for his crime and offered to accept Islam. The Prophet admitted him into the fold of Islam and forgave him. He joined in the fight against the false prophet Musaylimah during the caliphate of Abū Bakr. It was he who finally slew Musaylimah, with the very same weapon that had made a martyr of Ḥamzah.

13. Ka'b ibn Zuhayr, a famous poet, who used to write poems abusing the Prophet. He fled from Makkah when the city was conquered and his execution was ordered, but he then came to Madinah, asked forgiveness, and beseeched the Prophet to accept his allegiance. The Prophet did so, presenting Ka'b with his own sheet at the same time.

14. Ḥārith ibn Ṭalāṭil, a poet who used to pour scorn on the Prophet through the medium of his poetry. The Muslims were permitted to slay him, and 'Alī did so.

15. 'Abdullah ibn Zib'arī, yet another poet, who used to express his contempt for the Prophet in verse. When the Prophet ordered him to be killed, he fled to Najrān. Later on he came to the Prophet repented, and accepted Islam. The Prophet forgave him.

16. Hubayrah ibn Abī Wahab Makhzūmī, also a poet, who used to deride the Prophet's mission. He was also on the list of those to be killed. He fled to Najrān where he died an infidel.

17. Ḥind bint 'Utbah, the wife of Abū Sufyān. Her hatred of Islam was so great that, in the battle of Uḥud, she extracted Ḥamzah's heart and masticated it. She was to be killed, but she came before the Prophet, sought forgiveness

and accepted Islam. After the Prophet had forgiven her and admitted her into the fold of Islam she went home and broke all the idols in her house, saying: "Truly, you have misled us."

It is clear, then, that all the seventeen men and women who were sentenced to death after the conquest of Makkah were guilty of specific crimes. Yet whichever of them sought forgiveness, or had someone pleaded on his or her behalf, was forgiven. None of those who appealed for clemency was killed. Of the seventeen who were sentenced to death, eleven were forgiven, either directly or through some mediator. Five people who made no plea for clemency were put to death. One fled from Makkah, and died a natural death in a faraway land.

In the wake of the Conquest of Makkah, how was it that the Prophet forgave people who were guilty in the sight of God? When a woman named Fāṭimah belonging to the Banū Makhzūm tribe, had committed a theft, her kith and kin feared that her hand would be amputated. They approached Usāmah ibn Zayd who, they thought, being a close associate of the Prophet, would be in a position to ensure that their relative escaped punishment. Usāmah came to the Prophet and pleaded for clemency on behalf of Fāṭimah Makhzūmī. The Prophet was visibly upset when he heard Usāmah's words. "Are you trying to persuade me with regard to limits that God has set down?" he asked. The Prophet then called people together and delivered an address. "By the power who has control over my soul," he said, "if my daughter Fāṭimah were to steal, then I would certainly amputate her hand." Fāṭimah

Makhzūmī received her due punishment, after which she repented and became a righteous, upright person.[3]

This shows that no one is able to forgive a wrongdoer when punishment has been prescribed by God. How was it, then, that the Prophet forgave people with such magnanimity after the Conquest of Makkah? The reason was that there is a difference between war crimes and crimes committed under normal conditions. People cannot be accorded remission of punishment for the latter form of crime. Crimes committed during wartime, on the other hand, can be forgiven when the perpetrators renounce their antagonism and seek clemency. Crimes committed under normal conditions are nullified when the punishment God has laid down is meted out, while war crimes are neutralized through surrender and an appeal for mercy. The enemies of Islam in Arabia had committed the most heinous crimes against the Muslims. Even so, the Qur'ān announced that if they repented, what had gone before would be forgiven.[4] Furthermore, if the enemy sues for peace, peace should be made, even if there is a danger of the peace terms being broken.

> If they incline to peace, make peace with them, and put your trust in God. Surely He is the Hearing, the Knowing. Should they seek to deceive you, God is all-sufficient for you. He has made you strong with His help and rallied the faithfuls around you.[5]

One of those sentenced to death and then subsequently forgiven was 'Ikrimah ibn Abī Jahl. Along with his father, he had been an active opponent of Islam, and had subjected the Prophet and his companions to all forms of persecution. Yet, when news came that 'Ikrimah was coming to accept

Islam, the Prophet told his companions not to insult 'Ikrimah's father, "for abuse of the dead hurts the living."

It was magnanimity such as this, after the conquest of Makkah, that turned Islam's most implacable foes into staunch custodians of faith.

NOTES

1. *Al-Bidāyah wa al-Nihāyah.*
2. Ḥadīth, *Zād al-Ma'ad*, Ibn Qayyim.
3. Ḥadīth by al-Bukhārī and Muslim.
4. Qur'ān, 8:38.
5. Qur'ān, 8:61-62.

PART THREE

14

The Termination of Prophethood

In the early years of the Prophet Muḥammad's mission, a man who had come to Makkah on a pilgrimage was asked on his return to his country what was new in Makkah. "Muḥammad has claimed prophethood," he answered, but the only person of any distinction who has become a follower of his is the son of Abū Qaḥafah (Abū Bakr). From this answer one can tell what people thought of the Prophet in A.D. 610, when he commenced his mission. In those days, his opponents used to refer to him as if he were a village lad, calling him Ibn Abī Kabshah, i.e. the son of his village foster parents, simply in order to deride him. Those who preferred to be more polite would call him "a youth from the Quraysh."

This was how the Prophet was referred to in his own lifetime. Now, centuries later, things have changed. The prophethood of Muḥammad is no longer a controversial matter; it has become an established fact. Now, when one thinks of the Prophet Muḥammad, it is a great historical personality that springs to mind, one who has been a subject of discussion for generation upon generation over the last

1500 years. If this history were to be taken away from the Prophet of Islam, he would return to being "Ibn Abī Kabshah" in the eyes of men. Were this to happen, there is not a shadow of a doubt that the number of Muslims in the world today would be counted in scores rather than in hundreds of millions. It is very difficult to recognize a prophet of God when he comes in the guise of 'Ibn Abī Kabshah'. On the other hand, to accept one who has become an established historical personality is relatively easy. The Prophet of Islam has now secured what the Qur'ān calls a "position of praise and glory."[1] Small wonder, then, that those who sing his praises run into thousands of millions.

It was this factor which contributed more than anything to the denial of prophets by their peoples in previous ages. "This is just an ordinary person," people would say. "Up till now we knew him by his common name. How did he become a prophet of God all of a sudden?" "Whenever a prophet comes among his people, this objection is raised, posing a serious impediment to the acceptance by a prophet's contemporaries of his teachings.

All of the prophets, at the time of their emergence, were greeted with suspicion and scepticism. The psychological barrier preventing people from believing in one who, in their eyes, appeared like anyone else, proved insurmountable for most people. When they failed to believe in the prophets, however, they were punished according to the law of God.

Now God decided to send a prophet who would break down this barrier. There would be no room for doubt about whether his claim to prophethood was genuine or the result of over-zealous ambition. He would take his place in history as a prophet of God. His name would stand out in the seas of time, like a beacon beckoning people to belief. There would be no difficulty for people in recognizing him as God's Prophet, believing in him, and winning a share in God's eternal blessings.

There are several traditions according to which the Prophet is reported as saying that his followers would be more numerous than those of any other prophet. This is another way of making the same point. After Muḥammad, on whom be peace, there would be no other prophet. Never again would his followers have to choose between belief and disbelief. They would continue to grow in number until the coming of the Last Day.

A look at Israelite history will help to illustrate this point. The Jews who lived in the time of Jesus believed in God's law as revealed to Moses. Yet when a new prophet—Jesus, the son of Mary—arose amongst them, they denied him. They continued to believe in their own historic prophet and refused to believe in the prophet of their day. Seven hundred years later, the Prophet of Arabia was sent to the world. By this time the number of Christians in the world had increased considerably. History, however, was to repeat itself. Christians were not prepared to believe in an Ishmaeli, rather than an Israeli, Prophet. Again they retained their faith in an historically established Prophet—Jesus—but did not believe in a contemporary one—Muḥammad. Except for a few Christians who accepted Islam, those who had been believers in Jesus became disbelievers in his successor.

Thanks to the termination of prophethood, the followers of Muḥammad are never again going to have to choose between an ancient Prophet and a modern one. Never again—at least in the present world—will they be forced to opt for the old or the new—something which occurs in the community of an historic Prophet when a contemporary Prophet visits them. The installation of the Prophet Muḥammad on the pinnacle of history, on what the Qur'ān calls "a position of praise and glory,"[2] is one factor contributing to his being "a mercy for all nations."[3] Historically, the position of Muḥammad as a Prophet of God cannot be questioned; that is the nature of his position of praise and glory in this world. On the Day of Resurrection, it will be made manifest in the form of special divine favour being conferred upon him.

It would be a mistake to think that the Prophet Muḥammad's elevation to such a position was a simple matter of selection. It was to bring a revolution in human history. Only an individual of the highest moral calibre, only one able to perform unparalleled feats of self-sacrifice and steadfastness would be considered fit to be chosen. For this task the Lord saw fit to call upon Muḥammad:

> You who are wrapped up in your vestment, arise and give warning. Magnify your Lord, cleanse your garments, and keep away from all pollution. Bestow no favours expecting gain. Be patient for your Lord's sake.[4]

The great soul "wrapped up in his vestment' responded to the call and participated in the divine scheme with wholehearted dedication, although many were his trials and tribulations before the prophetic mission, which was to be a mercy for the whole world, reached completion. The coming of repeated prophets, one after the other, to the world, had been a severe test for humanity. Now this era had passed and there would be one acknowledged Prophet for all time, enabling people to enter into the sphere of God's mercy in an unending procession.

With God's choice of Muḥammad, then, prophethood was given historical credibility. This meant that no more prophets had to come to the world in future. But it was not merely a matter of divine proclamation. Certain conditions had to be fulfilled before this could happen. Firstly, God's commandments relating to every walk of human life had to be revealed. This was duly accomplished as the Qur'ān itself states: "It is He who has revealed the Qur'ān for you fully explained."[5] Secondly, a perfect pattern had to be presented before mankind. The Prophet Muḥammad provided mankind with just such a "good example,"[6] and this condition was fulfilled. Thirdly, there had to be arrangement for the permanent preservation of the Qur'ān. This task Almighty God took upon Himself: "It was We who revealed Qur'ān, and We will certainly preserve it."[7]

God's way with previous prophets had been to send them with certain signs and miracles. The prophets, for their part, left no stone unturned in discharging their duty to communicate the word of God to their peoples. In the process they proved that they had been sent by God by performing wondrous acts. If, in spite of all this, people did not believe, then there was no more that the prophets could do. It was now time for God's angels to take action, bringing down punishment on the disbelievers.

With the final Prophet, however, it was decided that the people he addressed should not be subjected to this form of divine punishment. Rather, the Prophet himself, along with his companions, were told that those who still did not believe and who actually attacked Islam would be punished at the hands of the Muslims.[8] In other words, the task which used to be performed by angels would be accomplished by the hands of men.

It was due to this divine verdict that even after emigration and after having fully communicated the word of God to them until there remained no rational ground for denial, yet, unlike the peoples in the times of the previous prophets, they were visited by no all-consuming manifestation of the wrath of God. Rather, the Prophet and his companions were made to confront them on the battlefield. God's succour assisted the believers against their foes, and they emerged victorious. So it was that God's religion was established on the Arabian peninsula in the form of a State.

It is God's way to reveal His commandments in the context of relevant circumstances. Since the religion the Prophet left to the world had to be complete in every detail, so had his mission to pass through every walk of human life. Only then would a correct pattern of life dealing with matters of both individual and general concern be established for coming generations. As Muslims continued to engage themselves in defuse against non-Muslims who refused to believe and attacked them, the granting of God's revelation was nearing completion. Commandments relating to different situations were being revealed, not all at the same time, but gradually, in accordance with the prevailing situations. The decision to have disbelievers punished at the hands of Muslims rather than by angels thus played an important part in the completion of *Shari'ah*, for only if the Prophet were made to face every form of human situation would he be able to display every facet of the Islamic way of life. The course that events themselves took enabled the Prophet to show, not only how one should live at home, but how one should conduct oneself on the battlefield, and in position of power. The model that he left for coming generations covers every walk of life, and stands preserved until the coming of the Last Day.

The provision that God made for the termination of prophethood also produced circumstances conducive to the preservation of the Qur'ān, the revealed word of God. If previous scriptures had not been preserved in their original form, it was because no protective power had emerged in support of them. But the Prophet and his companions fought against their adversaries and established Islamic rule in a substantial portion of the globe, so that the Book of God enjoyed state protection, its immunity from all attempts to change or destroy it being thus ensured. The Qur'ān was preserved for one thousand years in this way, with one generation passing it on to the next under the protective wing of an Islamic government. Then mankind entered the age of the printing press, and there was no further danger of the Qur'ān being destroyed.

It would be a mistake to think that all this was accomplished smoothly. In order to establish Islam as the ruling religion, thus ensuring the preservation of the Book of God, the Prophet and his companions had to suffer torments of unbearable intensity. The pagans wanted to see miracles. The Prophet, too, would have liked to have been able to produce miraculous signs of his prophethood. But it was not to be. Instead, the Prophet's character and demeanour had to take the place of miracles. The Prophet's opponents were not visited by any celestial or terrestrial punishment from God, as had been the case with those who denied the prophets of old. The Prophet and his companions had themselves to do what earthquakes and volcanoes had previously been used for — punish the disbelievers. The Book of God was not revealed all at once; the period of revelation extended over twenty-three years. During this time the Muslims, under the leadership of the Prophet, had to cross all the deep rivers and climb every high mountain of life, so that the path which God desired His servants to follow could be fully mapped out.

The trials which the Prophet and his companions underwent during this period reached a height of intensity called in the Qur'ān "a tremendous shaking."[9] The Prophet was given the immensely arduous directive not to compromise in any way with his oppressors.[10] However difficult the circumstances, he and his companions were given no leave to "stay behind,"[11] in face of the call of God. Were the Prophet's wives to demand as much as two meals a day, then they were given notice to choose between "this life and all its finery", on the one hand, or God and His Messenger on the other.[12]

The establishment of the prophethood which would become a subject of "praise and glory" was the most hazardous project in the entire annals of human history. Even the Prophet was forced to admit that he had been persecuted "as no other Prophet" had been. In the words of his wife 'Ā'ishah, he was "shattered" by the treatment meted out to him in spite of he and his companions having denied themselves the comforts, even the necessities of life, in order to make the prophethood of Muḥammad "a mercy for all nations."

This is the great favour which the Prophet Muḥammad bestowed upon the human race. Because of it his followers have been called upon to invoke peace and blessings upon him until the end of time. His family and his companions are also included in this invocation, for they stood by the Prophet through thick and thin, remaining with him throughout the most gruelling afflictions. It is only natural that those who acknowledge the favour of the Prophet of Islam should express their gratitude to him. The peace and blessings which Muslims invoke upon their Prophet are an expression of their gratitude in the form of prayer. As the Prophet himself said: "Miserly is the one who hears mention of my name, and does not invoke peace and blessing upon me."[13]

NOTES

1. Qur'ān, 17:79.
2. Qur'ān, 17:79.
3. Qur'ān, 21:107.
4. Qur'ān, 74:1-7.
5. Qur'ān, 6:114.
6. Qur'ān, 33:21.
7. Qur'ān, 15:9.
8. Qur'ān, 9:14.
9. Qur'ān, 33:11.
10. Qur'ān, 17:75.
11. Qur'ān, 9:119.
12. Qur'ān, 33:28.
13. Ḥadīth of Tirmidhī and Nasā'ī.

15

The Qur'an— The Prophet's Miracle

Every Prophet is given a miracle—a sign. The miracle of the Prophet of Islam is the Qur'ān. The prophethood of Muḥammad, on whom be peace, was to be valid until the Last Day. It was imperative, therefore, that his miracle also be one which would last for all time. The Qur'ān was, therefore, assigned to the Prophet as his everlasting miracle.

The Prophet's opponents demanded miracles, such as those performed by previous prophets, but the Qur'ān stated clearly that such miracles would not be forthcoming.[1] The Qur'ān even had this to say to the Prophet:

> If you find their aversion hard to bear (and would like to show them a miracle), seek if you can a burrow in the earth or a ladder to the sky by which you may bring them a sign. Had God pleased, He would have given them guidance, one and all. Do not be one of the ignorants.[2]

Instead, the revealed Book of God was made into the Prophet's miracle:

> They ask: "Why has no sign been given him by his Lord?" Say: "Signs are in the hands of God. My mission is only to give plain warning." Is it not enough for them that We have revealed to you the Book which is recited to them? Surely in this there is a blessing and an admonition to true believers.[3]

There are many different aspects of the Qur'ān's miraculous nature. Here we are going to concentrate on just three:

1. The language of the Qur'ān—Arabic—has, unlike other international languages, remained a living form of communication over the ages.

2. The Qur'ān is unique among divine scriptures in that its text has remained intact in the original form.

3. The Qur'ān challenged its doubters to produce a book like it. No one has been able to take up this challenge, and produce anything comparable to the Book of God.

The languages in which all the ancient scriptures were revealed have been locked in the archives of history. The only exception is Arabic, the language of the Qur'ān, which is still current in the world today. Millions of people still speak and write the language in which the Qur'ān was revealed nearly 1500 years ago. This provides stunning proof of the miraculous nature of the Qur'ān, for there is no other book in history which has been able to make such an impact on its language; no other book has moulded a whole language according to its own style, and maintained it in that form over the centuries.

Take the *Injil*, known as the New Testament, of which the oldest existing copy is in Greek and not Aramaic, the language which Jesus is thought to have spoken. That means that we only possess a translated account of what the Prophet Jesus said and did; and that too, in ancient Greek, which is considerably different from the modern language. By the end of the 19th century the Greek language had changed so much that the meaning of at least 550 words in the New Testament—about 12% of the entire text—was challenged. At that time a German expert, Adolf Deissman, discovered some ancient scrolls in Egypt. From them it emerged that biblical Greek was in fact a colloquial version of classical Greek. This language was spoken in Palestine during the first century A.D. Deissman was able to attach meanings to some of the unknown words, but there are another fifty words whose meanings are still unknown.[4]

Ernest Renan (1823-1894) carried out extensive research on Semitic languages. He wrote a book on their vocabularies, in which he had this to say about the Arabic language:

> The Arabic language is the most astonishing event of human history. Unknown during the classical period, it suddenly emerged as a complete language. After this, it did not undergo any noticeable changes, so one cannot define for it an early or a late stage. It is just the same today as it was when it first appeared.[5]

In acknowledging this "astonishing event of human history" Renan, a French orientalist, is in fact acknowledging the miraculous nature of the Qur'ān. It was the Qur'ān's phenomenal literary style which preserved the Arabic language from alteration, such as other languages have undergone. The noted Christian writer, Jurgī Zaydān (1861-1914) is one of the scholars to have recognized this fact. In a book on Arabic literature he writes:

> No religious book has had such an impact on the language in which it was written as the Qur'ān has had on Arabic literature.[6]

World languages have changed so much over the ages that no expert in any modern language is able to understand its ancient form without the aid of a dictionary. There have been two main causes of language alteration—upheavals in the social order of a nation and development of a language's literature. Over the centuries these factors have been at work in Arabic, just as in other languages. The difference is that they have not been able to change the structure of the Arabic language. The Arabic that is spoken today is the same as that which was current in Makkah when the Qur'ān was revealed. Homer's Ilyad (850 B.C.), Tulsi Das' Ramayan (A.D. 1623), and the dramas of Shakespeare (1564-1616), are considered literary masterpieces of their respective languages. They have been read and performed continuously from the time of their compilation until the present day. But they have not been able to keep the languages in which they were written from alteration. The Greek of Homer, the Sanskrit of Tulsi Das and even the English of Shakespeare, are now classical rather than modern languages.

The Qur'ān is the only book to have moulded a language in its own form, and maintained it in that form over the ages. There have been various intellectual and political unheavals in Arab countries, but the Arabic language has remained as it was when the Qur'ān was revealed. No change in Arab social order has been able to alter in any way the Arabic tongue. This fact is a clear indication that the Qur'ān came from a supernatural source.

One does not have to look any further than the history of the last 1500 years to see the miraculous nature of the Book revealed to the Prophet Muḥammad.

SOCIAL UPHEAVALS

The example of Latin shows how social upheavals affect languages. Though in latter days Italy became the centre of Latin, it was not originally a product of that country. Around the 12th century B.C., during the Iron Age, many central European tribes spread out into surrounding regions. Some of them, especially the Alpine tribes, entered Italy and settled in and around Rome. Their own language mixed with the language of Rome, and that was how Latin was formed. In the third century B.C. Lubus Andronicus translated some Greek tales and dramas into Latin, thus making it a literary language. The Roman Empire was established in the first century B.C., and Latin became the official language. The strength of Latin was even further reinforced by the spread of Christianity. With the support of religious and political institutions, and backed by social and economic forces, Latin continued to spread until eventually it came to cover almost the whole of ancient Europe. At the time of St. Augustine, Latin was at its peak, and right up to the Middle Ages it was considered the main international language.

The 8th century A.D. was an age of Muslim conquest. The Romans were forced to take refuge in Constantinople, which became the capital of the eastern half of the Empire, until in 1453 the Turks took Constantinople and banished the Romans from this, their last stronghold. The decline of the Roman Empire enabled various local languages to flourish, notably French, Italian, Spanish and Portuguese. Latin, the parent language, had a strong influence on all of them, but itself remained only as the official language of the Roman Catholic Church. No longer a living tongue, it retained only historic interest, and continued to be used to explain technical, legal and scientific terms. Without a good grasp of Latin, for instance, one cannot read Newton's Principia in the original.

Every classical language followed much the same pattern, changing along with social circumstances until, eventually, the original language gave way to another, completely changed one. Ethnic integration, political revolutions, and cultural clashes always left a deep mark on the language that they affected. These factors have been at work on the Arabic language over the last 1500 years, but, amazingly, it has remained intact. This extraordinary resilience of the Arabic language is entirely due to the miraculous spell the Qur'ān has cast on it.

In the year A.D. 70, some Jewish tribes left Syria and settled in Madinah, where the Arabic-speaking 'Amāliqah tribe lived. Along with the 'Amāliqahs, the Jews took Arabic as their language, but the Arabic that they spoke was different from common Arabic, retaining a strong Hebrew influence. After the coming of Islam, Arabs settled in many parts of Africa and Asia where other languages besides Arabic were spoken. Their intermingling with other races, however, did not have any effect on the Arabs' language, which remained in its original state.

In the very first century after the revelation of the Qur'ān, Arabic was exposed to the sort of forces which cause a language to alter radically. This was when Islam spread among various Arab tribes, who began to congregate in major Muslim cities. There was considerable variety of intonation and accent among the different Arab tribes. So much so that Abū 'Amr ibn al-'Ulā' was moved to remark that the "Himyar tribe do not speak our language; their vocabulary is quite different from ours." 'Umar ibn Khaṭṭāb once took before the Prophet an Arab whom he had heard reciting the Qur'ān. The Arab had been pronouncing the words of the Qur'ān in such a strange manner that 'Umar was unable to make out what part of the Book of God he was reading. The Prophet once spoke to a visiting delegation of some Arab tribe in their own dialect. It seemed to 'Alī as if the Prophet was speaking in a foreign tongue.

The main reason for this difference was variation in accent. For instance, the Banū Tamīm, who lived in the eastern part of Najd, were unable to say the letter 'j', (ج) and used to pronounce it as 'y' (ي) instead. The word for mosque (*masjid*), they used to pronounce '*masyid*', and instead of '*shajarat*' (trees), they would say '*sharat*'. 'Q' (ق) they pronounced as 'j', (ج) calling a '*tarīq*' (road) a '*tarīj*', a '*ṣadīq*' (friend) a '*ṣadīj*', '*qadr*' (value) '*jadr*' and '*qāsim*' (distributor) '*jāsim*'. According to normal linguistic patterns, the coming together of tribes who spoke such varying dialects should have initiated a fresh process of change in the Arabic language, but this was not to be. The supreme eloquence of the language of the Qur'ān guarded Arabic from any such transformation. What happened instead has been explained in the following words by Dr Aḥmad Ḥasan Zayyāt:

> After the coming of Islam, the Arabic language did not remain the monopoly of one nation. It became the language of all those who entered the faith.[6]

Then these Arab Muslims left their native land, conquering territory extending from Kashghar in the east to Gibralter in the west. Persian, Qibti, Berber, Hebrew, Greek, Latin, Aramaic and Suryani were among the languages spoken by the peoples they came into contact with. Some of these nations were politically and culturally more advanced than the Arabs. Iraq, bastion of an ancient civilization and the cultural centre of major tribes, was one of the countries they entered. They mingled with the Iranians, masters of one of the world's two great empires. The highly advanced Roman civilization, and an expanding Christian religion, were two of the forces that they clashed with. Among the countries they occupied was Syria, where Phoenician, Ghassanid, Greek, Egyptian and Cana'anian tribes had left behind outstanding traditions in literature and ethics. Then there was Egypt, the meeting place of oriental and occidental philosophy. These factors were more than enough to transform the Arabic language, as had been the case with other tongues exposed to similar forces. But they were rendered ineffective by the Qur'ān, a specimen of such unrivalled literary excellence that no power could shake the language in which it had been written.

With the conquests of Islam, Arabic no longer belonged to one people alone; it became the language of several nations and races. When the "*ajamīs*"[7] of Asia and Africa accepted Islam, they gradually adopted Arabic as their language. Naturally, these new converts were not as proficient in speaking the language as the Arabs of old. Then the Arabs in their turn were affected by the language spoken by their new co-religionists. The deterioration of Arabic was especially evident in large, cosmopolitan cities, where there was more intermingling of races. First it was the rank and file, those who did not pay much attention to the finer points of linguistics, who were affected. But the cultural elite did not remain immune either. A man once came to the court of Ziyād ibn Umayyah and lamented. "Our fathers have died, leaving small children," with both "fathers" and "children" in the wrong case. Mistakes of this nature became commonplace, yet the Arabic language remained essentially the same. Shielded by the Qur'ān's supreme eloquence, written Arabic was not corrupted by the degradation of the spoken version. It remained cast in the mould of the Qur'ān.

For proof of the Qur'ān's miraculous nature, one has only to look at all the traumatic experiences that Arabic has been through over the last 1500 years. If it had not been for the protective wing of the Qur'ān, the Arabic language would surely have been altered. The unsurpassable model that was established by the Qur'ān remained the immutable touchstone of standard Arabic.

The fall of the Umayyad dynasty in the second century

Hijrah posed a great threat to the Arabic language. The Umayyads had been a purely Arab dynasty. Strong supporters of Arab nationalism, they took their promotion of Arabic literature and language almost to the point of partiality. Their capital was situated in Damascus, in the Arab heartland. In their time, both the military and the civil administration were controlled by Arabs.

Now the Abbasids took over the reins of power. Iranian support had brought the caliphate to the Abbasids. It was inevitable then that the Iranians should maintain a strong influence on their administration. This influence led to the capital being moved to Baghdad, on the threshold of Persia. The Abbasids gave the Iranians a free hand in affairs of government, but looked down on the Arabs and their civilization, and made conscious efforts to weaken them, unlike the Umayyads who had always preferred Arabs for high posts.

With the wane of pro-Arab favouritism, Iranians, Turks, Syrians, Byzantine and Berber elements were able to gain control over all affairs of society and state. Marriages between Arabs and non-Arabs became commonplace. With the mixing of Aryan and Semitic civilizations, Arabic language and culture faced a new crisis. The grandsons of the emperors and lords of Persia arose to resurrect the civilization of their forefathers.

These events had a profound effect on the Arabic language. The state that it had reached by the time of the poet Mutanabbī (A.D. 915-965) is expressed in the following lines:

The buildings of Iran excel all others in beauty
As the season of spring excels all other seasons.
An Arab youth goes amongst them,
His face, his hands, his tongue, a stranger in their midst.
Solomon, they say, used to converse with the jinns,
But were he to visit the Iranians, he would need a translator.[8]

It was the Qur'ān's literary greatness alone which kept Arabic from being permanently scarred by these upheavals. The language always returned to its Qur'ānic base, like a ship which, after weathering temporary storms on the high seas, returns to the safety of its harbour.

During the reign of the caliph Mutawakkil (A.H. 207-247), large numbers of 'Ajamīs—especially Iranians and Turks—entered Arab territory. In 656 the Mongolian warrior Hulaku Khan sacked Baghdad. Later the Islamic empire received a further setback when, in 898, Andalusia fell to the Christians. The Fatimid dynasty, which had held sway in Egypt and Syria, did not last long either: in 923 they were replaced by the Ottoman Turks in large stretches of Arab territory. Now the centre of Islamic government moved from Cairo to Constantinople; the official language became Turkish instead of Arabic, which continued to assimilate a number of foreign words and phrases.

The Arab world spent five hundred and fifty years under the banner of Ajami (non Arab) kings. Persian, Turkish and Mughal rulers even made attempts to erase all traces of the Arabic language. Arabic libraries were burnt, schools destroyed; scholars of the language found themselves in disgrace. The Ottoman emperors launched an anti-Arabic campaign, fittingly called "*Tatrīk al-'Arab*" (Turkisation of Arabs) by the well-known reformer Jamāluddīn Afghānī (1838-97). But no effort was strong enough to inflict any permanent scar on the face of Arabic. Fierce attacks were launched on Arabic language and literature by the Tartars in Bukhara and Baghdad, by the Crusaders in Palestine and Syria, then by other Europeans in Andalusia. According to the history of other languages, these assaults on Arab culture should have been sufficient to eradicate the Arabic language completely. One would have expected Arabic to have followed the path of other languages and merged with other Semitic tongues. Indeed, it would be true to say that if Arabic had not come up against Turkish ignorance and Persian prejudice, it would be spoken throughout the Muslim world today. Still, its very survival in the Arab world was due solely to the miraculous effect of the Qur'ān. The greatness of the Qur'ān compelled people to remain attached to Arabic. It inspired some Arab scholars—Ibn Manzūr (A.H. 630-711) and Ibn Khaldūn (A.H. 732-808) being two that spring to mind—to produce, in defiance of the government of the day, works of great literary and academic excellence.

Napoleon's entry into Cairo (1798) ushered in the age of the printing press in the Middle East. Education became the order of the day. The Arabic language was invested with new life. Yet the centuries of battering that Arabic had received was bound to leave its mark: instead of pure Arabic, a mixture of Arabic and Turkish had been taken as the official language in Egypt and Syria.

The situation changed again with the British occupation of Egypt in 1882. They opposed Arabic with all their strength, prescribing compulsory English in schools and eliminating other languages from syllabi. The French did the same in areas over which they had gained control. With the colonial powers forcing their subjects to learn their languages, Arabic lived in the shadow of English and French for over one hundred years. Yet it still remained in its original form. Certainly, it assimilated new words—the word "*dabbabah*" meaning tank, for instance, which had previously been used for a simple battering ram. New styles of writing emerged. If anyone were to write a book about why people adopt Islam today, he might call it. "*Li madhā aslamnā*" (Why we accepted Islam?), whereas in the old days rhythmical and decorative titles were preferred. Many words were adopted by the Arabic language—the English word "doctor" for example. But such changes were just on the surface. Arabic proper still remained the same as it had been centuries ago, when the Qur'ān was revealed.

LITERARY ADVANCEMENT

Once in a while, writers of outstanding status appear on a language's literary scene. When this happens, the language in which they write undergoes some change, for their literary masterpieces influence the mode of popular expression. In this way languages are continually passing through progressive evolutionary stages, until eventually they become quite different from their original form. With Arabic this did not happen. At the very outset of Arabic history, the Qur'ān set a literary standard that could not be excelled. Arabic maintained the style set for it by the Qur'ān. No masterpiece comparable to the Qur'ān was destined to be produced after it; so Arabic remained cast in the mould of that divine symphony.

Take the example of English. In the 7th century A.D. it was just an ordinary local dialect, not geared to the expression of profound intellectual thought. For another five hundred years this situation continued. The Normans conquered England in 1066 and, when the founding father of the English language—Geoffrey Chaucer—was born around 1340, the official language of their court was still French. Chaucer himself had a command of Latin, French and Italian, besides his native English. This, along with his great gifts of scholarship, enabled him to make English into an academic language. To use Ernest Hauser's words, he gave the English language a "firm boost" with his Canterbury Tales. Chaucer transformed a dialect into a language, paving the way for fresh progress in times to come.

For two hundred years English writers and poets followed Chaucer's guidelines. When William Shakespeare (1558-1625) appeared on the scene, English took another step forward. His dramas and poems set a new literary standard, enabling English to march further forward. The coming of the scientific age two hundred years later had a tremendous impact on every stratum of society. Language now began to follow the dictates of science. Prose became more popular than poetry, factual expression more effective than story-telling. Dozens of poets and writers from

Jonathan Swift (1667-1745) to T.S. Eliot (1888-1965) were representative of this trend. They were the makers of the modern age of English literature through which we are now passing.

The same thing happened with other languages. Writers, or groups of writers, kept on emerging who became more popular than their predecessors. Whenever they appeared, they steered the language on a new course. Eventually every language changed so much that it became impossible for a person to understand the ancient form of his own tongue without the aid of dictionaries and commentaries.

There is only one exception to his universal trend, and that is Arabic. The claim of the Qur'ān, that no one would ever be able to write a book like it, has been borne out to the letter. For further proof of this fact, one need only look at the various attempts to produce a work equal to the Qur'ān that have been made over the centuries. All attempts have failed dismally. Musaylimah ibn Ḥabīb, Ṭulayḥah ibn Khuwaylid, Naḍr ibn al-Ḥārith, Ibn al-Rāwandī, Abū'l 'Alā' al-Ma'rrī, Ibn al-Muqaffa', Al-Mutanabbī, and many others, have tried their hand at it but their efforts, like Musaylimah's extraordinary reference to "God's blessing upon pregnant women, extracting from them a sprightly life, from between the stomach and the foetal membrane"[10] look ridiculous when compared with the literary majesty of the Qur'ān.

But the greatest substantiation of the Qur'ān's claim that no one would be able to write a work like it[11] comes from what Ernest Renan has called the "linguistic miracle" of the

Arabic language. As with every other language, masters of Arabic—great poets and writers—have appeared over the ages. But, in the 1500 years since the Qur'ān was revealed, no one has been able to produce a work that excelled the Qur'ān. The standard that the Qur'ān set has never been improved upon. Arabic has remained on the course that the Qur'ān set for it. If the Qur'ān had ever been bettered, Arabic would not have remained stable as it has. It would have received a new impetus, and set out on a fresh course.

The impact that the Qur'ān has had on Arabic is like that of a writer who produces a work of unsurpassable literary excellence at the very beginning of a language's history. After such a figure has made his mark, no lesser writer can change the face of the language. The Qur'ān was revealed in the Arabic current at the time, casting it in a more elevated literary mould than had ever been seen before or afterwards.

By making vital additions to traditional modes of expression, the Qur'ān opened the way for expansion of the Arabic language. The use of word "One" (*aḥad*) in the 112th chapter of the Qur'ān, entitled "The Unity," is a good example. Previously it had been used in the genitive to express "one of us" for example, or for the "first day' of the week, Saturday or *Yawm al-Aḥad*. It was used for general negations, as in *ma jā'nī aḥadun*—"no one came to see me." But in using *aḥad* as an attribute of Almighty God, the Qur'ān put the word to an entirely novel use. The Qur'ān brought many foreign words into Arabic usage, for instance *istabraq* from Persian, *qaswarah* from Abyssinian, *sirāt* from

Greek, *yamm* from Syrian, *ghassāq* from Turkish, *qisṭās* from Latin, *malakūt* from Armaic and *kafūr* from Hindi. The Qur'ān tells us (25:60) that the idolators of Makkah were baffled at the word *raḥmān*. They used to say "What is this *raḥmān*? This was because the word was not Arabic. It had been taken from the Sabaean and Hamiri languages. The Christians of Yemen and Abyssinia used to call God *raḥamnan*. The Makkanṣ considered the word foreign when it appeared in the Qur'ān in an arabicized form. They enquired what *raḥmān* meant, being unaware of its linguistic background. Over one hundred non-Arabic words of this nature were used in the Qur'ān, taken from languages as far apart as Persian, Latin, Nabataean, Hebrew, Syrian, Coptic and many others.

Although the Qur'ān was revealed mainly in the language of the Quraysh, words used by other Arab tribes were also included. 'Abdullah ibn al-'Abbās, a Qurayshi Muslim, was puzzled when the word *fāṭir* appeared in the Qur'ān. "I did not know what the expression 'Originator of the heavens and the earth' meant," he explained. "Then I heard an Arab saying that he had 'originated' a well, when he had just started digging it, and I knew what the word *fāṭir* meant." Abū Hurayrah said that he had never heard the word *sikkīn* until he heard it in the chapter, 'Joseph', of the Qur'ān. "We always used to call a knife (*mudiyah*)," he said.

As Jalāluddīn Suyūṭī has pointed out in *al-Itqān*, many words were pronounced differently by various Arab tribes. The Qur'ān took some of these words, and used them in their most refined literary form. The Quraysh, for instance, used the word *a'aṭā* for 'he gave,' while the Himyaris used to pronounce it *anṭā*. The Qur'ān prefered *a'aṭā* to *anṭā*. Likewise it chose '*aṣābi*' rather than *shanatir* and *dhi'b* instead of *kata'*. The general trend of preferring Qurayshi forms was sometimes reversed, as in the phrase *la yalitkum min a'mālikum*—"nothing will be taken away from your actions"—which was borrowed from the Banū 'Abbās dialect.

In giving old Arabic words and expressions new depth and beauty, the Qur'ān set a standard of literary excellence which no future writer could improve on. It revised certain metaphors, rephrasing them in a more eloquent form than had been heard before. This was how an ancient Arab poet described the impermanence of the world:

> Even if he enjoys a long period of secure life, every mother's son will finally be carried aloft in a coffin.

The Qur'ān put the same idea in the poignantly succinct words: "Every soul shall taste death."[12] Killing and plundering presented a major problem in ancient Arabia. Certain phrases had been coined to express the idea that only killing could put an end to killing, and these were considered highly eloquent in pre-Islamic days. "To kill some is to give life to the whole," one of them went. "Kill more, so that there should be less killing," and "Killing puts an end to killing," were some other examples. The Qur'ān expressed the idea in these words: "In retaliation there is life for you, oh people of understanding."[13]

In pre-Quranic days, poetry held an important place in Arabic, as in other languages of the world. Poetical expression of ideas was given pride of place in the literary arena. The Qur'ān, however, left this beaten track, and used prose instead of poetry. This in itself is proof that the Qur'ān came from God, for in the 7th century A.D. who save God—who knows the future just as He knows the past—could know that prose rather than poetry should be chosen as the medium for divine scripture that was to last for all time. The Qur'ān was addressed to future generations, and soon poetry was going to become less important as a mass medium of communication. Rhetorical language was also very much in vogue before the Qur'ān, but for the first time in literary history, the Qur'ān introduced a factual rather than rhetorical style. The most famous topics for literary treatment had previously been military and romantic exploits. The Qur'ān, on the contrary, featured a much wider spectrum, including matters of ethical, legal, scientific, psychological, economic, political and historic significance within its scope. In ancient times, parables were a popular mode of expression. Here too, the Qur'ān trod new ground, adopting a more direct method of saying things. The method of reasoning employed in the Qur'ān was also considerably different from that used in pre-Quranic times. Whereas purely theoretical, analogical proof was all that the world had known prior to this the Qur'ān introduced empirical, scientific reasoning. And to crown all its achievements, the Qur'ān expressed all this in a refined literary style, which proved imperishable in times to come.

There was an ancient Arab saying that "the sweetest poem was the one with the most lies." The Qur'ān changed this introducing a new mode of "articulate speech" (55:4) based on real facts rather than hypothetical fables. Now

Arabic followed the Qur'ān's lead. Pre-Islamic Arabic literature was collected and compiled with the preservation and understanding of that language of the Qur'ān in mind. Great departments of learning, facilitating understanding of the Qur'ān and explaining its orders and prohibitions, came into existence. The learning of Arabic grammar, syntax and etymology, Islamic theology and traditions, as well as Qur'ānic studies, were all aimed at helping us to understand the message of the Qur'ān. Even the subjects of history and geography were originally taken up us part of the Arabs' attempt to understand and practice the teachings of the Qur'ān. There is no other example in the history of the world of any single book having such an enormous impact on a people and their language.

Through its development and improvement of the Arabic language, the Qur'ān became known as a superb literary masterpiece. Anyone who knows Arabic can see the unique quality of the Qur'ān's style as compared to any other work of Arabic literature. The Qur'ān is written in a divine style totally different from anything humans can aspire to. We will close this chapter by relating a story which clearly portrays the difference between the work of God and that of man. It is taken from Sheikh Ṭanṭāwī's commentary of the Qur'ān:

> "On 13 June 1932," Ṭanṭāwī writes, I met an Egyptian writer, Kāmil Gilānī, who told me an amazing story. One day he was with an American orientalist by the name of Finkle, with whom he enjoyed a deep intellectual relationship. "Tell me, are you still among those who consider the Qur'ān

a miracle?" whispered Finkle in Gilānī's ear, adding a laugh to indicate his ridicule of such belief. He thought that Muslims could only hold this belief in blind faith. It could not be based on any sound, objective reasoning. Thinking that his blow had really gone home, Finkle was visibly pleased with himself. Seeing his attitude, Gilānī too started laughing. "Before issuing any pronouncement on the style of the Qur'ān," he said, "we should first have a look and see if we can produce anything comparable to it. Only when we have tried our hand, shall we be able to say conclusively whether humans can produce anything comparable to the Qur'ān or not."

Gilānī then invited Finkle to join him in putting a Quranic idea into Arabic words. The idea he chose was: Hell is extremely vast. Finkle agreed, and both men sat down with pen and paper. Between them, they produced about twenty Arabic sentences. "Hell is extremely vast," "Hell is vaster than you can imagine," "Man's intellect cannot fathom the vastness of Hell," and many examples of this nature, were some of the sentences they produced. They tried until they could think of no other sentence to express this idea. Gilānī looked at Finkle triumphantly. "Now that we have done our best, we shall be able to see how the Qur'ān stands above all work of men," he said. "What, has the Qur'ān expressed this idea more eloquently?' Finkle enquired. "We are like little children compared to the Qur'ān," Gilānī told him. Amazed, Finkle asked what was in the Qur'ān. Gilānī recited this verse from *Sūrah Qāf:* "On the Day when We will ask Hell: 'Are you full?' And Hell will answer: 'Are there any more?'"[14] Finkle was startled on hearing this verse. Amazed at the supreme eloquence of the Qur'ān, he openly admitted defeat. "You were right, quite right," he said, "I unreservedly concede defeat." '"For you to acknowledge the truth," Gilānī replied, "is nothing strange, for you are a man of letters, well aware of the importance of style in language." This particular orientalist was fluent in English, German, Hebrew and Arabic, and had spent all his life studying the literature of these languages.[15]

NOTES

1. Qur'ān, 17:59.
2. Qur'ān, 6:35.
3. Qur'ān, 29:50–51.
4. Xavier Lean-Dufour S.J., *The Gospels and the Jesus of History*, Desclee Co Inc., New York, 1970, pp. 79–80.
5. Ernest Renan (1823–1894).
6. Jurgi Zaydān (1861–1914), *Ādāb al-Lughāt al-'Arabiyyah.*
7. Dr. Aḥmad Ḥasan Zayyāt.
8. Non-Arabs.
9. Mutanabbī (A.D. 915–965), *Sharḥ Diwān al-Mutanabbī*, Beirut, 1983, p. 384.
10. *Tahzīb Sīrat ibn Hishām*, vol. 2, p. 121.
11. Qur'ān, 17:88
12. Qur'ān, 3:185.
13. Qur'ān, 2:179.
14. Qur'ān, 50:30.
15. Sheikh Tanṭāwī, *al-Jawāhir fī Tafsīr al-Qur'ān al-Karīm*, Cairo, A.H. 1351, vol. 23, pp. 111–112.

16

The Companions of the Prophet

The Companions of the Prophet—the *Ṣaḥābah*—stand alongside him in history just as they stood alongside him during his lifetime, for they were the ones selected by God to assist His messenger. They joined with him in seeing his divine mission through to its proper conclusion. As 'Abdullah ibn Mas'ūd said: "God chose them to accompany His Prophet, and to establish his religion."

Let us take a look at a few of the outstanding qualities of the Companions which gave them their place in history.

ISLAM WAS SOMETHING THEY LOVED

One of the qualities of the Companions described in the Qur'ān was their attachment to the Faith.[1] Of this, love is the ultimate expression; it is the highest feeling we can have for something; it replaces all else in our thoughts. Our attitude towards the beloved is something instinctive. We know what to do and what not to do, because real feeling has developed for the object of our love. Its joys and sorrows become our own. This was the intensity of feeling that the

Companions had for Islam. They rejoiced in the success of their faith as a father rejoices when his son is successful. When Islam received a setback, they would not rest until they had redressed it.

When one associates oneself with a cause—as the Companions did with Islam—one needs no telling about what one's attitude should be. Heartfelt enthusiasm shows the way. One is willing to give everything for it and place its interest above all else. Our losses on its behalf then become our gains, and there can be no feeling of the diminution of our personal worth in the face of its claims. The difficulties we encounter in its espousal are easily surmounted because of the fervour with which we are imbued.

There was nothing extraordinary or supernatural about the Companions. They were human beings like any other. What made them stand out from the rest of mankind was that the feeling of true love, which most people feel only for themselves, was felt by them for the faith of Islam. They built for the future of Islam as normal people build for their own personal futures. Just as people put all their energy and wealth into the pursuit of their own interests, so did they put their all into the pursuit of Islamic interests. It was the depth of their attachment to Islam which enabled them to establish the supremacy of the Faith.

RECOGNISING THE PROPHET AT THE VERY BEGINNING

One unique quality of the Companions was that they recognised a prophet who was their contemporary. It is very difficult to recognize and believe in a prophet of one's own day: this can be gauged from the fact that no group except for the Companions has ever managed to do so. At every stage of ancient history prophets were denied and ridiculed when they appeared among their peoples. "You thought nothing of My prophets," the Bible says. Who were these people who "thought nothing" of the prophets? They were the very ones who believed in both prophecy and divine revelation. They had set up great institutions in the name of prophets. It was with great enthusiasm that they included days for the remembrance of various prophets in their calendar. But it was only ancient prophets whom they revered in this manner. As for prophets of their own day, they made them objects of ridicule and scorn.

The Jews disbelieved in the Prophet Jesus, even though they believed in Moses. Despite their veneration for Jesus, the Christians denied the Prophet Muḥammad. Even the Quraysh of Makkah prided themselves on being heirs of Abraham; but when the heir to Abraham's prophetic legacy came among them, they attacked him and expelled him from the land.

Why was there this discrepancy between people's treatment of ancient prophets on the one hand, and contemporary prophets on the other? The reason for it was that ancient prophets were supported by the might of historical tradition. They become an essential part of a people's national heritage. People of later generations look back at prophets of old as upon sacred heroes—forgers of their national identity. Clearly, few will resist faith when there is so much added incentive to believe. With a contemporary prophet, however, the situation is quite different. His prophethood is still a controversial issue. His mission is surrounded in a cloak of doubt. In order to believe in him, one has to see through outward appearances. In order to follow him, one has to bury all thoughts of oneself. Doubt prevails over the truth of his mission. His prophethood has not yet received the verification of history. Under such conditions, it is the most difficult thing in the world to believe in a prophet, and actively participate in his mission. But it was this, no less, that the Companions were able to do: believe in a prophet of their own day as if he were a prophet of ancient times.

During the Battle of the Trench (A.H. 5) Madinah was besieged by the Quraysh and all of the Arab clans who had entered into an alliance with them. The siege was intensified until it became impossible for the Muslims to obtain even the basic necessities of life. At this time one of the Muslims said in desperation: "Muḥammad used to promise us that the treasures of Khusrau and Caesar would be ours, and now here we are—unable even to relieve ourselves in peace." When this battle took place the Prophet's promise was just that—a promise; it was nowhere near fulfilment, although now it is a matter of ancient history. The Companions, nevertheless acknowledged the Prophet's greatness before his promises had become history. Those who acknowledge his greatness today do so after the fulfilment of his promises, after history has put the stamp of greatness upon him. There is a world of difference between these two acknowledgements. One bears no comparison to the other.

Today, even non-Muslim historians have been compelled to allot pride of place in human history to the Prophet Muḥammad. But, during his lifetime, recognizing his greatness was a matter of extreme difficulty. So much so that this could only be done by those who had been granted special grace by God.

ADHERING TO THE QUR'ĀN WHEN IT WAS STILL THE SUBJECT OF CONTROVERSY

The Companions' way of preaching the faith was to take a revealed portion of the Qur'ān and recite it to the people. For this reason the Companions who went to Madinah to preach Islam were called *muqrīs*—reciters of the Qur'ān. In a modern environment, this would be nothing extraordinary. But when one leaves aside the 1400 years of history that stand between us and the Companions, and imagines the conditions that prevailed in their time, their action appears in an entirely new perspective. At that time it was a mammoth task to stand amongst the people and recite the Qur'ān, one that no group except for the Companions had ever performed.

The picture that springs to mind with the mention of the word "Qur'ān" today is that of a book that has, over 1400 years, established its greatness without the slightest shadow of a doubt. Millions of people the world over accept it as the Book of God. It has become a matter of personal pride to express belief in the Qur'ān. At the time of revelation, however, the Qur'ān did not enjoy this status. Many of the Ṣaḥābahs' contemporaries treated it as an object of derision. "We have heard them," said some speaking of the revelations. "If we wished, we could speak the like. They are but fables of the ancients."[2] "Fables of the ancients he has written," they used to say. "They are dictated to him morning and evening."[3]

To believe in the Qur'ān under such circumstances was like seeing future events as if they had already happened. It required vision enabling one to see a concealed truth before it had become established in the eyes of men. How difficult it must have been, then, to make the Qur'ān the basis of one's preaching mission. To do so amounted to a negation of personal greatness and the acceptance of the greatness of another—one whose greatness had not yet been accepted by the world. When the famous Arab poet Labīd accepted Islam, he gave up writing poetry. When someone asked why he had done this, he replied; "What? After the Qur'ān?" If a poet today was to relinquish his writing for the same reason, he would be accorded tremendous acclaim and popular respect. In saying, "How can I write poetry after the advent of the Qur'ān," he would be looking at a Qur'ān with a glorious history behind it. Labīd said these words at the very beginning of the Qur'ān's history. There is no comparison between acknowledging the greatness of something after history has cast a mantle of greatness upon it, and doing so beforehand. The Qur'ān has explained the difference in these words:

> Those of you that gave of their wealth before the victory and took part in the fighting are not equal (to those who gave and fought thereafter). Their degree is greater.[4]

SPENDING ONE'S WEALTH FOR THE SAKE OF A TRUTH WHICH HAS YET TO BE ESTABLISHED

The following incident has been related by Ibn Abī Ḥātim on the authority of 'Abdullah ibn Mas'ūd. When the verse of the Qur'ān—"Who will lend God a goodly loan; it will be doubled for him many times"[5]—was revealed, Abū Daḥdāḥ of the Anṣār asked the Prophet if God really wanted them to "lend Him a loan," The Prophet replied in the affirmative. "Give me your hand," Abū Daḥdāḥ said to the Prophet. The Prophet put his hand in Abu Daḥdāh's as the latter told him that he would lend his whole orchard—consisting of six hundred date palms—to his Lord. His wife Umm Daḥdāḥ was in the orchard with her children at the time. Abū Daḥdāḥ came and told her to leave it, for he had donated it to the Lord on High. "What a good deal you have made!" Umm Daḥdāḥ exclaimed, and immediately took her children and belongings out of the orchard. "How many trees—luxuriant and laden with fruit—Abū Daḥdāḥ will have in paradise," the Prophet said of this donation.

This incident is representative of a general eagerness among the Companions to donate their wealth for the sake of their faith. One must call to mind once again that this happened 1400 years ago. Were anyone to perform an act of similar charity in the name of their religion today, it is quite possible that they would have great honours conferred upon them by Muslims which far exceeded their expenditure. But things were quite different in the time of the Companions. To spend in the cause of religion in those days was to be condemned as insane by society. Far from raising one to a high pinnacle of fame, it was like burying oneself in a pit of self-oblivion. The cause to which the Companions devoted their lives and properties was one surrounded in doubt. Historical evidence had not yet accumulated in support of it. The truth of Islam had not yet become established in society at large. Yet the Companions donated their wealth for the sake of their religion at that uncertain period of Islamic history. Now, 1400 years later, the greatness of Islam has become an established fact, supported by centuries of history. To spend on a cause which has not consolidated its place in society is of a very different order from spending on a consolidated, established cause.

PLACING ONE'S OWN CROWN ON THE HEAD OF ANOTHER

Before the Prophet's emigration to Madinah, 'Abdullah ibn Ubayy had stood out as a natural leader in that city. His character, charisma and intelligence had led the people of Madinah to choose him as their king. They considered him the right person to put an end to the civil strife and conflict which had raged among them for so long. A ceremony was planned at which 'Abdullah ibn Ubayy was to be crowned king of Madinah.

Arrangements for 'Abdullah ibn Ubayy's coronation had been completed when Islam first came to Madinah. The people of Madinah took naturally to the new religion, and Islam won followers in every home. A delegation travelled to Makkah, where they met the Prophet and heard the teachings of Islam from his lips. The impression that they received was that the person they needed to reign over their society was—not 'Abdullah ibn Ubayy—but the Prophet Muḥammed. On behalf of the people of Madinah, they asked the Prophet to come to their town and take over as their leader. They swore allegiance to the Prophet at 'Aqabah, an event that proved a watershed in Islamic history.

Quite apart from its far-reaching historical implications, this act of allegiance was an extraordinary feat. It was as if the people of Madinah were taking the crown off their own head, and placing it on that of a stranger. People have always been highly reluctant to take someone from outside their own nation or tribe as leader. Such a move was unheard of in ancient Arabia. In this case it was rendered even more difficult by the fact that the "Muḥammad" whom they were taking in was not the great historical personality that we know today. He was a person who had been expelled by his own people. Not only was he a controversial figure, he was a homeless, destitute one as well. The people of Madinah were giving him everything, with the promise of nothing in return. In the 20th century we have heard some western thinkers—notably Bernard Shaw—mention what a fine leader of the western world a person like Muḥammad would make. To make an offer like this in the 6th century, however, was a very different matter, for at that time the unique qualities of leadership that the Prophet possessed had not become engraved on the pages of history.

REALIZING ONE'S OWN LIMITATIONS

The Prophet Muḥammad used to confer with his Companions over every matter that arose. He would call them together and, after explaining the situation, ask them for their opinion. Though he appeared to be consulting with everyone, what actually used to happen was that there would be silence for a while, then Abu Bakr would get up and briefly offer his opinion. 'Umar would do the same, and a handful others followed suit, before finally a unanimous decision was reached. Consultations followed the same pattern during Abu Bakr's term as Caliph. 'Umar would be the first to speak, then a few others would give their opinion. The final decision would have everyone's agreement. It was only during 'Umar's caliphate when the number of Muslims who had not seen the Prophet increased, that alternations took place in the consultation process.

This may appear to be a simple matter, but it is of great significance. It shows how humble the companions were, how aware of their own shortcomings and limitations. Such a procedure can be followed only by those humble enough to acknowledge another's worth at their own expense. This was one unique quality of the Companions: they looked objectively at themselves in the way that average people would look only at others.

One must remember that the Abū Bakr and 'Umar of whom we speak were not the historic personalities that we know today. It was vastly more difficult then to recognize the worth of Abū Bakr and 'Umar than it is now. The two men had then still to be appreciated when history was in its formative stage, whereas in the present day we are in a position to evaluate them with historical hindsight. For the companions, they were just two of their number; for us they have become two mighty pillars standing out in the landscape of history. For us to fail to acknowledge Abū Bakr and 'Umar would be to defy history. For the Companions to acknowledge these two amounted to abnegation of their own selves—an infinitely more difficult task, which the Companions accomplished in exemplary fashion.

TAKING RESPONSIBILITY UPON ONESELF

Dhāt al-Salāsil was a place in the Syrian desert, occupied by the Ghassānid and Kalb tribes to which the Prophet sent an expedition under the leadership of 'Amr ibn al-'Āṣ. When the latter reached there, and saw the preparations being made by the enemy, he realized that his own force was too weak to do battle with them. He thereupon set up camp, and sent a message to the Prophet asking for reinforcements. The Prophet then prepared an additional force of 200 *Muhājirs*, which was despatched under the leadership of Abū 'Ubaydah ibn al-Jarrāḥ.

When Abū 'Ubaydah's force joined with that of 'Amr ibn al-'Āṣ, the question arose as to who would be leader of the combined army. 'Amr ibn al-'Āṣ was in no doubt that he should be, as the reinforcements had been sent at his request. Abū 'Ubaydah's companions did not agree. They thought that Abū 'Ubaydah should be leader of the whole army, or otherwise the division should remain under separate command. When the quarrel escalated, Abū 'Ubaydah addressed 'Amr, telling him that the final promise the Prophet had taken from him was that the two of them should agree with one another, and work in unity. "Even if you disobey me," he said, "I promise to obey you."

Had Abū 'Ubaydah so desired, he could have remained obdurate and left it to Amr to give way. Substantial arguments in support of his position could have been found. But he eschewed such a course, and instead took it upon himself to put an end to the argument unilaterally. In community life, it is essential that people should be able to do this. Only when people are magnanimous enough to accept their own responsibilities, instead of arguing about their rights, can a community function harmoniously. It requires exceptional courage to do this, but there is no other way of preserving unity in a society.

NOT BEARING GRUDGES

Khālid ibn al-Walīd was an extremely brave and able soldier, who remained commander of the Muslim army in Syria from the time of the Prophet right throughout the caliphate of Abū Bakr. 'Umar, however, disapproved of some of Khālid's habits, and asked Abū Bakr to remove him from his command. Abū Bakr did not act on 'Umar's advice, but 'Umar was so set in his opinion that, on becoming Caliph, he dismissed Khālid. The commander of the Muslim army was demoted to the rank of an ordinary soldier.

When the order came, Khālid was laying all low before him as the Muslims' triumphant march through Syria continued. All of a sudden came the news of his dismissal, and the appointment of Abū 'Ubaydah ibn al-Jarrāḥ in his place. The news shocked Khālid's army, and a group of soldiers gathered in their leader's tent. They assured him of their support, and urged him to defy the Caliph's orders. Khālid sent them away, telling them that he did not fight for 'Umar's cause; he fought for the cause of 'Umar's Lord. Before he had fought as commander; now he would fight as an ordinary soldier.

Only a person who rises above grudges and rancour can act in this manner—one who has a positive attitude to life and refrains from reacting adversely. Khālid's words show how deeply involved he was in doing the will of God. So much so that he took 'Umar's decision completely in his stride.

DOING MORE THAN ONE IS LEGALLY BOUND TO

In the month of Sha'bān A.H. 6 the Prophet received news that a force of 1000 men had gathered under the leaders of the Quraysh, and was advancing on Madinah. Six hundred were clad in armour, and there was an elite cavalry unit consisting of one hundred men. Tension was running high in Madinah as the Prophet called a meeting of both the Muhājirs and the Anṣār, to ask them what should be done. As normally happened on such occasions, senior members of the Muhājirs rose to offer their opinion. "Prophet of God," they said, go ahead and do whatever your Lord commands you. We will stand by you. We are not going to tell you to go and fight along with your Lord, while we stay sitting here, as the Jews did before us.[6] Rather we say unto you: go and fight along with your Lord; we too will fight alongside you. We will not desert you as long as at least one of us has life in his body."

Yet despite such assurances from the Muhājirs, the Prophet kept on sounding people as to what he should do. Sa'd ibn Mu'ādh, one of the Anṣār, arose. "Perhaps we figure in your thoughts," he said to the Prophet. The Prophet said that they did. Then Sa'd ibn Mu'ādh, on behalf of his fellow Anṣārs, reassured the Prophet with these words: "We have believed in you, and acknowledged you as God's prophet. We have testified to the truth of your teachings. We have solemnly promised to listen to you and obey whatever you say. So do whatever you deem fit, Prophet of God. We will stand by you. We swear by the one who has sent you with the truth, even if you take us to the shores of the sea and plunge us into its waters, we too will follow you. Not one of us will stay behind. We have no qualms about joining you to do battle with the enemy tomorrow. We are resolute on the field of battle, true to our word in times of conflict. Perhaps God will enable us to prove ourselves in a manner which will be pleasing to you. Take us with you, trusting in the grace of God." When Sa'd ibn Mu'ādh had his say, a final decision was taken to advance to meet the enemy.

During the Battle of Badr (A.H. 3), the Prophet kept on looking towards the Anṣār. The background to his concern has been explained by Ibn Hishām. "When the Anṣār entered into the second oath of allegiance at 'Aqabah' he writes," they were not bound by their oath to accept the responsibility for his safety outside Madinah. 'While you are in our country,' they said, 'we will defend you as we defend our own wives and children.' This was all very well, but the Prophet was afraid that the Anṣār would consider themselves obliged to assist him only if the enemy entered Madinah, and would not feel themselves under any obligation to fight an enemy outside the precincts of the city.'

True, although the Anṣār had entered into a defence pact at 'Aqabah, according to its terms, they were not strictly bound to fight in Badr, 80 miles away from Madinah. But the Anṣār did not use this as an excuse. It redounds to their credit that they went far and beyond the strict terms of their agreement and, along with the Prophet, offered their life's blood on the field of Badr.

AVOIDING CONTROVERSY, AND CONCENTRATING ON ONE'S BASIC GOAL

The historian Ṭabarānī tells us on the authority of Masar ibn Makhramah, of how on one occasion the Prophet addressed the Companions with these words: "God has sent me as a mercy for all, so pass on what you have heard from me. God will make manifest His mercy. And do not quarrel with one another, as the disciples quarrelled over Jesus, the Son of Mary. He called on them to perform the same mission as I am entrusting to you now. But those who lived far away did not like the idea, and asked not to go, and Jesus remonstrated with his Lord over this matter." "We will pass on your message," the Companions assured him in response. "Send us wherever you please."

Internal friction is the greatest thorn in the side of a

community, preventing its members from pursuing a constructive course of action. The Companions did not let themselves sink into the quagmire of petty controversies. Fear of God had imbued them with a profound sense of responsibility. They concentrated on discharging these responsibilities, and had no time for quarrels which would have prevented them from doing so. Even during the Prophet's lifetime, they had taken Islam to the borders of the Arabian peninsula. After his demise, they continued to act as if at his behest. Blind to all thoughts of self-aggrandisement, they dispersed in the neighbouring lands. Their homes were just like small schools, in which they imparted to people knowledge of the Arabic language, the Qur'ān, and the Prophet's *sunnah*. In this way they passed on what they had heard from the Prophet. This was a time of great Islamic conquests, and a certain portion of the Muslim community had to shoulder the political responsibilities that came with an expanding empire. The Companions might have been expected to take their share in the political glory, but they showed no inclination for such things. The majority of them used the atmosphere created by the conquests of Islam to further their preaching mission. It was their, and their disciples' steady, unobstrusive efforts that created—within a space of fifty years—the vast expanse of territory now known as the Arab world. They not only changed the religion of people spread over three continents, but they brought to them a new language and culture as well.

BEING CONTENT TO REMAIN IN OBSCURITY

The first matter that had to be settled after the Prophet's death was the election of a Caliph. The Anṣār put forward their own candidate—Sa'd ibn 'Ubādah. When the Muhājirs learnt of the Anṣār's proposal, a group of them hurried to the Thaqīfah (shed) of the Banū Sa'dah, where the Anṣār were gathered. Abū Bakr addressed them. "There is no doubt that you are truly endowed with the qualities you have mentioned. But as for leadership of the Arab people, it is to the Quraysh we must look for that. Geographically and ethnically, they occupy a central place in Arab life. I will propose to you two names 'Umar and Abū 'Ubaydah ibn al-Jarrāḥ, swear allegiance to whomsoever of them you please."

'Umar arose after this and immediately swore allegiance to Abū Bakr as Caliph. The Anṣār followed his lead, but some of them took it so hard that they told the Muhājirs that they had as good as killed Sa'd ibn 'Ubaydah.

The Anṣār had made enormous sacrifices for the cause of Islam. They had given shelter to the stranded ship of Islam when it had been forced to leave its own waters. Yet despite their sacrifices, they agreed to make another one. They disowned a share in power, and united behind a Qurayshī caliph. There was good reason for the appointment. The Quraysh, to which clan the Muhājirs belonged, had been considered leaders of Arabia for centuries. A leader from any other tribe would not have commanded the support needed to administrate a burgeoning empire. The Anṣār were realistic enough to acknowledge their own shortcomings in this respect, and accept the Muhājirs' unilateral decision. It is hard to find a comparable example of such selfless realism in the history of the world.

RATIONAL DECISIONS, DURING EMOTIONAL CRISES

The Battle of Uḥud (A.H. 4) was the severest battle in Islamic history. All the warriors of the Quraysh, thirsty for revenge after their defeat at Badr, descended on the Muslims. Just when the fighting was at its fiercest, the Prophet drew his sword and asked his companions which one of them would take it and exact its full worth. To the first few who volunteered, the Prophet did not give the sword. Then Abū Dujānah came forward, and asked the prophet what was the full worth of the sword. "That you should strike the enemy with it until it bends," the Prophet replied. "That is how I shall wield it," Abū Dujānah said, as he offered to take the sword. The Prophet gave it to him. Abū Dujānah's pride was visible as he strode off with the sword in his hand. "Such strutting cannot be pleasing to God," said the Prophet, "But the occasion excuses it." Abū Dujānah tied a red cloth around his head, signalling his readiness to fight to the death. He did indeed conduct himself with incredible bravery, striking all who came before him. Then an astonishing incident occurred, which was later described by Abū Dujānah himself, "I saw someone inciting the enemy in a particularly violent way. I rushed towards him and raised my sword to kill him. The person screamed and I saw that it was a woman. I refrained from debasing the Prophet's sword by slaying a woman with it."

Another companion has described the incident like this. "I saw that Abū Dujānah had raised his sword to kill Hind bint 'Utbah. Suddenly he removed the sword from above her head." One of the orders that the Prophet used to issue in times of battle was that women, children and old men should not be slain. Abū Dujānah remembered the Prophet's orders in the heat of the battle and, even as his sword was plunging down on its victim, he withdrew it when he saw that it was a woman.

From this one can see how strong was the Companions' control over their emotions. Even in moments of overwhelming passion, they were able to take reasoned decisions, and were able to judge matters dispassionately, no matter how extreme the provocation they faced. Even when feelings of anger and vengeance had gone beyond all bounds, they were able to adopt the correct frame of mind. Changing direction when travelling at full speed may appear easy enough, but in practice it is extremely difficult. Only one can accomplish such a task who goes so in fear of God that it is as if God were standing before him in all His power and glory.

GROWING LIKE A TREE

The Qur'ān refers to both the Torah and the Injīl (The Old and New Testaments) in order to describe two qualities of the Companions. Quotations from the Torah explain their individual qualities, while the Injīl provides illustration of their qualities as members of their community:

> Thus they are described in the Torah and in the

> Gospel: like the seed which puts forth its shoot and strengthens it, so that it rises stout and firm upon its stalk, delighting the sowers. Through them God seeks to enrage the unbelievers. God has promised those of them who will believe and do good works forgiveness and a rich reward.[7]

The simile is presented like this in the New Testament:

> And he said, So is the kingdom of God as if a man should cast seed into the ground;
>
> And should sleep, and rise night and day, and the seed should spring and grow up, he knoweth not how. For the earth bringeth forth fruit of herself; first the blade, then the ear, after that the full corn in the ear.
>
> But when the fruit is brought forth, immediately he putteth in the sickle, because the harvest is come.
>
> And he said, Whereunto shall we liken the kingdom of God? or with what comparison shall we compare it?
>
> It is like a grain of mustard seed, which, when it is sown in the earth, is less than all the seeds that be in the earth:
>
> But when it is sown, it groweth up, and becometh greater than all herbs, and shooteth out great branches; so that the fowls of the air may lodge under the shadow of it.[8]

This parable, told in both the Qur'ān and the Bible, tells how the social evolution of the Companions of the Prophet would be like that of a tree. Starting as a tiny seed, the pillar of their society would develop as a tree trunk, gradually consolidating its roots in the ground and stretching its branches out in the air above. They would grow up gradually in natural stages, finally reaching a peak in their growth. Their splendid development would cause gratification to men of faith and frustration to enemies.

The Companions of the Prophet were chosen to carry out Almighty God's wish that Islam should thrive like a tree. The fact that God wished it did not mean that the task would be easy. They were required to eschew the easy, quick way of doing things and follow the path of patience. They had to bury their desires and personal preferences, always giving precedence to the will of God. The Companions had to give everything to bring the tree of Islam into existence, not caring for any return in this world. They had to involve themselves unconditionally in God's scheme. As a result of their effort, Islam grew into a permanently flourishing garden, which no power in the world was able to destroy.

NOTES

1. Qur'ān, 49:7.
2. Qur'ān, 8:31.
3. Qur'ān, 25:5.
4. Qur'ān, 57:10.
5. Qur'ān, 57:11.
6. Qur'ān, 5:24.
7. Qur'ān, 48:29.
8. Bible, Mark, 4.26-32.

PART FOUR

17

Manifestation of Prophethood in the Present Day and Age

God decreed that the final prophet, Muḥammad, on whom be peace, should establish the dominance of true religion over all other religions.[1] This special task entrusted to the Prophet of Islam has also been entrusted to his followers. The dominance of religion that Muḥammad brought about was the culmination of a grand divine scheme, with the groundwork having been laid over the previous 2,500 years. All the Prophet had to do was bring it to completion. So it has been with the Prophet's *ummah*—his community. Over the last 1000 years the ground has been prepared for the re-establishment of the dominance of true religion. If the followers of Muḥammad make wise and conscientious use of the opportunities available to them, the mantle of God's succour will indeed fall on them, in the same way as it fell upon the Prophet. That is the promise of God.

The article, *"Man and His Gods,"* in the *Encyclopaedia Britannica,* tells of the Islamic revolution brought about by the Prophet Muḥammad as having "changed the course of human history."[2] The author, a Christian orientalist, has no choice but to acknowledge the unique, historic impact of Islam. What Islam brought about was no less than the spiritual liberation of mankind. Without the burden of superstition and idol worship to weigh them down, people were able to advance in every walk of life. Themselves products of the Islamic revolution, these advances can once again be used to the benefit of Islam. The conditions are perfect for a revival of Islamic dominance. It could become a reality as easily as growing a healthy crop from moistened, fertile soil.

The revolution brought about by the Prophet and his Companions was essentially a spiritual one, solidly based on belief in one God and the hereafter. Yet there were far-reaching worldly repercussions as well. The preaching of true religion became considerably easier than it had been in the past. Major obstacles which had stood in the path of one who called mankind to God were submerged in a wave of great social change.

When the *sūrah* of the Qur'an entitled "Repentance" was revealed, the Prophet sent 'Alī to Makkah with the message that no idolator would be allowed to perform Ḥajj in future. With such force and persistence did he issue the proclamation that his voice became hoarse. Nowadays he could have done the same thing much more easily with a loudspeaker. This is just a simple example, but it illustrates quite well the way modern facilities can be utilized for the proclamation of truth.

There have been two main eras in the preaching of true religion, the first prior to the mission of the Final Prophet, and the second afterwards. Before the coming of Muhammad, on whom be peace, the onus of preserving the divine scriptures had been put upon the followers of prophets. In the words of the Qur'an, they had been "required to guard the Book of God."[3] With the Qur'an, however, God has Himself made it plain that "it was We who revealed the Qur'an, and We will certainly preserve it."[4]

It was God's will that, with the mission of the Prophet of Islam, polytheism should be vanquished and monotheism reign supreme in the world.[5] Only He can bring about circumstances conducive to such a transformation in human thought. So it was that, over the 2,500 years preceding the coming of Muḥammad, the groundwork for the Islamic revolution had been laid. It was for the Prophet Muḥammad to work on this foundation and bring about the domination of monotheism over polytheism.

The Islamic revolution of the Prophet's time forever vanquished polytheism. Through the work of the Prophet and his companions the possibility vanished of polytheism ever again ruling the world. Yet, in the present age, monotheistic thought has once again forfeited its dominance. In the world today atheistic thought holds pride of place, and monotheism has in practice been relegated to a position of secondary importance.

God indeed had full knowledge of the fact that atheism was going to rear its head in the world. Accordingly, He sent down His succour, preparing conditions in the world which would counter atheism, and re-establish the dominance of monotheistic thought. This process has been continuing for the last one thousand years. Now it has reached its climax. Though atheism still holds sway in the world, the conditions are perfect for a reassertion of the supremacy of monotheistic thought.

Nearly 4000 years ago, the Prophet Abraham preached the word of God in Ur, the capital of ancient Iraq. He impressed on people that God was the sole controller of loss and gain. He has no partner. From Him should one seek help, and He alone is worthy of being worshipped. This message of monotheism proved too much for the reigning king, Nimrod, to bear. So violent was his reaction to Abraham's preaching, that he ordered God's prophet to be burnt at the stake, a fate from which he was saved by divine intervention. Though there is still idolatry in the world today, no modern ruler would react so violently to the message of Abraham were it to be preached in his land.

The reason for this is the change that has occurred in the philosophy of government. In Nimrod's time polytheism was a political creed; now it only has the status of a limited religious creed. Government in the ancient world was generally based on a polytheistic foundation. Nimrod, like other monarchs of his day, was a figurehead of this system. He was meant to be an incarnation of the sun god, endowed with a supernatural right to rule over others. No modern ruler would base his rule on such a claim. Now it is popular support, not supernatural strength, which entitles a person to govern. That is why the pure message of *tawhīd* (monotheism) would present no challenge to any ruler nowadays. For Nimrod and his contemporaries, on the other hand, it amounted to a cutting off of the very source of their power.

At the very outset of their missions, ancient prophets used to come up against the active resistance of the custodians of power. The preaching of the prophets was anathema to them for it directly contradicted the divine powers they claimed for themselves. The denial of these meant an end to their right to rule. The only way that anyone could be elevated to kingship in those days was by making himself out to be an offspring or incarnation of God. Any individual who introduced the teachings of monotheism to such a society, appeared to be attacking the pillars of this polytheistic power structure. The establishment rose to resist the threat. With Islam, the world was shown that no human being is endowed with supernatural powers: God alone is the source of all strength. Islam proclaimed to the world the equality of human being. It taught that no one has any inherent superiority over others. Political institutions were then separated from the realm of religious creeds. A ruler's power base would in future come from below, from among the grassroots of popular opinion. Laying claim to celestial powers would no longer qualify a person to rule over others.

Similar was the case of the antique 'supernatural' doctors. If anyone intended to succeed as a physician in ancient times, he might well pretend that he had subdued occult forces, and received knowledge about the mysteries of medicine from a supernatural source. Imagine that someone were to say, in such a society, that medicine was learnt, not from communion with supernatural sources, but in medical colleges. The first people to oppose such a theory would be those who made a living out of "supernatural medicine." Doctors in the modern age show a very different reaction. Far from opposing the call to learn medicine in universities, they encourage it, and follow the same practice themselves.

The 7th century A.D. marked the beginning of a period of historical change, made possible by the Islamic revolution of the Prophet Muḥammad. Now, that process of change is reaching its culmination. Preachers of true religion can call upon a mass of supporting evidence from within the range of human knowledge itself. Legal and social modifications have enabled the free and open preaching of religion. No Nimrod or Pharaoh can rise to stamp out the call of truth now. Massive inroads have been made into the world of nature, and our knowledge of the way it functions has increased considerably. This knowledge provides solid intellectual support for the teachings of true religion. The ground on which people who violently opposed the call to truth used to stand has vanished from beneath their feet.

An enormous intellectual revolution, known as the scientific revolution, has taken place in modern times. The changes it has brought about in people's outlook are completely supportive to the call of truth. If present opportunities are utilized properly, the domination of monotheistic thought can be established by appealing, through written and spoken efforts, to people's good sense. There is no need to resort to force of arms, as one had to in ancient times.

The scientific revolution of modern times is in fact a by-product of the Islamic revolution of the Prophet's time. Through the revolution brought about by the Prophet, God brought certain factors into play. A process of historic change, finally culminating in the scientific revolution of modern times, was initiated. While establishing the dominance of monotheistic thought over polytheism at the onset of the Islamic era, God also created factors which would in later times enable monotheism to triumph once more, this time over atheistic and agnostic thought.

Before the coming of Islam, polytheistic thought had reigned supreme the world over. What polytheism really comes down to is worship of forms. The polytheistic urge in people used to make them turn in worship to any particularly striking or spectacular worldly phenomenon, whether it was the sun in the sky, or the king on earth. For this reason scientific research could not be conducted during the polytheistic era. As the historian Arnold Toynbee has pointed out, natural phenomena were considered objects of worship, so they could not possibly become objects of investigation. With Islam and the advance of monotheism, the awe in which worldly phenomena had been held collapsed. People realized that all things besides God were objects of His creation. There was no cause to consider worldly phenomena as sacred: their natures could be analysed and investigated. The liberation of the human intellect which Islam brought about started at the very beginning of the Islamic era, in the time of the Prophet. On the occasion of a lunar eclipse, the Prophet Muḥammad pointed out that lunar and solar eclipses were signs of God. They were not signs of the birth or death of any human being, as had been thought during the age of superstition that preceded Islam. In this way the Prophet refuted both human and material greatness, asserting the greatness of God alone. In so doing, he initiated a trend in human thought which eventually reached Europe and resulted in the scientific revolution of modern times.

One significant advantage of the Islamic revolution was that it put an end to the age of superstition. Superstition is the basing of one's beliefs on vague notions and speculations, rather than upon solid facts, as, for example, had been the case in pre-Islamic Arabia, when people thought that solar and lunar eclipses were a sign of the death of some great person. Superstition was the greatest obstacle to accepting Islam. A person whose mind is ruled by superstitious notions cannot objectively compare Islam with other creeds. Rather than judge matters on the basis of real, tangible evidence, he accepts certain set ideas, and rejects anything that is not in accord with them. Take, for instance, the historical aspect of religion. Anyone who objectively considers the historical credentials of Islam as compared with other religions will find that the authenticity of Islam cannot be doubted from an historical point of view; other religions, however, are shrouded in mystery and legend.

But historical credibility was not considered an important factor during the age of superstition, while in our modern age the utmost importance is attached to it. Higher criticism has now been given the status of a separate branch of learning. Its findings reveal conclusively that the only religion with impeccable historical credentials is Islam. Other religions are based more in myth than in real history.

The scientific mind sought to understand the universe in the light of experiments and observations. As a result of scientific research, mysteries of the universe which confirm Islamic teachings on a high intellectual level were unravelled. Human research has revealed, for instance, that throughout the entire universe, one law of nature applies. Both celestial and terrestrial circumstances are determined by the same set of everlasting rules. This shows that the Lord of the Universe is one. If there were many gods, then there would also be many laws at work in nature.

Another obstacle to acceptance of monotheism had been ancient philosophy. In pre-Islamic times the minds of educated people were conditioned to think in philosophical terms. Philosophers have always sought to discover ultimate reality, but five hundred years of splendid history have not brought them any nearer their goal. The main reason has been the failure of philosophers to understand human limitations. Their efforts to reach a comprehension of ultimate reality were doomed because human, with their limited intellectual capacity, cannot on their own fathom a reality which is infinite and unlimited in nature. For this, prophetic wisdom is required, but human's attachment to philosophical thinking had prevented them from responding positively to the message taught by prophets.

For centuries theologians, influenced by the predominant philosophical pattern of thought, sought to define and specify the basic tenets on which the whole concept of monotheism lies. What they failed to realize was that these are all unseen realities. Our present intellects are simply not geared to fully comprehend such realities. From a religious point of view, the greatest achievement of modern science has been to remove the mistaken notion that truth is something that can be seen with one's eyes. Our range of understanding has been conclusively exposed as limited. Under the influence of science, philosophy has been forced to take second place, leaving science to guide our intellectual course. In the process monotheism's path has been cleared. It has become clear — at least indirectly — that there is only one way left for us to discover reality: we must heed the call of the prophets. People may still have a tendency to desire to see something before they believe it, but the philosophical frame of mind that they represent is on the defensive in today's scientific age. The demand to actually see invisible realities, like God, revelation and the world of eternity—the basics of monotheistic religion—has become academically untenable.

For the first time in known history, the inherent limitations in the scope of human knowledge have been conclusively established. Scientific research into the mysteries of the universe has showed us one truth with staggering clarity: that it lies beyond the powers of our limited intellect to fully encompass the world of realities. This discovery is highly important from an Islamic point of view, for it highlights the need for prophethood. On the one hand we have scientists desperately anxious to gain an understanding of ultimate reality. On the other we have them, owing to built-in limitations, incapable of doing so. There is a vacuum in our spiritual make-up which only divine guidance, or prophethood, can fill. In acknowledging our intellectual limitations, science points, on a purely academic level, to the need for revelation. There is nothing else that can make up for what humanity lacks.

In ancient times, people were not generally allowed freedom of expression. The basic reason for this was the veneration in which monarchs and leading personalities were held. People who for some reason reached an elevated position in society used to be considered sacred and blessed. Their opinions were respected far above those of others. The inordinate awe in which they were held gave them the ability to force others to comply with their wishes. The monotheistic revolution of Islam laid waste this myth of human greatness, putting all human beings on a level at par with each other. A new philosophical trend emerged, one that was finally to develop into democracy in western countries. One of the main principles of democracy is that all people are equal. It gives all people the right to express, in words or in writing, what is in their consciences. Under the democratic system it became possible, for the first time in history, to preach divine religion without fear of suppression or reprisal.

Science has brought out into the open countless material blessings, which for centuries had remained concealed from our sight. As far as Islamic preaching is concerned, the most important of these has been the development of modern methods of communication. The mass media, quick, efficient means of transport, the computer and video revolutions—all these things can be used to the advantage of Islam, enabling its teachings to be imparted to people on a universal scale.

These opportunities are highly conducive to furtherance of the Islamic cause. At the beginning of the Islamic era God had created—after a period lasting 2,500 years—conditions which would assist the establishment of Islamic dominance. So it is now. A process has been continuing over the last 1000 years, out of which conditions conducive to the re-establishment of Islamic dominance have emerged. There is no lack of opportunities, but they have to be utilized properly if they are to reap positive results. A dynamic community is needed for this task, one which is able to make the most of the opportunities available, as the Prophet and his Companions did with the opportunities available to them. If a community of this nature emerges, it will not take long for Islamic dominance over atheistic and irreligious thought to be re-established, just as it was made to dominate over polytheism at the beginning of the Islamic era.

For over one hundred years, these possibilities have been awaiting a community of this nature, but unfortunately no such community has emerged. True, countless Muslim groups and movements have sprung up over this period, but it has to be said that these groups have come into existence as a result of reactions to events. Political conditions have played a particularly important role in giving birth to them. What is needed, on the other hand, is a group of people intensely aware of the opportunities that God has created over the last one thousand years, a group that will fit in with God's scheme and exploit the complete range of possibilities that God has prepared for the resurgence of Islam that he desires.

One of the incidents that occurred during the Battle of Badr is related in biographies of the Prophet as follows. The infidel force vastly outnumbered the Muslims. When their powerful army bore down on the Prophet and his companions, the Prophet—overwhelmed by the intensity of his own emotions—cast himself at the feet of his Lord. "Lord," he cried, "if you destroy this group, you will never be worshipped again on earth." This was no exaggeration on the Prophet's part. The fact was that those 313 souls who took the field at Badr were no ordinary group of people. Outwardly weak and ill-equipped, they represented the culmination of 2,500 years of history. A group like them is required today. The only ones who can make up such a group are people who are intensely aware of the divine scheme which has been developing over the last one thousand years, and have set their hearts on playing their role in it; who are so strong and unwavering in their commitment to the task in hand that they will go to any lengths, and make any sacrifice, in order to see it through to completion. Such is the true "party of God." And it is the party of God that shall triumph.[6]

In his book, *History of the Arabs*, Professor Philip K Hitti has written that "after the death of the Prophet, sterile Arabia seems to have been converted as if by magic into a nursery of heroes the like of whom both in number and quality is hard to find anywhere."[7]

For Islam to reign supreme in the world, people's entire way of thinking has to change. Islamic thought has to gain ascendancy over every other system of thought. This was the task that God chose the Prophet and his companions to perform, and its immensity should not be underestimated. If the Prophet's successors were also capable of continuing to perform this task, it was precisely because they had been reared in this "nursery of heroes", for it was only after surmounting numerous and hazardous obstacles that they succeeded in establishing the dominance of Islamic over polytheistic thought. Today Islam has lost its former dominance—this time to atheistic thought. For its ascendancy to be re-established, another "nursery of heroes" shall have to emerge. If the Prophet and his immediate successors were obliged to undergo such a rigorous phase of initiation, his latter-day successors should show no reluctance to do likewise.

Just as the followers of the Prophet in his day suffered all kinds of privations and courted every danger to bring Islam into a position of supremacy in the world, so, in fact, have Muslims of the present day engaged in titanic struggles for its restoration. They have sacrificed their lives and properties, expended time and energy on preparing literature and lectures in support of Islam; they have travelled great distances in furtherance of the Islamic cause. As far as the quantum of effort is concerned, the struggle of present-day Muslims in the path of Islam has far surpassed that of the Prophet's contemporaries and his immediate successors. But as far as results are concerned, the story is very different. While the efforts of the Prophet and his companions changed the whole course of human history, the efforts of present-day Muslims have served only to aggravate their own plight.

This paradox stems from the differing psychologies that lay behind the struggle of the first Muslims on the one hand, and that of modern Muslims on the other. While the former were moved by a sense of discovery, the latter have been moved by a sense of loss. For example, when the Quraysh sent two men to try to secure the return of those Muslims who had felt forced to emigrate to Abyssinia, the Negus (the King) called the Muslims to his court and questioned them about their religion. Ja'far's response provides a vivid picture of the feelings which moved the companions. He said: "O king, we were a people steeped in ignorance, worshipping idols, eating unsacrificed carrion, committing abominations, and the strong would devour the weak. Thus we were, until God sent us a Messenger from out of our midst, one whose lineage we knew, and his veracity, his trustworthiness and his integrity. He called us unto God, that we should testify to his Oneness and worship Him, and renounce the stones and idols, that we and our fathers had worshipped; and he commanded us to speak truly, to fulfill our promises, to respect the ties of kinship and the rights of our neighbours, and to refrain from crimes and from bloodshed. So we worship God alone, setting naught beside Him, counting as forbidden what He has forbidden and as licit what He has allowed. For these reasons have our people turned against us, and have persecuted us to make us forsake our religion and revert from the worship of God to the worship of idols. That is why we have come to your country, having chosen you above all others; and we have been happy in your protection, and it is our hope, O king, that here, with you, we shall not suffer wrong."

We can see from Ja'far's words how much Islam meant to him, and to those on whose behalf he was speaking. Islam was for them a life of enlightenment as opposed to a life of ignorance; it was a discovery of One God, and abandonment of idols. They had abandoned an unruly life for a life of divine guidance, revealed to them through the Prophet Muḥammad. They now sought eternity, not the world. Gone was the permissiveness of yesteryear; what they had discovered now was the joy of an upright moral bearing—the path of justice as opposed to oppression, of kindness as opposed to cruelty.

A sense of discovery imbues one with unquenchable spirit, putting vitality into one's thoughts and an irresistable dynamism into one's actions. A sense of loss on the contrary dooms all one's efforts to failure. One plagued by such a feeling becomes incapable of constructive thought or action. The first Muslims were moved by a sense of discovery. That is why they produced an incomparable example of dynamic action. Modern Muslim movements have sprung from a feeling of loss, and for this reason have given rise to an unprecedented saga of misconceived policies and ill-fated initiatives.

This sense of having lost out in life is a sentiment which is unequivocally voiced by their leaders:

> We have lost all our forefathers' legacy. Heaven has thrown us down from the high Pleiades to the earth.

Practically all Muslim movements of modern times have arisen out of this feeling of loss and persecution. They may differ from one another in the way they put their point across: some use the language of nationalistic politics, while others confine themselves to religious terminology. But, in essence, they are all the same, being derived from a feeling of having lost their past glory.

When the Greek mathematician Archimedes (287-212 B.C.) discovered the law of specific gravity, his ebullience knew no bounds. He quite literally forgot himself in the joy of his discovery. In more recent times, the Shah of Iran had lost just his throne, but this purely material loss deprived him of even the will to live. Such is the nature of both discovery and loss. All one sees is the object that one has discovered, or lost.

There is no doubting the fact that a feeling of discovery engenders positiveness of character, while negativity is all that can come from a feeling of loss. The elevated and noble manner in which the first Muslims conducted their affairs was a result of their sense of discovery. They were high-minded enough to bow low before truth, magnanimous enough to acknowledge the worth of others. People of their word, they did exactly what they said they would. They were forgiving to others, in the hope that God in turn would be forgiving to them. So constant was their vision of truth that they would not waver from it; nor would they allow their own feelings to cloud their vision of it. Their decisions were based on sound reason. They did things — not to retaliate for the way they had been treated — but because they were the right things to do.

This is how a positive character works. The functioning of a negative character is totally different. Negativity is to follow impulse rather than truth. The hesitant and suspicious nature that it fosters prevents one from taking meaningful initiatives, or cooperating with others. A lack of realism dominates one's attitudes, both towards oneself and to others. Unable to see things in terms of truth, one sees them through one's own tainted vision. One's own ability is inflated in one's view, while that of others is minimized. One's defeats turn into victories in the fairy-tale world of one's own imagination, while in reality even one's successes turn into failures. It is here that present-day Muslims differ from the founding fathers of their religion.

The Prophet of Islam brought an unprecedented revolution to the world, one that was inititated by a profound feeling of spiritual discovery, and accomplished by a unique display of positive virtues. Should anyone wish to achieve the same revolution from the negativity that comes from a sense of loss, he should have to find another God—for it is not God's will that this should happen. He should also have to find another prophet—for that was not the way of the Prophet.

NOTES

1. Qur'ān, 61:9.
2. *The Encyclopaedia Britannica* (1984), Article on "Man and his God," p. 389.
3. Qur'ān, 5:44.
4. Qur'ān, 15:9.
5. Qur'ān, 8:39.
6. Qur'ān, 58:22.
7. Philip K. Hitti, *History of Arabs* (1979), p. 142.

Goodword English Publications

The Holy Quran: Text, Translation and Commentary (HB), Tr. Abdullah Yusuf Ali

The Holy Quran (PB), Tr. Abdullah Yusuf Ali

The Holy Quran (Laminated Board), Tr. Abdullah Yusuf Ali

The Holy Quran (HB), Tr. Abdullah Yusuf Ali

Holy Quran (Small Size), Tr. Abdullah Yusuf Ali

The Quran, Tr. T.B. Irving

The Koran, Tr. M.H. Shakir

The Glorious Quran, Tr. M.M. Pickthall

Allah is Known Through Reason, Harun Yahya

The Basic Concepts in the Quran, Harun Yahya

Crude Understanding of Disbelief, Harun Yahya

Darwinism Refuted, Harun Yahya

Death Resurrection Hell, Harun Yahya

Devoted to Allah, Harun Yahya

Eternity Has Already Begun, Harun Yahya

Ever Thought About the Truth?, Harun Yahya

The Mercy of Believers, Harun Yahya

The Miracle in the Ant, Harun Yahya

The Miracle in the Immune System, Harun Yahya

The Miracle of Man's Creation, Harun Yahya

The Miracle of Hormones, Harun Yahya

The Miracle in the Spider, Harun Yahya

The Miracle of Creation in DNA, Harun Yahya

The Miracle of Creation in Plants, Harun Yahya

The Moral Values of the Quran, Harun Yahya

The Nightmare of Disbelief, Harun Yahya

Perfected Faith, Harun Yahya

Quick Grasp of Faith, Harun Yahya

Timelessness and the Reality of Fate, Harun Yahya

In Search of God, Maulana Wahiduddin Khan

Islam and Peace, Maulana Wahiduddin Khan

An Islamic Treasury of Virtues, Maulana Wahiduddin Khan

The Moral Vision, Maulana Wahiduddin Khan

Muhammad: A Prophet for All Humanity, Maulana Wahiduddin Khan

Principles of Islam, Maulana Wahiduddin Khan

Prophet Muhammad : A Simple Guide to His Life, Maulana Wahiduddin Khan

The Quran for All Humanity, Maulana Wahiduddin Khan

The Quran: An Abiding Wonder, Maulana Wahiduddin Khan

Religion and Science, Maulana Wahiduddin Khan

Simple Wisdom (HB), Maulana Wahiduddin Khan

Simple Wisdom (PB), Maulana Wahiduddin Khan

The True Jihad, Maulana Wahiduddin Khan

Tabligh Movement, Maulana Wahiduddin Khan

A Treasury of the Quran, Maulana Wahiduddin Khan

Woman Between Islam and Western Society, Maulana Wahiduddin Khan

Woman in Islamic Shari'ah, Maulana Wahiduddin Khan

The Ideology of Peace, Maulana Wahiduddin Khan

Indian Muslims, Maulana Wahiduddin Khan

Introducing Islam, Maulana Wahiduddin Khan

Islam: Creator of the Modern Age, Maulana Wahiduddin Khan

Islam: The Voice of Human Nature, Maulana Wahiduddin Khan

Islam Rediscovered, Maulana Wahiduddin Khan

Words of the Prophet Muhammad, Maulana Wahiduddin Khan

God Arises, Maulana Wahiduddin Khan

The Call of the Qur'an, Maulana Wahiduddin Khan

Building a Strong and Prosperous India and Role of Muslims, Maulana Wahiduddin Khan

Islam As It Is, Maulana Wahiduddin Khan

Sermons of the Prophet Muhammad, Assad Nimer Busool

Bouquet of the Noble Hadith, Assad Nimer Busool

Forty Hadith, Assad Nimer Busool

Hijrah in Islam, Dr. Zafarul Islam Khan

Palestine Documents, Dr. Zafarul Islam Khan

At the Threshold of New Millennium, Dr. Zafarul Islam Khan

Islamic Sciences, Waqar Husaini

Islamic Thought..., Waqar Husaini

The Qur'an for Astronomy, Waqar Husaini

A Dictionary of Muslim Names, Prof. S.A. Rahman

Let's Speak Arabic, Prof. S.A. Rahman

Teach Yourself Arabic, Prof. S.A. Rahman

Islamic Medicine, Edward G. Browne

Literary History of Persia (Vol.1 & 2), Edward G. Browne

Literary History of Persia (Vol.3 & 4), Edward G. Browne

The Soul of the Quran, Saniyasnain Khan

Presenting the Quran, Saniyasnain Khan

The Wonderful Universe of Allah, Saniyasnain Khan

A-Z Ready Reference of the Quran (Based on the Translation by Abdullah Yusuf Ali), Mohammad Imran Erfani

The Alhambra, Washington Irving

The Encyclopaedic Index of the Quran, Dr. Syed Muhammad Osama

The Essentials of Islam, Al-Haj Saeed Bin Ahmed Al Lootah

Glossary of the Quran, Aurang Zeb Azmi

Introducing Arabic, Michael Mumisa

Arabic-English Dictionary, J.G. Hava

The Arabs in History, Prof. Bernard Lewis

A Basic Reader for the Holy Quran, Syed Mahmood Hasan

The Beauty of Makkah and Madinah, Mohamed Amin

A Brief Illustrated Guide to Understanding Islam, I.A. Ibrahim

The Concept of Society in Islam and Prayersin Islam, Dr. Syed Abdul Latif

Decisive Moments in the History of Islam, Muhammad Abdullah Enan

The Handy Concordance of the Quran, Aurang Zeb Azmi

The Hadith for Beginners, Dr. Muhammad Zubayr Siddiqui
A Handbook of Muslim Belief, Dr. Ahmad A Galwash
Heart of the Koran, Lex Hixon
A History of Arabian Music, Henry George Farmer
A History of Arabic Literature, Clément Huart
How Greek Science Passed to Arabs, De Lacy O' Leary
Humayun Nama, Gulbadan Bano
Islam and the Divine Comedy, Miguel Asin
Islam and Ahmadism, Muhammad Iqbal
The Islamic Art and Architecture, Prof. T.W. Arnold
The Islamic Art of Persia, Ed. A.J. Arberry
Islamic Economics, Sabahuddin Azmi
Islamic Thought and its Place in History, De Lacy O' Leary
The Life of the Prophet Muhammad, Mohd. Marmaduke Pickthall
Life of the Prophet Muhammad, B. Salem Foad
The Most Beautiful Names of Allah (HB), Samira Fayyad Khawaldeh
The Most Beautiful Names of Allah (PB), Samira Fayyad Khawaldeh
The Moriscos of Spain, Henry Charles Lea
Muhammad: The Hero As Prophet, Thomas Carlyle
Muhammad: A Mercy to All the Nations, Qassim Ali Jairazbhoy
The Muslims in Spain, Stanley Lane-Poole
One Religion, Zaheer U. Ahmed
The Pilgrimage to Makkah, Sir Richard F. Burton
Principles of Islamic Culture, Dr. Syed Abdul Latif
The Sayings of Muhammad, Sir Abdullah Suhrwardy
Selections from the Noble Reading, Tr. T.B. Irving
A Simple Guide to Islam, Farida Khanam
A Simple Guide to Islam's Contribution to Science, Maulvi Abdul Karim
A Simple Guide to Muslim Prayer, Muhammad Mahmud Al-Sawwat
Spanish Islam (A History of the Muslims in Spain), Reinhart Dozy
The Spread of Islam in France, Michel Reeber
The Spread of Islam in the World, Prof. T.W. Arnold

The Story of Islamic Spain, Syed Azizur Rahman

The Travels of Ibn Battuta, Tr. H.A.R. Gibb

The Travels of Ibn Jubayr, Tr. J.C. Broadhurst

What is Riba?, Maulana Iqbal Ahmad Khan Suhail

Concerning Divorce, Maulana Wahiduddin Khan

The Concept of God, Maulana Wahiduddin Khan

Conversion: An Intellectual Transformation, Maulana Wahiduddin Khan

The Creation Plan of God, Maulana Wahiduddin Khan

The Fire of Hell, Maulana Wahiduddin Khan

The Good Life, Maulana Wahiduddin Khan

The Garden of Paradise, Maulana Wahiduddin Khan

Hijab in Islam, Maulana Wahiduddin Khan

Islam and the Modern Man, Maulana Wahiduddin Khan

Islam in History, Maulana Wahiduddin Khan

Islam Stands the Test of History, Maulana Wahiduddin Khan

Islamic Activism, Maulana Wahiduddin Khan

Islamic Fundamentalism, Maulana Wahiduddin Khan

Man Know Thyself, Maulana Wahiduddin Khan

Muhammad: The Ideal Character, Maulana Wahiduddin Khan

The Man Islam Builds, Maulana Wahiduddin Khan

Manifesto of Peace, Maulana Wahiduddin Khan

Non-Violence and Islam, Maulana Wahiduddin Khan

Polygamy and Islam, Maulana Wahiduddin Khan

The Revolutionary Role of Islam, Maulana Wahiduddin Khan

The Road to Paradise, Maulana Wahiduddin Khan

Search for Truth, Maulana Wahiduddin Khan

The Shariah and Its Application, Maulana Wahiduddin Khan

Spirituality in Islam, Maulana Wahiduddin Khan

The Teachings of Islam, Maulana Wahiduddin Khan

Uniform Civil Code, Maulana Wahiduddin Khan

The Way to Find God, Maulana Wahiduddin Khan

A Case of Discovery, Maulana Wahiduddin Khan.